RESPECTABLE BURIAL

RESPECTABLE BURIAL
MONTREAL'S MOUNT ROYAL CEMETERY

BRIAN YOUNG   Colour photographs by GEOFFREY JAMES

McGill-Queen's University Press   Montreal & Kingston • London • Ithaca

© McGill-Queen's University Press 2003
ISBN 0-7735-2529-7

Legal deposit second quarter 2003
Bibliothèque nationale du Québec

Colour photographs © Geoffrey James

Printed in Canada

This book has been published with the help of a grant from the
Mount Royal Cemetery.

McGill-Queen's University Press acknowledges the support of the Canada Council for
the Arts for our publishing program. We also acknowledge the financial support of the
Government of Canada through the Book Publishing Industry Development Program
(BPIDP) for our publishing activities.

National Library of Canada Cataloguing in Publication

Young, Brian, 1940–
  Respectable burial : Montreal's Mount Royal Cemetery / Brian Young ; photographs
by Geoffrey James.

Includes bibliographical references and index.
ISBN 0-7735-2529-7

  1. Mount Royal Cemetery (Montréal, Quebec)–History.
2. Protestants–Quebec (Province)–Montréal–History. 3. Burial–Quebec
(Province)–Montréal–History. 4. Death–Quebec (Province)–Montréal–History.
5. Montréal (Quebec)–Social life and customs. 6. Montréal (Quebec)–History.
I. James, Geoffrey, 1942–II. Title.

FC2947.61.Y68 2003   971.4'28   C2003-900321-3   F1054.5.M862M68 2003

Colour photographs throughout the frontmatter are by Geoffrey James

This book was designed and typeset by David LeBlanc in Bembo 11/14
in Montreal, Quebec

To Elizabeth and Edgar Andrew Collard, historians and lifelong friends of the cemetery

CONTENTS

MAPS

ACKNOWLEDGMENTS

My list of thanks is substantial, cutting across teaching and research worlds at McGill University and professionals in publishing, photography, and burying. In the United Kingdom, particular thanks are due to Julie Rugg of the Cemetery Research Group, University of York, and historians Colin Coates and Robert Morris of the University of Edinburgh. Brian Treggett, superintendent of Mount Hermon Cemetery in Quebec, opened his archives and walked his grounds with me. In Montreal, Mary Anne Poutanen of the Montreal History Group helped train researchers and sat in on multiple discussions of the meaning of Protestantism, respectability, and cemetery space. Peter McNally helped with documentation on the Old Protestant Burial Ground. I benefited from the input of members of my McGill seminar on Quebec institutions, a class that focused on the history of the cemetery. Tramping the cemetery with me, working in the archives, and presenting their material culture essays, Brian Fitzgerald, Darcy Ingram, Julie Lassonde, John Papageorgiou, Olivier Peri, and Caroline Schoofs helped me understand essential elements of stone, architecture, and place. Students Anny Duchaine, Walter Forsberg, and Marie-Laure Mahood researched superbly on the forgotten – those buried in the free ground. Meticulous archival research was done by Sophie Mathieu and Caroline Schoofs; much of the work on the charity lots and Chinese concession was done by Darcy Ingram. Jadwiga Dunin Borkowska and Jarrett Rudy contributed important newspaper research. Rosalyn Trigger and Janice Harvey, both specialists on the Protestant community, helped me with their insights. Mia Webster brought order to my photo and image research. Donald Roy, retired manager of the Cemetery Company and Crematorium, was gracious with my questions, leading me through institutional history as well the Roy family's private life on the mountain. Landscape architect Malaka Ackaoui shared her enthusiasm for the cultural and physical meaning of the cemetery.

At McGill-Queen's University Press, Aurèle Parisien was an innovative, hands-on editor, dogged in cajoling from me the best book possible. Editing the manuscript, Barbara Tessman combined empathy for the author's work with a ferocity of exactitude. Behind the scenes at the press, Joan McGilvray and Susanne McAdam applied both the steel of e-mail and the balms needed to help an author to the finish line. Working with Geoffrey James helped me adjust the historian's perspective to the mind's eye of the photographer. At Mount Royal Cemetery, director of public relations Myriam Cloutier provided enthusiastic help at every turn. The cemetery's executive director, Merle Christopher, was essential in the writing of this history, generous with both company records and his own knowledge of the human and business implications of burial. I greatly enjoyed my contacts with the trustees. Their sense – old-fashioned I suppose – of culture and community, their attendance in a non-profit institution whose daily fare is death and burial, and their openness to my work gave me pause. Through the whole process of writing this book, Rod MacLeod played a central role, researching in cemetery archives, reading drafts, and offering insights into cemetery culture. The work owes much to all of these individuals: responsibility for the final result, however, rests entirely with me.

It is fitting that this book is dedicated to historians Elizabeth and Edgar Andrew Collard. Elizabeth Collard's works on Canadian pottery and porcelain stand as models of how the history of material culture can be written and researched. Editor emeritus of the *Montreal Gazette*, Edgar Andrew Collard had a lifelong interest in the Mount Royal Cemetery. His unpublished history of the cemetery, "Garden in the Sun," is available at the cemetery and was an important source in writing this history. His several books and his Gazette columns, written from 1944 to 2000, remain valuable sources for the history of English Montreal. Edgar Andrew Collard died in 2000 and Elizabeth Collard in 2001; both are buried in Mount Royal Cemetery.

IN THE CEMETERY

Walking up Mount Royal Boulevard from Park Avenue, one leaves behind the skyscrapers of downtown Montreal and, depending on the season, softball players or tobogganers in Olmsted's Mount Royal Park. A ten-minute ascent past elegant homes and forest brings you to the gates of Mount Royal Cemetery, nestled in a valley beneath the summits of Mount Royal and Outremont, and its careful contours of lawn, trees, and winding roads.

The oldest sections of the cemetery, with occasional wrought-iron fences and seemingly haphazard organization, have the comforting scale and rhythm of an English country church-yard. Later sections, further up the slope, are laid out broadly with reassuring, imperial expanses of manicured lawn. Inscriptions on piously plain or elaborately Romantic monuments memorialize Scots parentage, wealth, war, benevolence, and the domesticity of 'good wives.' Reminiscent of a thousand services in Protestant churches across Montreal, they preach the importance of work, service, family, and Britishness or resign themselves to the understatement of simple words: Father, Mother, Husband, Daughter.

The mood changes toward the back of the cemetery. The opulence of the Victorian section, with its strong sense of confidence, entitlement, and immortality, seems far away as graves of immigrant, infant, soldier, and pauper crowd the fence separating Mount Royal from the neighbouring Catholic cemetery.

What is this place, this thing, this idea called Mount Royal Cemetery? Is it a burying ground, established simply to deal with the grim realities of death and decay? A visible expression of the Victorian union of Nature and the human soul? A dignified vestige of Protestant benevolence? For some, it is a finely tuned business operation, whose professional superintendents have had to look beyond feeling and Protestant culture to deal with the realities of dirt, public health, efficiency, and the provision of a modicum of decency for all. In an echo of earlier debates over cremation or in-ground burial, the modern cemetery has been seen by some as a monument to human narcissism and reproached for abusing the natural environment. As a product of urban society, the cemetery will always be a site of competing technologies and ideologies.

The cemetery founders brought Victorian exuberance to their plans for a new burial site in Montreal. They chose the "rural" cemetery model and set out to create a site of natural beauty in juxtaposition to the city below. Above Montreal's industrializing grey, they sought controlled green loftiness and monuments mindful of the inspiration poets such as Wordsworth found in death. Although their cemetery was open to the public, it was governed by the strict codes of Protestant respectability and ideas of mourning and private grief. Mores and aesthetic sensibilities may have changed, but the deceased and their mourners continue to try to tell the stories they need to tell: beyond the exactness of death and chiseled dates, epitaphs and mementoes unite memory, tradition, and history, creating landscapes of fiction.

The photographs of Geoffrey James capture the conflicting notions of the cemetery, its past and its modernity, its inherent tensions. Spring blossoms are always the precursors to autumn foliage, and it is the essence of the cemetery that the ordered, lush beauty of perpetual care gives way to the sudden, transient disruption of earth, planks, waiting shovels, and the open grave. A stark mound of earth, black-backed anonymous mourners, a fleeting cyclist, and an exuberantly decorated grave mediate the cemetery trustees' vision of beauty and natural peace with the social and physical reality of their enterprise. The meshing of these visions is central to the history captured in this book.

The cemetery makes us aware of distance, silence, and seasonality and of nature's inexorable encroachment on worked stone, the human, and the built. James reminds us of the poetic link between sensuality and death, between beauty and reality, between fragile and solid. The restlessness and the stark, lonely beauty of his photographs lead into the cemetery's story, its mystery, and its meaning.

CHRONOLOGY

1760 Capitulation of Montreal; Anglican clergy arrive in Quebec

1786 Presbyterian congregation formed in Montreal

1799 Protestant cemetery opens

1801 chapel erected in Protestant cemetery

1803 Methodists organized in Montreal

1804 Père Lachaise, first "rural" cemetery, opens in Paris

1814 establishment of Military Burial Ground on Papineau Road in Montreal

1815 Papineau Cemetery, adjacent to the Military Burial Ground,
     established as second Protestant cemetery

1831 Mount Auburn Cemetery founded in Cambridge, Massachusetts;
     Baptists form congregation in Montreal

1832 cholera epidemic "fills" Protestant Burial Ground

1836 Laurel Hill Cemetery founded in Philadelphia

1843 Anatomy Act legislates delivery of unclaimed bodies to medical
     schools in United Province of Canada

1847 incorporation of Montreal Cemetery Company

1852 cemetery site on Mount Royal purchased from Dr Michael McCulloch;
     first burial (William Squire); Richard Sprigings named superintendent

1853 receiving vaults completed at new cemetery

1854 consecration of Mount Royal Cemetery (MRC) by Anglican Bishop Francis Fulford

1855 first mausoleum entombment at MRC; Notre-Dame-des-Neiges Cemetery opened

1861 embalming techniques become widespread; MRC introduces perpetual care

1862 superintendent's house built, along with gates

1864 trustees purchase additional twenty-eight acres, including what would become
     Mount Murray

1868 space granted for burial of firemen killed on duty

1874 cremation societies established in England and New York

1875 Protestant Burial Ground closed; burial of Joseph Guibord

1876 opening of first crematorium in the United States; two cottages at MRC built for employees; Mount Royal Park opens; the undertakers' journal, *The Casket*, established

1877 funeral of Orangeman Thomas Lett Hackett

1882 Funeral Directors' National Association of the United States founded

1886 incline railway built up Mount Royal

1887 founding of Association of American Cemetery Superintendents; cremation raised by MRC trustees for first time

1890 Frank Roy named superintendent

1891 opening of new Free Ground at MRC

1895 construction of Royal Victoria Hospital

1897 mechanized lawn mower introduced

1898 Ormiston Roy becomes superintendent; John H.R. Molson leaves cemetery $10,000 to establish crematorium; opening of children's section

1899 establishment of American Society of Landscape Architects

1900 construction of conservatory and new vaults at MRC; crematorium opened at Mount Auburn

1902 first cremation at MRC (Senator Alexander Walker Ogilvie)

1903 The Crematorium Limited granted federal charter separate from Mount Royal Cemetery Company; telephone system installed on grounds

1910 first burial in Hawthorn-Dale; inauguration of Last Post Fund plot in MRC

1912 railway tunnel built under Mount Royal

1913 resignation of George Durnford as secretary-treasurer; establishment of Forest Lawn Memorial Park in Glendale, California

1914 Ormiston Roy's title changed to landscape architect and general superintendent

1915 cemetery office moves to site on grounds of cemetery on Papineau Road

1917 establishment of the Imperial War Graves Commission; winter burials increasingly common

1918 Spanish influenza epidemic

1919 MRC office moved back to centre of city

1921 military burial lots in MRC purchased by federal government

1923 cemetery office opens in building bought at 1207 Drummond;
construction of Memorial Road from entrance to crematorium

1924 Ormiston Roy becomes landscape architect; John F. Roy becomes manager; St Joseph's
Oratory built; tram built from Côte-des-Neiges to Mount Royal Park

1927 last run of funeral tram to Hawthorn-Dale

1930 streetcar service to Mount Royal Park opens from intersection of Park and Mount Royal

1936 Unveiling of Cross of Sacrifice monument at Sir Arthur Currie's grave

1949 Conservatory demolished at MRC

1951 sale of second military lot to Department of Veterans' Affairs

1952 Bell Telephone tower built on land purchased from cemetery

1958 Ormiston Roy dies; cemetery administration transferred from downtown to cemetery
grounds; opening of automobile access to top of Mount Royal

1964 Vatican II permits cremation of Roman Catholics

1966 John F. Roy resigns as manager and is replaced by W. Wallace Roy; Donald Roy joins
company as assistant manager; strike by cemetery employees

1967 Donald Roy becomes manager

1970 FLQ crisis; army camped at south gates of cemetery

1974 Merle Christopher named as assistant to Donald Roy

1975 sales of memorials, bronze plaques, and inscriptions begin; opening of crematorium
in Notre-Dame-des-Neiges Cemetery

1976 Saint-Jean-Baptiste celebrations held in Mount Royal Park

1978 remains of sixty British soldiers moved to cemetery from excavation site
of Guy Favreau building

1979 clear-cutting by cemetery on Mount Murray

1984 crematorium extended, second chapel added along with small
mausoleum and columbarium

1986 establishment of Les amis de la montagne, an association established to protect environment of Mount Royal

1990 Donald Roy retires; Merle Christopher named as first executive director; master development plan for Mountain View produced; Elsie Norsworthy named as first female board member; company begins offering funeral services

1992 purchase by Mount Royal Cemetery Company of M.A. Blythe Bernier Funeral Home; expropriation of southern part of Hawthorn-Dale to Montreal Urban Community for incorporation into regional park

1995 new funeral and burial complex, Complexe Commémoratif Hawthorn-Dale, opened; communications coordinator Myriam Cloutier hired

1998 new logo adopted and company reorganized as Mount Royal Commemorative Services; completion of funeral complex at MRC; charitable association, the Friends of the Mount Royal Cemetery, established to encourage historical and educational activities

1999 pre-planning division established

2002 cemetery celebrates 150 years of its history since first burial in 1852; cemetery is designated "National Historic Site" by the Historic Sites and Monuments Board of Canada

2003 government of Quebec designates 7,500 hectares on Mount Royal, including the cemetery, as a protected historical and environmental site

INTRODUCTION

If there is an easy time in Mount Royal Cemetery, it is spring. Of course, in the burial business every day is a working day, and, even with lilacs in bloom, anonymous vans move through the gates to rendezvous at the funeral complex and crematorium. But the Mount Royal Cemetery has developed into an institution that is more than just death, bereavement, cremation, and burial, and this is never more evident than in the spring and summer months, when the cemetery is alive with activity. Lists drawn up by birdwatchers are posted on the gatehouse noticeboard alongside invitations for gospel-singing concerts and walking tours. Visitors are encouraged, their tours aided by pamphlets that speak of rare trees, buried tavern-keepers, and famous politicians. Even the closing of the gates at 7:00 P.M. seems casual – an employee idles in a truck, waiting for the last cars of stragglers to head home across the city. After closing, cyclists, dog walkers, and loiterers from around the Molson mausoleum continue to pass through the pedestrian gate, which is always open.

Organized activities at this time of year strike a balance between the many functions of the cemetery. On the evening of 6 May 1999, for example, the cemetery organized music, a candle-light walk, and the planting of a memorial rose bush to aid people trying to cope with Mother's Day and Father's Day, those busy Sundays when visitors tend to focus on their sense of bereavement. On 15 May, the cemetery held an Information Day, offering seminars on estate planning, preplanning, the grieving process, cremation, and memorialization trends. Accompanying the seminars were hourly concerts as part of the Montreal Chamber Music Festival as well as presentations on funeral traditions around the world by specialists on Hinduism, Judaism, Islam, and Buddhism. At 8:00 the next morning, the cemetery's natural environment became the

Opposite The Mount Royal Cemetery today.

With the installation of bluebird boxes, large numbers of bluebirds have returned to the cemetery.

focus, as ninety-two birdwatchers responded to the cemetery's invitation to a field trip and the annual spring count on the grounds. Thick foliage prompted by an early spring reduced sightings to 52 species, but these included 5 different species of hawks in addition to the song birds such as mocking birds, northern orioles, scarlet tanagers, and bluebirds nesting in the cemetery. Since boxes were put up for them in 1992, the bluebirds, after decades in decline, began breeding in ever increasing numbers. Over the years, 145 species of birds have been identified, including 25 different species of brilliantly coloured warblers. Later in the summer, the emphasis shifts again, to the rich historical tradition of the cemetery. In August, walking tours of the grounds are organized around the theme of the history of McGill University and the cemetery, including the monument in the cemetery to those who donated their bodies to the university for scientific research. Other historical facts await the interested visitor. It was a century and a half ago, on 19 October 1852, that Methodist minister and cholera victim William Squire had the distinction of being the first person buried in Mount Royal Cemetery. Fifty years later, on 19 April 1902, Canada's first cremation – that of Senator Alexander Walker Ogilvie, member of a prominent milling family and himself a cemetery trustee – took place in the cemetery's newly opened crematorium.

McGill Donors' Monument
(F1770, Section F7).

In 1992, the cemetery offered to provide McGill University with a commemorative site for the families of individuals who had donated their bodies for research at the university. The monument, which was unveiled on 16 November 1994, symbolizes the cycle of life: the small dove on the left matures into the larger one on the right, with the "broken" end representing death.

How did a cemetery that deals daily with death, burial, cremation, and sorrow come to link its image to birds, chamber music, and history? Mount Royal Cemetery's current orientation to community identity, history, and environmental issues is part of an attempt to counteract competition from death-care conglomerates that began buying up Montreal's mortuaries, cemeteries, and crematoria in the mid-1980s. Mount Royal's recent alignment with the forces of heritage and the environment forms part of the cemetery's "new respectability." A non-profit company with roots deep in the history of Montreal, the cemetery in the 1990s expanded its business activities to encompass a full range of funeral services, broadened its community involvement, and recognized an environmental responsibility.

If death, as wags put it, is one of the few certainties of life, disposal of corpses is a necessary act that occurs at the crossroads of delicate civic, religious, and private imperatives. Funerals, cremations, and burials are intense, defining moments for families, loved ones, and, if the deceased was a public figure, for the larger community. In May 2000, for example, people waited in seemingly endless lines to pay their respects to Canadiens legend Maurice Richard, whose body was laid out in Montreal's largest arena; a few months later, thousands queued outside City Hall to pay homage to former prime minister Pierre Elliott Trudeau. One of the most important burial processions in the history of Montreal occurred in December 1933, when Arthur Currie, First World War general and principal of McGill University, was buried in Mount Royal Cemetery.

In western society, cemeteries are the usual places to dispose of bodies. For the historian, they are laboratories in material culture. Their landscape, architecture, buildings, monuments, and epitaphs are profound cultural expressions pointing squarely to conceptions of religion, social position, nation, childhood, gender, and ethnicity. They also reflect imbalances of power. Clearly, the ability to have a voice in running the cemetery, to imagine, define, and shape burial space, and to provide for one's death and that of one's family by purchasing a family lot is the prerogative of the powerful and those with a sense of entitlement. In contrast, those down the pecking order of society – the hapless, the helpless, and the homeless – leave few physical markers of their passage, either through life or in death. Still, the poor, the unimportant, and – in the case of

Mount Royal – the non-Protestant were not entirely voiceless or powerless. Their determination to escape physical degradation on medical-school dissection slabs and to obtain the dignity of an individual grave, the memento of their name on a common grave marker, or, failing all else, a mound of dirt identifying their burial place, speaks clearly within the archives of Mount Royal Cemetery.

The cemetery is also a sort of permanent museum exhibition on how different generations face catastrophes, infant mortality, or old age. Dealing in a rapidly perishing commodity – corpses – the cemetery necessarily expands rapidly during epidemics, changes its marketing to suit new populations and clienteles, and reinvents its landscape as public perceptions of nature and environment evolve. In the offices of cemetery managers, the struggle to provide "perpetual care" clashes with the ravages that time exacts on corpses, memorials, and memory. The cemetery in fact offers important reflections on Time. Even casual visitors cannot be to the temporal theme of the epitaphs of those underfoot: "As you are now, so once was I," ; "Till we meet again"; or "Your time on earth will not be long." The Mount Royal Cemetery's attentiveness to greenery and landscape speak to a particular view of beautification and nature, while headstones serve as barometers marking how generations expressed their identity. Victorians had a view of memorialization profoundly different than that of Montrealers who lived through the First World War, for example. Ethnicity is also an important factor, with Buddhist, Jewish, and differing Protestant traditions easily discernible.

The founders of Mount Royal Cemetery succeeded in creating an institution that corresponded to the cultural imagination. Green, spacious, and moral, their "cemetery" – as apposed to a burial ground or graveyard – would differ from its ruder, urban predecessor. And, unlike other British manifestations that their community had built in Montreal – Nelson's Monument, Christ Church, the Crystal Palace – cemetery founders were able to combine a rural as well as an urban vision, building in an isolated space, set back from the city, and with access limited to those of their choosing. Inspired by their own estates and gardens, their libraries and travels, and by multiple examples across the Protestant world, the trustees constructed an institution that would impress by its classical architecture, its romanticized nature, and its strict codes of behaviour. Built in a commanding location on the city's highest point, the cemetery, with its urns, celtic

crosses, cut stone gates and buildings, and English-garden landscapes, represented a conservative and Protestant version of memory, the environment, and society – a conceptualization of space that might stand as a bulwark against Roman
Catholicism, nationalism, republicanism, and democratization percolating in the
city below. At the same time, although utopian, the cemetery was too critical to
issues of public health and public peace and too urban in its functions to remain
apart from social issues and technological change: its compromises with modernity were apparent in its design, its equipment, its system of record keeping, and
the evolution of its management.

The first trustees, although strongly British in their tendencies, relied heavily on American models in laying out their rural cemetery on Mount Royal. A
generation later, Ormiston Roy, the cemetery's most important superintendent,
was even more influenced by American cemetery culture and attitudes to landscapes. Early in the twentieth century, Roy brought the lawn-plan concept to
Montreal cemeteries. Both in Mount Royal Cemetery and in the new suburban cemetery, Hawthorn-Dale, opened in 1910, the stone and sentimentality of
the rural cemetery were replaced by a landscape of shrubs, perennial plants, and,
particularly, grassy vistas: death became less visible and burying almost inciden-
tal in the creation of a naturally harmonious and egalitarian public space. Two
other sea changes in cemetery operations occurred in this period. First, in 1902,
the opening on the cemetery grounds of Canada's first crematorium challenged
religious beliefs and traditional attitudes to burial. A powerful symbol of modernity, cremation emphasized the efficiency of the industrial furnace over the
naturalness and slowness of in-ground burial. Second, the cemetery's sense of
hierarchy and exclusivity was shaken by the democratization of death that
resulted from the First World War, and by the declining political place of English Montreal. One result of these transformations was that until the 1970s, the
trustees, philanthropic and occasional in their attendance, tended to subordinate
themselves to strong superintendents armed with on-site expertise in cremation, technology, horticulture, and records management.

Providing burial for destitute Protestants – recent immigrants, inmates from
asylums, prisons, and barracks, or victims of epidemics or work accidents – was
a Christian duty. While rural cemeteries were sometimes spared this responsibility by the construction of cheaper, segregated, and often municipally owned
burial sites, authorities at Mount Royal Cemetery willingly shouldered this

obligation. By continuing to bury the poor, cemetery fathers and their partners in charitable and ethnic societies demonstrated Christian responsibility and provided real evidence of social solidarity in Montreal's Protestant community. Along the cemetery's corners and back fences – and occasionally in surprisingly prominent locations – are the graves of the foot soldiers of urban society, reminders that the Protestant community included army privates, servants, labourers, sailors, and poor immigrants. Reaching back into the legacy of the Reformation and the Anglican churchyard, this Protestant responsibility to provide decent burial remained broad, and included Jews, errant Catholics, Protestants without any church attachment, or the anonymous unfortunate who was

Map of Mount Royal, show‐ing the two major cemeteries

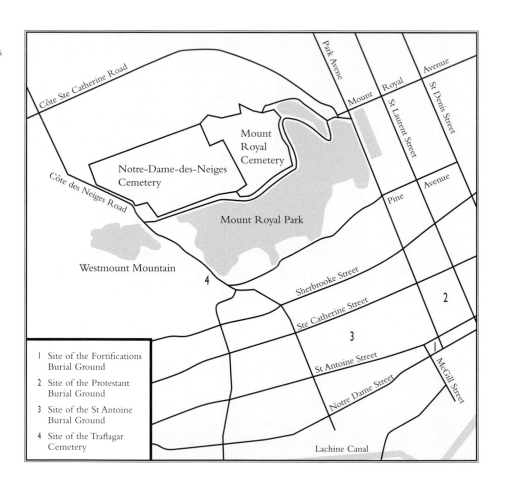

presumed Protestant. As Montreal's demography changed early in the twentieth century, the cemetery also became the final resting place for Orthodox Christians and Protestants of non-British origin. And in a transformation away from its focus on the family and individual memorials, the cemetery accepted memorialization of the social contribution of particular groups: firemen, the military, Masons, and members of fraternal societies.

Given the centrality accorded to Protestantism in this book, it may seem contradictory to also emphasize the cemetery's broad secular role. Yet, the cemetery's founding coincided with the pre-Confederation period in which state activity – in taxation, education, public health, and in the collecting of information about citizens – dramatically increased. The cemetery provides a good example of how elite groups were charged by the state to carry out public functions, often through organizations based on religion and with roots in the old world. As early as 1665, for example, the St Andrew's Society was organized in Scotland to bury epidemic victims. An awareness of the resonance of these cultural practices in Montreal, and the ways in which in an industrial society private corporations like the Mount Royal Cemetery assumed public functions like the burial of the poor, is critical to our understanding of Canadian history.

By persisting in their historic mission of burying the non-Catholic poor, the trustees were able to impose their vision of respectable burial across an entire Protestant community, from paupers to bank presidents. In the first decades of the cemetery's history, this vision brought the trustees into sharp conflict with a broad range of popular leaders from Joe Beef to Orangemen and the leaders of the Chinese community. The advance of the welfare state, secularization, and the Quiet Revolution in Quebec after the Second World War encouraged the stripping of the educational and social functions historically assigned to the Roman Catholic Church and its Protestant counterparts. For Mount Royal Cemetery, the confusion in the mind of both its managers and the public between its private-property rights and its civic responsibilities was at the root of the environmental and public-relations crisis surrounding its decision in 1970 to clear cut trees on its property. In 2002 the cemetery was designated a "National Historic Site" by the Historic Sites and Monuments Board of Canada. A year later it was included by the Quebec government as part of a larger protected historical and environmental site on Mount Royal.

Nor were issues concerning modernization restricted to the cemetery's relations with the public. Within the cemetery grounds itself, emerging professions – landscape gardener, landscape architect, superintendent, manager, and executive director – brought about new contradictions between modern professional, scientific, and technological interests and older traditions. New forms of transportation, industrial equipment, and consumerism outside the walls also brought change to the cemetery. It was not always easy for cemetery authorities to catch the right technological or transportation wave. In 1908, they built their satellite cemetery, Hawthorn-Dale, on the eastern outskirts of Montreal with a view to the tramway as the principal means of transporting both coffin and mourners; by the 1920s, however, the motorized hearse and the private automobile had revolutionized cemetery transport. Industrial change brought important labour savings and modifications to the organization of work. Across the cemetery's first decades, hundreds of labourers were hired to dig graves, to pull bodies from the winter mortuary, and to clear new sections of the mountain. After the First World War, the development of the gasoline tractor, the power lawnmower, stone drills, and the back hoe allowed the cemetery to bury year-round, to abandon its winter mortuary, and to reduce its seasonal labour in favour of a smaller, more rational workforce.

By the late nineteenth century, institutions like the funeral parlour and hospital were challenging the power of the Protestant clergy and the cemetery's traditional means of doing business. Visitation and funerals were increasingly displaced from the deceased's home or church to the funeral parlour. Another new professional, the funeral director, benefiting from a monopoly over the technique of embalming, took charge of laying out corpses, negotiating burial times and the presence of clergy, and orchestrating the committal service at the cemetery. Indeed, the purchase of the cemetery lot itself might be organized by the funeral director.[1] Dying itself was increasingly segregated from daily life, and death in bed at home was increasingly replaced by death in hospital. The Royal Victoria Hospital, embarrassed by recurring makeshift funerals held in its medical amphitheatre, opened a chapel in its new pathology wing in 1902 to meet the new demand for funerals from families who "could not make suitable arrangements." After the hospital funeral service, bodies were transferred directly to the cemetery for burial.[2]

Almost from its inception, then, Mount Royal Cemetery has been subject to social, technological, and economic pressures from the outside world. In inviting me to write this history and in opening their archives, the trustees asked me to think about the complex ways that these pressures have been addressed, how the Mount Royal Cemetery[3] evolved from a "lugubrious place, impregnated with the idea of death and mourning,"[4] to a natural and historical treasure, while continuing to be a successful business enterprise. Envisaging more than a corporate history, a survey of the rich and eccentric buried in their grounds, or a tour of curious epitaphs, they encouraged me to link the cemetery with broader developments in Canadian society; I think they hoped that in learning the history of their cemetery, readers would better understand their community. This, it turns out, is quite in keeping with the cemetery's original mission.

RESPECTABLE BURIAL

ONE

ABANDONING URBAN

BURIAL GROUNDS

In the early nineteenth century, following the Napoleonic Wars, Montreal was home to an ethnically diverse and rapidly expanding population. Average growth rates of 4 per cent a year pushed the city's population to some 34,000 by 1831.[1] This expansion meant an increasing number of births and, inevitably, deaths. Between 1831 and 1844, almost 18,000 births and 7,254 deaths were registered in Montreal. In dangerous years, death challenged birth as the dominant statistic: for example, in the typhoid year of 1849, Montreal registered 2,355 births and 1,522 deaths.[2]

At mid-century, when the Mount Royal Cemetery was established, the city's English-speaking population formed a majority, although it was sharply divided into Catholic and Protestant sectors and by fractious ethnic histories imported from the British Isles. About a third of Montreal was Protestant, usually English or Scot but also American and Irish Protestants. French Canadians, who were virtually all Catholics, represented 44 per cent of the city's inhabitants. Another 25 per cent of the population were English-speaking Catholics, mostly Irish.[3]

The casual reader of newspapers of the period might conclude that Death struck the city's population randomly or as the result of bad luck – a train accident or shipwreck, a runaway horse, a tavern brawl, a drunken husband. The popular press avidly covered the many coroners' inquests held in the city. In 1848, 323 inquests were held in Montreal to determine the cause of unusual or violent deaths. Confirming the hazards of the fast-flowing St Lawrence, the danger of work on its banks and in boats, and undoubtedly that period's sensitivity to suicide, inquests rendered 136 verdicts of "drowned," along with 15 suicides, 9 "found dead," 8 cases of "intemperance," and one of "want of food." "Unknown" was not a common term, coroners and juries choosing instead to describe 94 deaths as occurring from "the visitation of God."[4]

Cemetery archives belie the centrality of the spectacular deaths described in newspapers. They speak instead to age, health breakdown, disease, epidemics, class realities, dangerous working conditions, and the particular dangers of being an infant or mother in Montreal.[5] Like that of most cities, Montreal's public health system was rudimentary, and the lack of city-wide sewer or running-water systems produced a steady harvest for burial grounds. While our society views the death of children as "unnatural," it was all too common an occurrence before the First World War. In both Europe and America, early death punished both the middle and lower classes. In 1846, almost two-thirds of

Catholic burials in Montreal were of children under four. Statistics for Protestants were similarly grim: over a third of the burials in Toronto's Protestant cemeteries in 1850–54 were of infants under one year of age.[6] Mount Royal's own statistics confirm the vulnerability of children. In 1859, for example, 47.7 per cent of burials were of children under ten years of age. Epidemics were particularly devastating for children: in the 1885 smallpox epidemic in Montreal, 57 per cent of the Protestant victims were under fifteen.[7]

Cemeteries do more than reveal death's predilection for the very young and old, they are also clear markers of status and identity – attempts, through the medium of the dead, to suggest social coherence and stability: in fact, gravediggers have rarely succeeded in narrowing the gap, so evident in life, between privileged and pauper. Throughout history, pharaohs, lords, bishops, and other wealthy individuals have left instructions for the positioning of their graves near altars and other holy places and have commissioned lavish funeral monuments that proclaim their standing. In Quebec, the Catholic clergy, along with seigneurs and merchants, were buried in crypts under their churches and chapels. Underneath the parish church of Saint-Jean-Port-Joli, for example, 216 clergy and notables were buried. Montreal's parish church, Notre Dame, was built in the 1820s with three vaults in its crypt: one for Christian Brothers, a second for the nuns of the Congregation of Notre-Dame, and a third for the priests of the Seminary of Montreal. In 1861, with construction of their new hospital and convent on the slopes of Mount Royal, the Hôtel-Dieu nuns transferred the remains of 178 sisters buried beneath the choir floor in the old convent to a new vault in their chapel.[8] Ordinary people received no such distinction. Although most found a resting place in a graveyard, some were unceremoniously buried in fields around Montreal, as a contemporary press account attests.

On Wednesday a Coroner's inquest was held on the body of Elizabeth Thompson wife of one Hibberts, a soldier of the 10th Reg. The verdict of the inquest was that she came by her death by intoxication and the effect of the cold. The body was found in one of the king's bateaux on the side of the river about 8 in the morning, when notice was immediately given to the Coroner, who by three o'clock in the afternoon had the Jury assembled. We have been informed, a certificate was asked of the Coroner to be presented to the Roman Catholic clergy, that the body might be interred in Christian like manner. Instead of a certificate, a reply was given, that all that was necessary would be to dig a hole in some place or other and put the body into it. The corpse, however, lay in the Bateau until 4 in the afternoon of Thursday, exposed to beasts and birds of prey, when Mr. F. Bouche, a Mr. Roy, and a woman, humanely deposited the body wrapped in a sheet, into a deal chest and interred it in a neighbouring field.[9]

Protestants of different denominations had a wide variety of burial rites and traditions. For members of the Church of England, burial in consecrated ground was important; consequently churchyard burial grounds were established when churches were built in colonial cities like Halifax and New York. In New York City, literally thousands of people had been buried in the churchyard of Trinity Church by the mid-nineteenth century. Although occasional conflicts arose over the rights of dissenting clergy to perform burial services in these Anglican churchyards, they were the usual burial places for Protestants. For their part, Presbyterians strongly opposed burial under churches or in church walls as well as bell-ringing or singing at funerals and burials. In the villages or countryside, many Protestants organized family lots or inter-denominational burial grounds. An isolated gravesite, in a farmer's field, for example, could be specifically consecrated by an Anglican clergyman, as the following account of the burial of an infant by an Anglican missionary in 1852 suggests.

I reached a place at which I had made an arrangement of the previous day to turn aside from my round in order to inter the corpse of an infant child. Arrived at the school house in which the funeral service was to be performed I awaited the coming of the parents and friends of the deceased child with the body. Upon their arrival the customary psalms and lessons were read and an address given, according to the almost universal practice of the country, from Amos iv.12. The body was then committed to the ground in a corner of the farm belonging to the family, not far from the schoolhouse, the same place I had sometime before interred the mortal remains of the Grandmother of the infant. A strikingly picturesque spot is that sequestered burying place, and one which could not fail to carry back the mind of the observer to primitive times and remind him of the case of Macpelah (I think I have it right), the burying place of the Patriarchs and their wives. Sheltered upon one side by a craggy rock surmounted by a few stunted bushes, the lofty eminence upon which this unwonted burial took place was situated commanded on all other sides a most extensive view of the surrounding country – comprizing for the greater part large tracts of the un-reclaimed forest dotted here and there by distant settlements. Two or three different mountains at various distances bounded the prospect and gave a variety of light and shade. The sun shone brightly forth, the clear blue sky overhead broken by intervals by fleecy clouds and the balmy air of coming spring imparted an inexpressible feeling of elevated enjoyment and could not fail to raise the reflective mind in contemplation to that bright and glorious world beyond the grave and which by the Redeemer's death and resurrection is opened out to each believer.[10]

By necessity, Protestant burial in Quebec City and Montreal was different from that in other cities in the

Abandoned Free Presbyterian Church, La Guerre, Huntingdon County.

This photo, taken in 2000, emphasizes the out-migration of Protestants in rural Quebec and gives poignancy to the issue of perpetual care.

British Empire. Established as French and Catholic, Montreal in the period of New France had five different Catholic burial grounds.[11] After the British capture of Montreal in 1760, the city's most important burial ground was inside the walls between St François Xavier Street and what is today Victoria Square. There was, of course, no Anglican Church in pre-Conquest Montreal, and until they built Christ Church on Notre Dame Street in the first decade of the nineteenth century, Anglicans worshipped in the Jesuit chapel. The only permanent Protestant church in the city in the 1790s, when discussions began of establishing a Protestant burial ground, was the St Gabriel Street Presbyterian Church. Since it was without a churchyard, Protestants, in the decades between the Conquest and the opening of their own cemetery in 1799, were buried in a section of the Catholic burial ground near the present corner of St Jacques and St Pierre Streets.[12]

By the 1790s, overcrowding and public health concerns about contamination from the burial grounds within the walls led local politicians to consider constructing cemeteries outside the city walls. Both the Catholic community and the city's small Jewish congregation looked to sites among the orchards and estates in the St Antoine suburb. The Roman Catholic or St Antoine burial ground was built on what is now Dominion Square.[13] At the same time, the city witnessed a sharpening of ethnic and religious self-consciousness. The growing wealth of the city's Protestant merchants reinforced their determination to impose British culture and institutions on Montreal – what Murray Greenwood has aptly called the "garrison mentality" of the English elite.[14] Thus, by late in the decade, representatives from the principal Protestant denominations formed a committee to examine establishment of a burial ground outside the city walls.

In 1797, committee members James McGill, John Richardson, Thomas Forsyth, Charles Blake, and Isaac Winslow Clarke, all prominent leaders in the Anglican and Presbyterian communities, paid £200 for a site north of the city's walls in the St Laurent suburb (the present site of the Guy Favreau federal government complex on René Lévesque Boulevard). Described later by the *Montreal Gazette* as "decent and convenient," the Protestant Burial Ground was initially a small site measuring 161 feet by 262 feet with access via a lane from Craig Street.[15] By 1824 it had been enlarged to include important frontage and access via Dorchester Street, and in 1842 it was expanded again.

Of great significance in the structure of the new burial ground was its inter-denominationalism, a goal commonly sought by Protestant leaders. In Glasgow, for example, the

Necropolis was established by Merchants' House as a non-denominational cemetery and its first burial was of a Jew. In Montreal, this broad conception of a burial ground as an institution that might serve to integrate and unify the community, whatever the deep differences among faiths, meant that individuals would be buried in grounds "common to all Protestants of Montreal and the vicinity." Drawn originally from the Anglican and Presbyterian congregations to which a Wesleyan Methodist was later added, trustees were named from among subscribers to lots: as vacancies occurred on the board, the trustees themselves appointed successors from among lot-holders. In 1801 a chapel, or "burial house" for "the convenience of persons attending funerals," was constructed on the grounds.[16] Again, this was apparently used by all denominations.

From the opening of the burial grounds, important Protestants moved to acquire lots and to transfer their loved ones from the old burial ground within the walls. When judge and burial-ground trustee Arthur Davidson died in 1807, he was buried in the new ground. His first wife, a McCord, had, at age twenty-three, predeceased him in 1790 and, as her headstone reads, her remains had been "interred within the walls." In 1811 she was moved to a grave alongside her husband in the new grounds. A half century later, her remains would be moved yet again, this time to Mount Royal.[17]

The Protestant Burial Ground was just one institution established by an expanding Protestant Montreal. The city's Protestant leadership, in organizing a hospital, schools, churches, and asylums, wanted to signal the presence of their community, its stability, persistence, and history. These leaders looked to institutions in which they could codify behaviour, manners, dress, and the relations expected in refined society. In particular, the new burial ground would pay respect to deceased elders while protecting the living

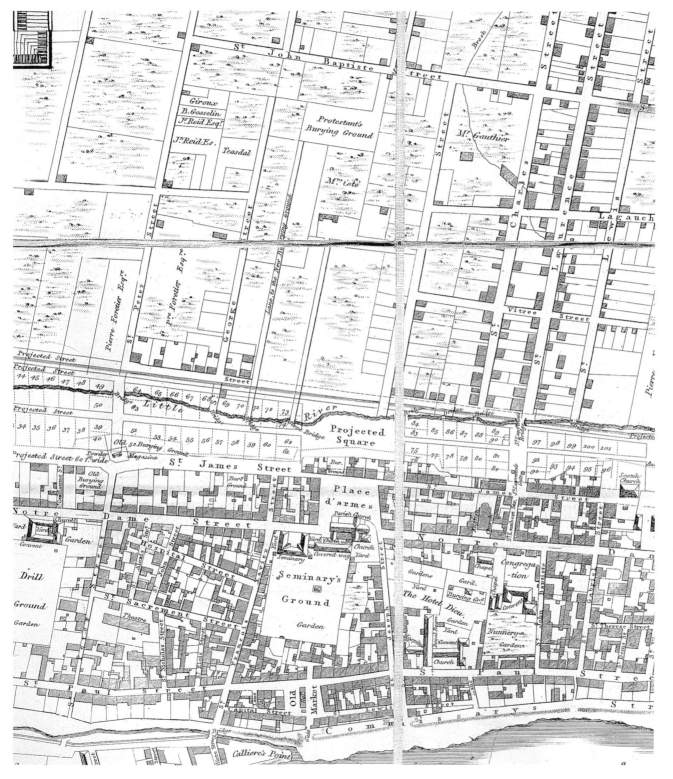

Location of the Protestants' burying ground, 1815.

Montreal's Protestants opened their burial ground north of the walled town in 1799. It can be seen here near the top of the image, a vacant piece of land reached via a narrow road marked "Lane to the New Burying Ground." In 1815 the trustees purchased the land immediately north of the original burial ground, doubling its size and giving them an entrance on Dorchester Street (then known as St Jean Baptiste Street). Until the opening of this burial ground in 1799, Prostestants had been buried in the "Old Burying Ground" just within the fortifications near what became St James Street (now St Jacques Street), visible here on the middle left. Note also the "Church Yard" lying beside Notre Dame Church, on the south side of Place d'armes.

through a growing sensitivity to public health and hygiene issues. It would also emphasize the importance of Memory in a changing urban society and serve to instruct the public in moral, religious, and cultural issues ranging from architecture, to epitaph texts and verdure. The burial ground was on the fringe of the city – a new semi-public space open to the public for visits but subject to rules drawn up by the trustees. Its regulations spoke to the trustees' concern for order and decorum; the presiding clergy were reminded of their obligation to maintain authority in the grounds, to control burial ceremonies, and to keep accurate statistics. No burial could occur without the presence of a Protestant minister: he was to officiate and to enter the burial in the official register of his church. Entries were to include the day of death, the occupation of the deceased, and the signatures of two witnesses. Although the Roman Catholic and Anglican Churches had particular privilege in Lower Canada as established churches – that is, as officially recognized to perform civil functions such as marriage or burial – legislation passed over the first decades of the nineteenth century enabled Jewish, Baptist, Methodist, Congregationalist, and Presbyterian congregations in Montreal to keep burial registers.[18]

In the past, as today, regulating the flow of funerals, assuring a disciplined labour force, and controlling activities on the grounds are essential to the well-run cemetery: one can easily imagine the distress of a funeral party arriving to find preparations incomplete. Nineteenth-century cemetery manuals urged sextons to keep a grave open at all times to avert such emergencies. "To prevent confusion," ministers were to give the sexton or superintendent twenty-four hours' notice of a burial.[19] Successive cholera and typhoid epidemics shortened the notice required for burials, which by 1853 had been reduced to eight hours "daylight notice."[20] The burial ground's chapel was to remain locked; officiating clergy obtained the keys at the registrar's office in the old grounds. Collecting fees from the bereaved could be difficult, especially once the body was in the ground and the family had dispersed. For this reason, regulations stipulated the payment of burial fees in advance.

While family lots for the monied remained available in the newly constructed burial ground, the provision of graves for the Protestant poor was an important, ongoing issue. Historical myth may attribute almost universal wealth to English Montrealers, but the trustees, bound to make the burial ground "common to all Protestants," faced the reality of burying ever larger numbers of indigent Protestants. While there was never any question of shirking this responsibility, two practical issues had to be considered – who in the Protestant community was to shoulder the actual costs, and what was the definition of a minimal burial? Responding to questions that would persist into the twentieth century, trustees had to decide if pauper burial included an individual grave, a religious service at graveside, and a grave marker or mound of dirt that family members could recognize.

In October 1818, a common grave was dug in preparation for Protestant paupers who would die over the coming winter. This large, eight-foot-deep trench was constructed to hold two tiers of coffins. A temporary shed kept snow out of the hole. With the spring thaw, the common grave was filled in and the shed moved to the next winter's site.[21] Burying several bodies on top of each other in a single grave was another acceptable space saver. Where graves could be dug to a depth of six feet three inches, two tiers of adults could be buried in a single grave and, if necessary, a child added on top.[22] When paupers could be identified as belonging to a specific congregation, their burial costs were assumed by the members of that church. In 1816, for example, the elders of St Andrew's Presbyterian Church met to purchase a cemetery lot for burial of their poor parishioners. Yet, whatever their social necessity, free burials went against the Protestant grain of individual responsibility and were granted only on issuance of a certificate of pauperism by a minister or elder whose congregation then assumed the costs of the grave and gravedigger.[23]

Although industrialization is often dated as a later phenomenon, the construction of canals, large churches, and manufactures in the post-Napoleonic period dramatically changed the face of cities like Glasgow and Montreal, bringing them immigrants, a more mobile labour force, and men, women, and youth workers without family networks. In these expanding industrial cities, workers, ex-soldiers, and other poor died without any formal church affiliation. In Glasgow, the dying were taken to the Royal Infirmary and, when dead, were laid out in common pits covered by planks: "the stench emitted in hot weather was insufferable."[24] In Montreal, by contrast, to address this new social need, clergy from four Protestant churches, including St Andrew's, met in 1820 to establish a burial fund for the poor, and in 1823, St Andrew's voted £7.10.0 as its share for burying Protestants unclaimed from the morgue of the Montreal General Hospital.[25] The modesty of that sum can be judged in relation to other burial costs in the same decade. Family lots in the Old Burying Grounds cost £3 10s, a single grave £1. At the more distant Papineau Burial Ground, family lots sold for £2, large single graves for 13s., and small graves for 7s. 6d. Adult graves were to be at least four feet deep and a child's grave at least three feet. The superintendent was authorized to charge 2s. 6d. for a burial and 5s. for installing a headstone.[26] In addition to these expenses were gravediggers' fees for a variety of services.

The mortality of the Protestant poor overwhelmed measures of open winter pits, multiple burials in a single grave, and collaborative benevolence among different denominations. Opening a new Protestant burial ground, essentially for humble Protestants, offered the dual attraction of inexpensive land and of distancing the flagrantly poor from established lot-owners. As they would do a century later in opening Hawthorn-Dale Cemetery, the trustees looked east to cheaper land. In 1814, a Military Burial Ground had been established on Papineau Road; a year later, the Protestant trustees bought the adjacent site for £400. Near the present ramps to the Jacques Cartier Bridge, the "new" burial ground – commonly known as the Papineau Burial Ground – measured 425 feet by 158 feet.[27] Within just a few years, the demographics of Protestant death rendered both sites insufficient.

The cholera epidemic of 1832 claimed 1,950 victims in Montreal and brought issues of public health, burial space, and social responsibility to the trustees' doorstep. Within

Burial costs (1825).

Adult graves were to be at least four feet deep and a child's grave at least three feet. Aside from gravedigging fees, families paid £3 10 for a lot in the Old Burial Ground and £1 for a single grave. At the more distant Papineau Ground, family lots sold for £2, single graves for 13s. and children's graves for 7s. 6d. The superintendent also charged 2s. 6d. for a burial and 5s. for installation of a headstone.

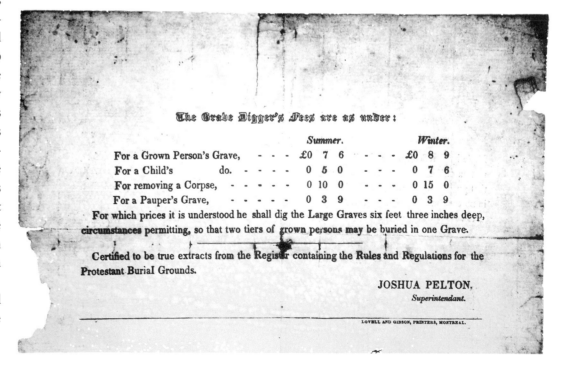

The Grave Digger's Fees are as under:

	Summer.		Winter.
For a Grown Person's Grave, - - -	£0 7 6	- - - -	£0 8 9
For a Child's do. - - - -	0 5 0	- - -	0 7 6
For removing a Corpse, - - - - -	0 10 0	- - -	0 15 0
For a Pauper's Grave, - - - - -	0 3 9	- - -	0 3 9

For which prices it is understood he shall dig the Large Graves six feet three inches deep, circumstances permitting, so that two tiers of grown persons may be buried in one Grave.

Certified to be true extracts from the Register containing the Rules and Regulations for the Protestant Burial Grounds.

JOSHUA PELTON,
Superintendant.

LOVELL AND GIBSON, PRINTERS, MONTREAL.

Cholera Plague, Quebec, c. 1832.

Epidemics such as cholera and typhoid spread rapidly, particularly in urban areas. The poor – who lived close together and had poor diets and rudimentary water and sanitation – were especially vulnerable. Joseph Légaré's painting shows the loading of Quebec City cholera victims onto carts bound for cholera pits. Cholera and typhoid epidemics in the 1850s, smallpox in 1885, and Spanish influenza in 1918 were the most important epidemics faced by Mount Royal Cemetery.

two years, cholera struck again (882 victims), as it did in 1849 (with 496 dead), 1851, 1852, and 1854. In 1847, the worst typhoid epidemic in the city's history killed 3,862. Montreal's burial crisis stemming from epidemics mirrored that of other cities. In Quebec City, a cholera burying ground for Catholics, later St Patrick's Cemetery, was hastily opened in 1832.[28] In Scotland, Glasgow witnessed 158 cholera deaths in a single day; in England, authorities in York opened a cholera burial-ground in which 185 victims were buried in the cholera season of 1832.

In the 1832 epidemic, Montreal's first cholera case was detected on 9 June. Three days later, over a hundred bodies had been piled in the Catholic burial ground and doctors threatened to burn them if they were not buried within the hour. Volunteers, hastily organized by priests, dug pits into which bodies were dumped by carters hired by public health officials. On 19 June, the worst day of the epidemic, 149 people were buried in what medical student Joseph Workman described as cholera's "death carnival."[29] In this haste, burial certificates and reliable death statistics often depended on the memory of carters and the record keeping of frantic burial-ground officials. Because of the fear of contaminating mourners, public health regulations suspended funerals by denying the entry of epidemic victims into churches for funerals: to encourage what one law called "speedy" interments, even graveside religious services were suspended along with the ringing of funeral bells.[30]

With the city's Protestant and Catholic burial grounds unable to meet demand, plague pits were opened near the emigrant sheds in Point St Charles. Eyewitnesses, like young immigrant Alfred Perry, had dreadful memories of burial scenes during the epidemic. Soon after the family's arrival in Montreal his father fell ill with cholera. He was sinking under the disease [when] a man with a cart came to the house and insisted he was dead, and, in spite of my mother's remonstrances, carried him away, put him in the cart and conveyed him to Point St Charles where a trench had been dug for the burial of immigrants. Mrs. Perry followed, still protesting that her husband was not dead. He was just about to be flung into the trench when he moved and was found to be alive. While the party was returning to town, Mr. Perry died. The only way Mrs. Perry could persuade another carter to take her husband's body to the English burial ground was to give him the suit from the corpse.[31]

The burial pit near the immigrant sheds was reopened for typhoid victims in 1847. Newspapers reported that 437 people, 65 per cent of whom were immigrants, died in Montreal in the week ending 24 July. While 80 immigrants were accommodated in the Protestant and Catholic burial grounds during this epidemic, at least 202 were buried in the Point St Charles pits; grave sites for the remainder are unknown. Near the Victoria Bridge, a stone marker denoting the common grave of 3,862 Irish immigrants can still be seen.[32]

These epidemics only accentuated the inadequacy of the city's burial grounds. In 1843, the Protestant trustees voted £12.10 to construct a "dead house" at the Papineau Burial Ground "for the reception of Strangers dying at Hotels or on Board Steam Boats."[33] Two years later, worried authorities reported that only 125 unoccupied lots were left in the old burial ground and 20 in the Papineau Burial Ground.[34] Nor was the problem just demographic. In the last two decades before construction of the Mount Royal Cemetery, the inability of religious and burial-ground authorities to provide a simple ceremony or a grave raised sensitive issues concerning class harmony, the competence of the city's Protestant fathers, and individual entitlement to decency in death. Hasty and Sunday burials were a particular source of conflict. In 1831, the superintendent of the Protestant Burial Grounds, responding to pressure from the clergy, informed the public that Sunday burials were henceforth forbidden "except during hot weather in the summer season ... and in such a case no funeral shall be permitted."[35] In a period when the largely Protestant medical community was professionalizing, expanding, and raising fees, newspaper cartoons began mocking the impotence of the medical establishment in combating epidemics. Reports in the local English press of the gruesome burial of three children in the same grave raised unexpressed fears of anonymous burial and disrespect for the vulnerable, the poor, and the sick.[36] Nor did the bereaved easily accept the disfiguration that resulted from regulations requiring that the cholera dead be covered with twenty-five pounds of lime. Rules concerning churchyard burials were even more stringent: twenty pounds of slaked lime was to be placed in the bottom of the coffin and another twenty pounds in the winding sheet.[37]

The increasing disfavour in which the old burial grounds was held did not stem only from the inadequacy of it size in the face of multiple deadly epidemics. As the St Laurent suburb expanded around it, the burial ground came to be used as park, playground, and pedestrian shortcut. Given the lack of public space in the nineteenth-century city, the community treated the burial ground as recreational space and pedestrian thoroughfare, but Victorian sensibilities were offended by such activities in a place supposedly dedicated to death, mourning, and decorum. Yet, even practices surrounding death and interment could

The Protestant Burial Ground.

Opened in 1799, Montreal's original Protestant burial ground was closed in 1854, two years after the opening of the new cemetery on Mount Royal. The old ground's crowded graves and congested appearance, so distasteful to Victorians, is evident from this undated photograph, probably from the 1860s. Although many families removed bodies from the old ground for reburial in family lots in the new cemetery, thousands of graves and monuments remained when the cemetery was dismantled in the 1870s to make way for Dufferin Square, a municipal park. The small stone building at centre-left is the mortuary chapel, built in 1801. Even after the closure of the grounds the building was used as an office by the Mount Royal Cemetery's registrar, Joshua Pelton. On his retirement in 1858 it became the first home of the Church of St John the Evangelist, and, in 1869, it was used – to the horror of many – as a school.

generate the disapproval of the authorities. The cemetery's unique connections with death and horror and its existence as a largely unsupervised public space could encourage risky behaviour. Funeral parties sometimes lingered, and graveside wakes could be riotous:

We are informed that on Monday morning, a shot fired from the Old Burying Ground passed through the window of the house of Mr. Ralston, 54 Chenneville Street. Mr. Ralston proceeded at once to the ground, and saw a man, whom he has every reason to believe, was the cause of the accident. That person, however, denied having fired at all. We trust that this may prove a caution to parties engaged in watching the graves of their friends, for it is within our knowledge, that shots are constantly fired, for the purpose, probably, of discharging the arms, but also with but little regard to the direction the ball may take.[38]

Aesthetic aspects of the graveyard also offended Victorian attitudes to purity and cleanliness. The new awareness of odours illustrates changing sensitivities.[39] Along with municipal regulations controlling the stench from cesspools and pigs, the poor drainage of overcrowded burial grounds came to public attention. In Saint John, New Brunswick, incorporators of the Rural Cemetery Company (1848) spoke "painfully" of the "unsightly and confined spots" and of the "crowded conditions of the Cemeteries now in use." Across the continent in British Columbia, citizens in Victoria objected to the smell of the Hudson's Bay Company graveyard, in which "remains partially exposed are exceedingly offensive to the passers by and to persons residing and holding property in the neighbourhood … These remains becoming more and more decomposed as the heat of summer increases are likely to infect the air, produce malaria, and breed disease."[40] American authorities wrote of "masses of putrefaction in one spot" near where "thousands of citizens sleep and contract diseases," and they didn't hesitate to associate foulness with race: "A southerly breeze blowing over a too densely packed graveyard towards a city must be not only offensive but unhealthy. If inquiry were instituted in Philadelphia, it would be found, beyond all question, that the black population are interred in such a manner as to render the air which blows over their graves extremely unwholesome."[41]

Graverobbing was yet another indignity associated with the old burial grounds contributing to the impression that they were dangerous places and that the Protestant dead deserved a more respectful setting. As part of their anatomy courses, medical students were required to practice dissection on human cadavers. By legislation of 1844, the destitute – people who died in the streets, jails, hospitals, or other institutions – might be delivered to a medical school unless claimed within twenty-four hours by relatives or friends. The act also allowed that, if the person had directed it, the body should be "decently interred."[42] In Montreal, where McGill University's Faculty of Medicine dated from 1829, an inspector of anatomy was to supervise the transfers, to collect the $5 fee for each body delivered to a medical school, and to provide official forms to the deceased's parish priest or Protestant minister that would replace the normal certificate that appeared in burial registers. Under the same act, medical schools were to ensure the "decent" internment of "used bodies."

This legal supply of cadavers rarely met demand, and until the 1890s, when the expanding use of embalming changed pathological practices, medical students in Montreal – or their suppliers, at prices ranging from thirty to fifty dollars a body – resorted to graverobbing. Bodies in transit that disappeared mysteriously from train stations, corpses dug up from fresh graves, and the contents of coffins that arrived at the cemetery with ballast instead of human remains, were all part of a night trade that culminated at the back doors of medical schools in Kingston, Toronto, and Montreal. An ability to obtain bodies might figure in a student's recommendation. A rural doctor in Ontario praised two of his students not only for their skills, but for the fact that "both seemed fond of the odour of a graveyard and I assure you will be among the most expert in obtaining dissecting material."[43] In the 1850s, theft of bodies from the Montreal General Hospital was of such proportions that, until it built a secure morgue, the hospital asked cemetery authorities to open coffins arriving from the hospital, particularly in winter, to ensure that their human cargo had not been replaced by rocks.[44] The delayed putrefaction of corpses in winter made it high season for McGill students. The preferred targets were the barely covered graves of the poor as well as the area's dead houses, with their unprotected frozen contents awaiting spring burial: "The dead poor, not being able to pay expenses of the vaults, were buried in winter in very shallow graves in a certain corner of [Notre-Dame-des-Neiges] cemetery, and those freshly made graves were marked by the guardian [in return for a bribe] and students went up at night, dis interred the bodies, buried usually the previous morning, removed all clothing, wrapped them in blankets and tobogganed them down Côte des Neiges Hill."[45] In January 1861, Montreal's chief constable, armed with a warrant, searched the McGill Medical School for six bodies stolen from graves in Longueuil: Dr. William Edward Scott, Professor of Anatomy at McGill, was subpoenaed to explain in court what he knew of the matter.[46]

In Montreal, burial ground president Judge John Samuel McCord was active in a broad range of civic issues that concerned beautification, respectability, and public health. A member of the city's sanitation committee, he was concerned by flooding in the Protestant Burial Ground and of the dangers of contamination: "no one who has seen the imperfect drainage of present ground," he wrote, "could hesitate" to support a new cemetery.[47] His personal papers include an 1852 parliamentary report on urban burial: the parliamentarians had asked witnesses if they had "known coffins to be burnt or removed and the bones they contained deposited elsewhere, or sold, to clear ground for further graves." "What kinds of diseases," they continued, "is the gas diffused from dead bodies most likely to produce, whether inhaled with the atmosphere, or drank with the water which has passed through a burial ground?" Parliamentarians were concerned that burial-ground gases might lead to drinking among gravediggers, and witnesses were asked if "the inhaling of the noxious gas escaping from crowded graveyards has any moral influence, inducing the use of stimulants by gravediggers."[48] These concerns for hygiene and efficient burial had clear links to the sanitarian movement associated in England with reformers such as Edwin Chadwick.

One result of the civic concerns of people such as McCord was the migration of the wealthy to estates on the slopes of Mount Royal. Completion in the city centre of the mammoth parish church of Notre Dame in the 1820s and, two decades later, of its Irish counterpart, St Patrick's, in the St Laurent suburb reminded Montreal Protestants of the city's deep religious fault lines. Along with these expanding Catholic institutions, Montreal had experienced the growth of French-Canadian nationalism, the rebellions of 1837–38, and development of the Saint-Jean Baptiste Society. For their part, English Montrealers saw the crushing of the Patriotes as a major victory and, in the 1840s, with wind in their sails and money in their pockets, they exerted their cultural preferences, and their vision of beauty and the sacred, on the city's landscape.

The imagination of English Montrealers owed much to British and American reading material, which was easily available in bookstores and libraries, and through periodicals and reading societies. Popular among such imports, particularly British touring books and alpine club literature, were accounts of the Highlands, Wales, and the Alps. In Montreal, the mountain emulated these European models and, at the same time, became associated with a northern, Anglo-Saxon element of an emerging English-Canadian nationalism. Soon after his marriage, John Samuel McCord, president of the Protestant Burial Ground, was swept up in this passion for Mount Royal. Eschewing the commercial district and the family home on the flats near the Lachine Canal, he built a summer home, which soon became his permanent residence, on Mount Royal. Whereas his father, Thomas – himself a trustee of the Protestant Burial Ground in 1815 – had used his estate in a practical way, producing vegetables and hay for consumption, John Samuel had a different image of masculine refinement and domesticity. Even as he commanded the Montreal militia in tracking down the Patriotes in 1837, he was expressing another, more domestic, form of manhood in his flower beds, his channelling of the mountain brook on his property, and his construction of a garden gazebo. McCord and his peers – with their culture of Britishness, their sense of social responsibility to their lessers, and their attraction to the area of Mount Royal – were critical forces in shaping the Mount Royal Cemetery.[49]

The effects of the Romantic movement on the development of Mount Royal Cemetery are clear. McCord, his wife, Anne Ross, and their neighbours were part of a colonial world influenced by British letters. As young people they read Walter Scott's *Ivanhoe* and studied the paintings of landscape artists such as John Constable. William Wordsworth was a particular favorite. The McCords chose their estate's classical name, Temple Grove, from a Wordsworth

John Samuel McCord

Anne Ross McCord

poem and shared the sense of beauty and sacredness that the poet perceived in Nature. In poems like "Tintern Abbey," Wordsworth gave huge support to the rural cemetery ideal, advocating the removal of graveyards to natural and isolated places where, in peaceful, well-drained, and safe surroundings, the dead could be honoured and moral lessons imparted to the living:

… that serene and blessed mood,
In which … the breath of this corporeal frame,
And even the motion of our human blood,
Almost suspended, we are laid asleep
In body, and become a living soul:
While with an eye made quiet by the power
Of harmony, and the deep power of joy,
We see into the life of things.[50]

Table 1 The establishment of rural cemeteries

Name of cemetery	City	Date of establishment
Père Lachaise	Paris	1804
Mount Auburn	Cambridge, MA	1831
Necropolis	Glasgow	1833
Laurel Hill	Philadelphia	1836
Green-Wood	Brooklyn	1838
Highgate	London	1839
Albany Rural Cemetery	Albany, NY	1841
Swan Point	Providence, RI	1847
Mount Hermon	Quebec City	1848
Cataraqui Cemetery	Kingston, ON	1850
Mount Royal	Montreal	1852
Notre-Dame-des-Neiges	Montreal	1855
Graceland Cemetery	Chicago	1861

In profound cultural ways, these new cemeteries built on urban fringes and euphemistically called "rural cemeteries" reflected a Romantic vision of landscape. In the late eighteenth century, garden designer Capability Brown had contoured a soft British vista that emphasized the cheerful and soothing, the grove and the winding road, the slope and the pond. This vision of an inspirational Nature was central to the rural cemetery movement. Cemeteries like Mount Royal were the first recreational areas designed to inspire city dwellers: their mission was moral and educational. Writing *The Layout, Planting and Management of Cemeteries in 1843*, landscape gardener John Claudius Loudon described them as schools "of instruction in architecture, sculpture, landscape gardening, arboriculture, botany, and in those important parts of general gardening, neatness, order and high keeping."[51]

Mount Auburn Cemetery, founded in 1831 in Cambridge, Massachusetts, was the immediate inspiration for the Mount Royal Cemetery; its twisting paths that followed the natural landscape, its park-like qualities, and its streets named after trees and plants, would be copied directly in Montreal. Modelled on the English garden, Mount Auburn was established by the Massachusetts Horticultural Society as a tranquil setting for the dead and, equally important, a place of consolation for the living. With its five artificial ponds, its miles of carriage and pedestrian paths, and its attractive rural location near Harvard University, Mount Auburn was laid out as an "ornamental burial place" and a "garden." Its setting was enhanced by a "cottage" for its resident gardener.[52] Hugely influential in the rural cemetery movement in America, it was described by Andrew Jackson Downing, the first professional consulted by the Montrealers, as the "Athens of New England." In its advertisements, Mount Auburn

View of Montreal from Mount Royal, c. 1840.

Commissioned by cemetery president John Samuel McCord and drawn from the site of his estate, this James Duncan painting with its vista, classicism, and landscaped nature could have formed a model for the rural cemetery that would be built on the other side of the mountain.

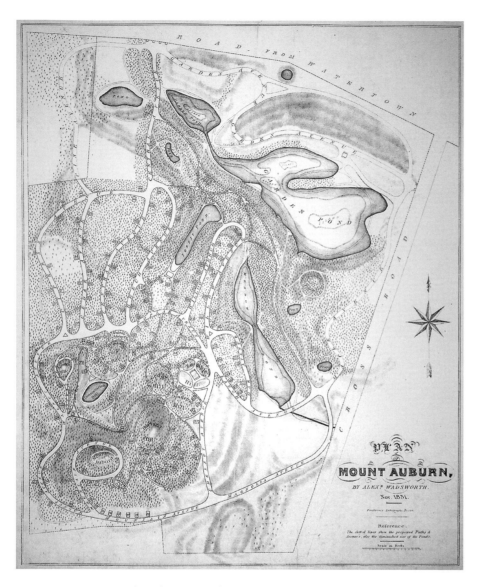

Plan of Mount Auburn Cemetery, 1832.

Mount Auburn's layout formed the prototype for most North American rural cemeteries, including Mount Royal. Designed by Henry A.S. Dearborn, it featured a utopian nature landscaped with ornamental ponds, curved roads, and peaceful burial terraces.

described itself as a place of "beauty" in which the "repulsive features" of earlier cemeteries had been removed.[53]

Trustees of the Protestant cemetery in Montreal were well aware of Mount Auburn and of the rural cemetery movement that had begun in France and then spread to Britain, the United States, and Canada. In 1847, the year the cemetery company was chartered in Montreal, James Smillie, a Scots engraver who had lived in Quebec before moving to New York in 1830, published illustrated volumes of Mount Auburn and Green-Wood Cemeteries. About 1845, the artist William Bartlett, well known for his Canadian landscapes, published an engraving of the Forest Pond at Mount Auburn.[54] These works found ready Canadian markets as city local politicians in several cities planned new cemeteries. In Kingston, the Cataraqui Cemetery was chartered as a non-profit corporation in 1850. "Necessary to the health of the city of Kingston" and planned as "an ornament to the neighbourhood," the cemetery was built on rolling hills on the city's outskirts, incorporating the ponds, superintendent's cottage, and winding roads characteristic of rural cemeteries.[55]

In Montreal, John Samuel McCord's functions as corresponding secretary of the Natural History Society, and president of both the Horticultural Society and the Protestant Burial Ground ensured his familiarity with the Massachusetts Horticultural Society and its development of Mount Auburn. He corresponded with officials at the Toronto Necropolis; from Quebec City, where his brother lived, he received a copy of the regulations of newly established Mount Hermon Cemetery as well as the suggestion to take the publications of the Mount Auburn and Green-Wood cemeteries as "guides."[56] Located four kilometres outside the walls of Quebec, Mount Hermon's terraced thirty-two acre site featured picturesque views of the St Lawrence River and distant mountains. For Protestants

William Bartlett engraving of Forest Pond, Mount Auburn Cemetery, 1839.

Books on rural cemeteries found ready markets. Works by engravers such as W.H. Bartlett and James Smillie illustrating Mount Auburn and Green-Wood cemeteries represented the coffee-table books of their day.

of all denominations, its grounds were purchased in 1848 and a year later the cemetery's plan was laid out by West Point professor David B. Douglass, already well known for his design of New York's Green-Wood Cemetery and the Albany Rural Cemetery. Debate in Quebec over construction of an Anglican chapel on the grounds (it was ultimately built across the street from the cemetery) and consecration of separate ground in Mount Hermon for Anglicans was instructional for the Montrealers as were its tastefully designed gates and superintendent's cottage.

At Mount Auburn, the Massachusetts Horticultural Society envisaged their cemetery as the site of an institute to train gardeners: in Glasgow, officials from the Royal Botanic Garden were consulted in the laying out of the city's Necropolis.[57] An 1846 cemetery manual published by one of the founders of Philadelphia's influential Laurel Hill Cemetery described the new cemeteries as "historical records," the tomb as "a chronicler of taste," and the setting as "the labourers' only library."[58] Like the grounds of McGill University, a new cemetery might serve as a natural laboratory to instruct the public in subjects ranging from botany to behaviour and religion. Significantly, the first Mount Royal charter utilized the terms "public cemetery and garden." For his part, cemetery president John Samuel McCord saw the cemetery as an important educational site for mourners, visitors, and his own children.

TWO

ESTABLISHING A "RURAL"
CEMETERY

Among anglophone Montrealers, the collapse of the French-Canadian nationalist movement in the abortive rebellions of 1837–38 strongly confirmed British cultural superiority. Such feelings were expressed most symbolically and given political form in the report of Lord Durham in 1839, which advocated the union of Upper and Lower Canada and the assimilation of the French Canadians. In trade, the professions, and industry, Protestant Montrealers remained forcefully in control, and their wealth and sense of identity encouraged expansion of institutions like McGill University, the Montreal General Hospital, the Protestant Orphan Asylum, the Ladies Benevolent Society, the Natural History Society, several ethnic societies, and the denominational churches. And yet, behind the spires, estates, and trappings of respectable Protestant society, was deep concern as to the permanence of the social order they had put in place. For its part, the mother country, rethinking mercantilism, the cost of empire, and changing relationships with the United States, shocked English Montreal with its questioning of the principle of preferential trade with its colonies and with its willingness to consider political reorganization in British North America. English Canadians also had to adjust to the realities of American economic power and republicanism. In Montreal itself, as we have seen, epidemics, immigration, and rapid urbanization were tearing at traditional hierarchies. The uneasy democratization of Lower Canadian society in the 1840s was marked by election riots, the stoning of the governor general's coach, the development of a movement advocating annexation to the United States, and in 1849 the sacking of the parliament buildings for the United Province of Canada – that political entity spawned by the Durham report – which were located in Montreal. The turbulence troubled the city fathers concerned with maintaining order and social peace. Thoughtful observers such as judge John Samuel McCord and industrialist John Redpath were concerned by what they interpreted as the breakdown of traditional authority and by the relevance of observations such as the following by John Stuart Mill: "the masses do not now take their opinions from dignitaries in Church or State, from ostensible leaders or from books."[1]

Religious and ethnic struggles continued to reverberate. While an older generation led by Louis-Joseph Papineau may have been spent, younger nationalists such as Louis-Hippolyte LaFontaine and George-Étienne Cartier were testing the political waters after 1841, looking for means to capitalize on their control of the French-Canadian vote.

Building on the city's overwhelming Catholic majority, successive Roman Catholic bishops of Montreal constructed competing social and educational institutions. Important among these would be the new Catholic cemetery, Notre-Dames-des-Neiges. An older generation of Catholic hierarchy had been more French-born, more aristocratic, and more willing to cooperate with British authorities. By the 1840s religious riots, attempts to proselytize the "other," and intolerance from both Orangemen and Papal Zouaves challenged longstanding alliances among the English and French-speaking elites.

Given the sacred, civil, and familial functions of burial grounds, building a cemetery was a critical moment in defining a community: space had to be attributed, collaboration among religious partners achieved, and rules established. All this had to be done even as the state expanded its authority in jurisdictions previously controlled by religious authorities – education, colonization, and social services like asylums and prisons. Through codification of the civil law, for example, the state was increasing its visibility in matters concerning the family and marriage. The cemetery was one possible way to offset the intrusion of the state into matters with public and private implications. If established as a private company, it could serve to impose a Protestant moral and social vision on urban society.

Protestant leaders in Montreal faced unique religious and political circumstances. In comparison to Toronto, where Protestant culture easily dominated, and Quebec City, where Roman Catholicism had only minor demographic challenge from the Church of England, Montreal's church spires were permanent reminders of competing visions. In addition its expanding Catholic infrastructure, by 1852 the city counted five Anglican churches, six Presbyterian churches, two Congregationalist churches, three Methodist chapels, a Baptist church, and a Unitarian congregation.

Despite the trustees' sectarian convictions and their ambivalence to Catholicism, their burial grounds were marked by an inclusiveness that offered burial to all Protestants and, in a larger sense, to all Montrealers – suicides and the excommunicated, for example – who did not find place in a consecrated Catholic burial ground. Between 1822 and 1846, the trustees oversaw the burial of 10,273 bodies, most of whom were poor.[2] Faced with the need for new burial facilities, the Protestant trustees reached out for broad interdenominational collaboration, and for a brief moment in 1845 it seemed as if Roman Catholics would join Protestants and Jews in a broadly based cemetery project.

Protestantism was changing in mid-century Montreal. Anglicans, proud of their status as an established church, had been forced to water their wine: they had, for example, lost the battle to make McGill University a sectarian, Anglican institution. Other Protestant denominations were increasing their numbers and, as congregations like the Methodists became more urban and respectable, they downplayed their traditional evangelicalism. Cemetery trustees hoped that a rallying point for Protestants of all social backgrounds could be found in Romanticism, as represented in the landscape, physical forms, and monuments of a new cemetery. Protestant culture in the mid-Victorian period, William Westfall has suggested, "relied upon a highly romantic appeal to impress a grand system of moral ideals directly upon the heart of a society."[3]

Montreal's experience had parallels in other centres. New Brunswick's past had long been marked by battles between Saint John's Protestant and Catholic Irish. Despite this bloody tradition, founders of the Saint John Cemetery sent their prospectus to each of the city's Christian denominations asking for participation: while Anglicans, Presbyterians, Congregationalists, and Baptists agreed to participate, the Methodists and Catholics did not respond.[4] In New

Brunswick's other major centre, the Moncton Rural Cemetery was open to Christians of all faiths, although few Catholics chose to be buried in its unconsecrated ground.[5]

In Montreal, the impetus for a new burial ground on the model of the "rural cemetery" came from the trustees of the Protestant Burial Ground, who towards the end of 1845 began to promote the idea of building a new non-denominational cemetery well outside the city's suburbs. A spot should be chosen, the *Montreal Gazette* argued, that was far enough away from town to be out of sight and large enough to meet the needs of Montrealers for a century or more. Such a place "must be sought out to be seen; and where, when seen, it would be admired as much for its retired position as for its beauty."[6] This description clearly fits what was to become the Mount Royal Cemetery.

On 7 April 1846 the trustees of the Protestant Burial Ground met, as always, in the offices of the Montreal Assurance Company. This time, however, they were joined by A.A. David, representing the Jewish community, and A. Laroque, from the Roman Catholic parish church. Laroque's mission and official status are clear from minutes kept of the meeting: he had been "deputed by his church wardens … to meet this committee and co-operate with them in their endeavour to procure a sufficient public cemetery for the wants of the City."[7] The subsequent charter makes clear that the cemetery envisioned at these meetings would have been decentralized, with segregated sections in which Roman Catholics, Jews, Anglicans, and others might have consecrated land and their own chapels. Individual congregations could have named their own administrators and kept registers for their particular section. Over the spring and summer of 1846, ecumenism was apparent, with both David and Laroque joining their Protestant counterparts on a search committee for a suitable site.[8] In an important circular issued by the sexton of the Protestant Burial Ground, on 24 October 1846, ministers of the "various congregations of Montreal" were requested to name a lay member to attend a meeting concerning the establishment of a "Public Cemetery for the use of all denominations."[9]

As was the case in Saint John, it was at the point of actually establishing a cemetery company that collaboration with Roman Catholic officials collapsed. While the actual motives for Roman Catholic withdrawal are unclear, it may have been related to the church's deepening conservatism, to suspicions of Protestant ambitions to proselytize, and to hardening attitudes concerning interfaith relations. Minutes of a meeting of the Protestant Burial Ground trustees on 3 January 1847 emphasize the absence of the Roman Catholic representative and the decision to purchase a new cemetery site "for the use of the Protestant and Jewish congregations, combining ornament with salubrity and safety."[10] A site on the northeast side of the mountain was clearly favoured: the trustees asked city officials about opening Bleury Street north to Côte Ste Catherine Road and sent surveyor John Ostell to dig practice graves on a potential site.[11]

This activity took place in the face of an upstart, private company that promised to build a competing Protestant rural cemetery on the crest of Côte des Neiges Road. Although apparently not incorporated, the Mount Trafalgar Cemetery began seeking subscriptions in April 1846 and conducted at least eight burials between 8 August 1846 and the onset of winter. Supported by a prominent provisional board of directors that included John Young, Luther Holton, William Workman, William Lyman, and Jacob DeWitt, the owner of the sixteen-acre site, Frederick B. Matthews, announced that as resident superintendent and gardener, he would be "in constant attendance to ensure order and decorum." Advertisements reiterated the ideals of the rural cemetery: "The extreme natural beauty of the

West Mount, William Murray's estate, 1899.

Born in Scotland, Murray made his fortune in shipping and insurance. His estate stretched from Ste Catherine Street to the summit of Westmount and included what is today Murray Hill Park. His benevolent interests were a checklist of associational life in Protestant Montreal: the Montreal General Hospital, the Ladies Benevolent Society, and the presidency of both the St Andrew's Society and the Protestant House of Industry and Refuge. At the Cemetery, he was a Presbyterian trustee (1851–74), the first secretary (1851), and the third president (1858–74): for years, the trustees met in his offices at the Montreal Assurance Company. In 1877, two years after his death, the cemetery's highest summit was renamed Mount Murray in his honour. More recently the summit has been known as Outremont Mountain and Section Mountain View while the lower part remains Murray Hill.

situation, the vast picturesque and diversified views it affords, the present advanced artificial improvement of the grounds, with clumps of trees and plants, beds of flowers, natural terraces and winding path to the TRAFALGAR TOWER peering from the summit of the MOUNT, clothed with luxuriant arbours – contribute to render this spot peculiarly adapted to the purpose of a CEMETERY."[12]

Despite this setting and the two dwellings that might serve immediately as a chapel, superintendent's residence, and burial vault, the Mount Trafalgar Cemetery was not a success, and Matthews was soon trying to sell his property to the trustees of the Protestant Burial Ground for £3,000.[13] Though generous for a private estate, his sixteen acres was clearly too small to accommodate the needs of the city's growing Protestant population: "though a good thing," one commentator remarked of the Mount Trafalgar Cemetery, "there is too little of it."[14] Potential purchasers of lots may also have been put off by the private, for-profit nature of the new cemetery. The Protestant Burial Ground's project, by contrast, although to be organized as a joint-stock company, was linked to the reputation, built up over half a century, as a trust rather than a commercial enterprise.[15] As such, it seems to have struck the right chord in the Protestant community – a private enterprise, operating autonomously from the state, but geared to public service.

In July 1847, fifteen members of the Protestant elite – John Samuel McCord, John Torrance, John Smith, William Murray, James Ferrier, Benjamin Holmes, J.H. Maitland, George Moffatt, David Brown, John Redpath, John Molson, Benjamin Lyman, John Mathewson, John Birks, and Henry Vennor – chartered the Montreal Cemetery Company; joining them as the sixteenth founder was A.A. David, a Jew. Besides their prominence in trade, industry, politics, and the judiciary, these men shared membership in

Montreal's national and benevolent societies. Most had been members of the Constitutional Association, which had taken up arms to contest the Patriotes, and many served as militia officers in the rebellions of 1837. Many shared a wide range of amateur intellectual interests in science and the arts. As estate owners, several had strong interests in gardening, landscaping, and the work of the Montreal Horticultural Society.

For four years, the Montreal Cemetery Company charter remained inactive; it was only in 1851 that a sufficient number of subscriptions were raised to organize the company. Its board was formed in a different fashion from that of the Protestant Burial Ground, which historically had five trustees – two trustees representing the Anglicans, two the Presbyterians (one from St Andrew's and one from St Gabriel's), and one the Methodists. The opening meetings of the Montreal Cemetery Company in 1851 were attended by trustees delegated by denominations in proportion to the value of the subscriptions they held in the new cemetery. This structure gave the Presbyterians nine trustees, the Anglicans five, the Wesleyan Methodists two, the Congregationalists two, and the Baptists and Unitarians one each. The Jewish community had one trustee, on the basis of the payment of £3.6.8 for lots (1852), but the community was in the process of deciding whether or not to withdraw from the project. For most of this time their trustee, A.A. David, was the only Jewish lot-holder (his wife belonged to the Church of England) and effectively represented himself.[16] By 1853, he had left the board. At their meeting on 8 April 1851 the trustees convinced Judge McCord to transform his mandate at the Protestant Burial Ground into presidency of the new cemetery. With an active board, an experienced president, and £1,401 subscribed on its books, the company advertised that it was looking for a cemetery site.[17]

After rejecting several tenders for reasons of price or unsuitability, the trustees established a committee consisting of Hugh Allan, William Murray, and surveyor J.H. Springle to find a site. They examined dozens of possibilities over the summer of 1851, including the Rolland farm in the flat east-end suburb of Ste Marie. Although the farm was to be sold at a cheap price at public auction, the committee rejected it after Springle's inspection.[18] Their preference remained the mountain, and particularly McGill medical professor Michael McCulloch's Spring Grove Farm on its northeast side.[19] On 8 November, the trustees agreed to purchase fifty-seven acres from McCulloch, at a cost of £50 an acre. Subsequently, to give a view of the east-end of the city, to provide space for a projected lake, and to improve entrance access, a further thirteen acres were purchased from McCulloch.

Adopting the rhetoric of the defunct Mount Trafalgar Cemetery, the cemetery's first annual report (1852) utilized the word "beautiful" twice in the same paragraph and expressed the trustees' pleasure at obtaining "a tract of land admirably adapted for their purpose; possessing sufficient depth of soil, rivulets and springs to make ponds and lakes, well wooded, and with an undulating surface and beautiful for situation, – retired from the bustle and heat of the City, and yet near and convenient of access. A spot capable of being made one of the most beautiful and finest Cemeteries in America."[20] The trustees also moved to associate the cemetery with the mountain, changing its name from the Montreal Cemetery Company to the Mount Royal Cemetery. But, while it fulfilled their criteria of public health, isolation from the city, and natural beauty, Spring Grove Farm came with significant disadvantages as a cemetery site. It was largely covered by forest, and its stream presented spring run-off problems. Its rocky terrain and steep slopes would make burial difficult and would necessitate

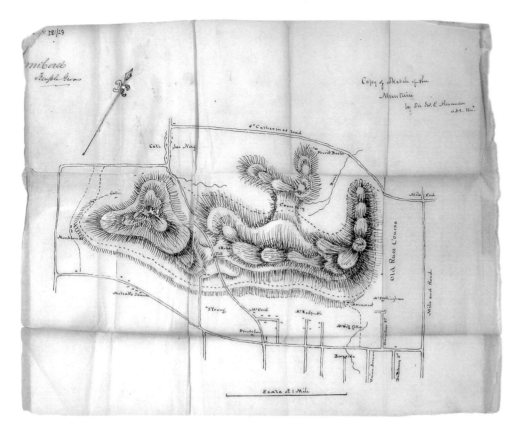

The mountain.

This nineteenth-century sketch map illustrates the cemetery's location, the steepness of the slopes, the original road network, and the locations of the McCord and Redpath estates.

the grading of whole sections. Nor was there an access road, although McCulloch agreed to use £500 of the purchase price to construct a road to the cemetery from Côte Ste Catherine Road.

The founders' ambitions and clear understanding of the wider rural-cemetery movement became evident when they sought the advice of American specialists. While a local contractor was hired to build a fence around the property, the trustees passed over Montreal's nascent architectural and landscaping professionals, writing instead to Andrew Jackson Downing, the continent's pre-eminent landscapist, for advice on planning their cemetery. When he did not reply promptly, they consulted the superintendent of Philadelphia's prestigious Laurel Hill Cemetery, who

suggested James Sidney. In this period when burgeoning professionalism still left opportunities for generalists, Sidney was reputed among rural-cemetery advocates for his varied skills in cartography, surveying, civil engineering, and landscaping. He designed the Woodlawn Cemetery in the Bronx and Easton Cemetery in Easton, Pennsylvania, as well as planning additions to Mount Auburn and Laurel Hill, the two most important American rural cemeteries. For neophytes in cemetery construction like the Mount Royal trustees, he had the added advantage of offering the services of the construction company he had established in Philadelphia with James P.W. Neff. The announcement of Sidney's commission to design their cemetery was made at the annual meeting of April 1852, the trustees asking him to lay the grounds out with particular care "to display, to the best advantage, its great natural beauties."[21]

In just a matter of weeks, Sidney visited Montreal and produced a plan closely modelled on that of Mount Auburn. Impressed by his speed and professionalism, and probably by the plan's similarity to the best American model, the trustees accepted Sidney's construction firm's tender of £1,468. For this fee, Sidney and Neff were to lay out the carriage drives, burial lots, the lake, receiving vaults for the winter, and the superintendent's house and office. Accepting the importance of a grandiose entrance area with a lake and substantial gates, the trustees bought an additional strip along the front of the property and a triangular section to the east. Concurrent with this construction in the summer of 1852, work also began on the access road leading down the mountain from the entrance. This eighty-foot avenue would provide a dignified, reliable all-weather road for funeral parties originally forced to take a "circuitous and inconvenient" path that snaked up from Côte St Catherine Road. To give the road a more direct descent, a right of way

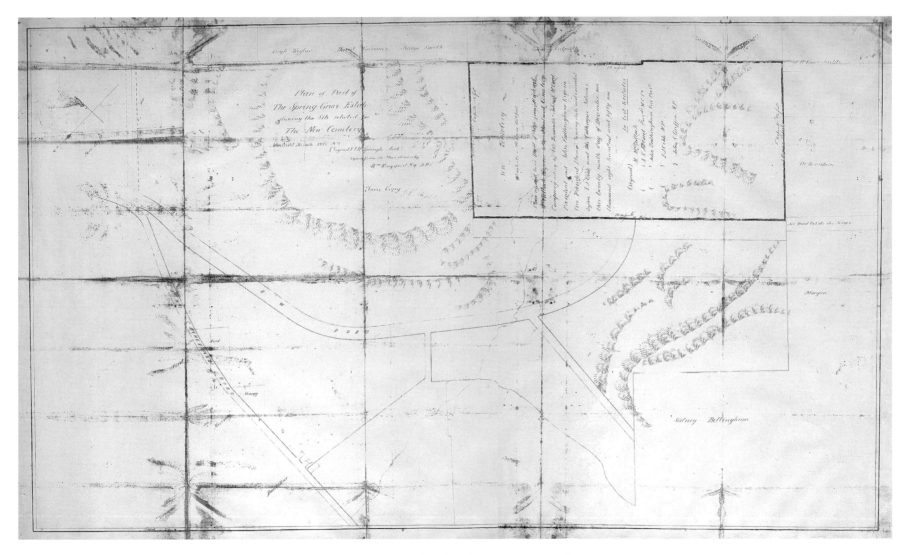

Map of Spring Grove Farm, December 1851.

James Springle, a Montreal architect and surveyor as well as a cemetery trustee, drew this map of the McCulloch estate at the time of the trustees' first purchase of land in 1851. It shows the limited extent of the cemetery at that time, the proposed road connecting it with Côte St Catherine Road, and the adjoining estates. Most of the land to the north of Spring Grove Farm remained in the hands of the McCulloch family.

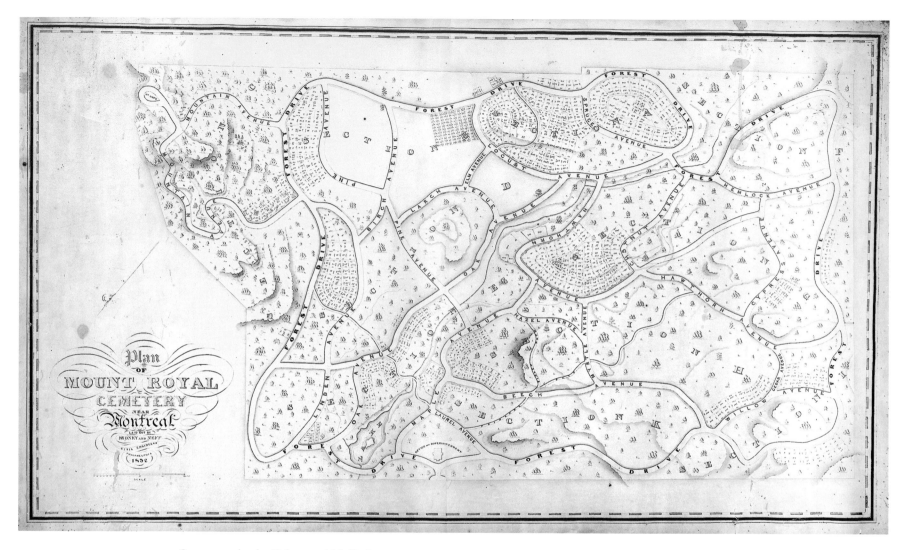

Cemetery plan by Sidney and Neff, 1852.

James Sidney's layout had great similarities to Mount Auburn, giving full play to nature and the contours of the mountain. In the grounds and beyond the superintendent's house and the artificial lake, the visitor climbed by the winding Maple street towards the lofty views and first grave subdivision of Section A. Maple Street was among the most popular village street-names in English Quebec and, in the cemetery, was joined by Oak, Pine, Hemlock, Beech, and Cedar, to give a sense of familiar nature. Note how some lots are drawn on the plan with Section A, the highest part of the cemetery at that time, fully sketched out as an elite section.

was purchased across the property of Benjamin Hall. This permitted Mount Royal Avenue, as the road was christened, to continue directly down the mountain.[22]

With construction underway, the trustees had to face immediate practical and sensitive issues that would test the inter-denominational collaboration evident five years earlier in the chartering of the cemetery company: the consecration of the grounds, the assignment of burial sections and the allotment of poor sections, the rights of different religious groups to segregated space within the grounds, and the integration of differing monument, literary, spatial, and funerary traditions among the cemetery's constituents. As they looked at the resolution of these problems in other cemeteries, the trustees faced conflicting options. In Toronto, the Toronto General Burying Grounds had been established as a non-sectarian, non-profit organization in 1826. In York, England, half of the chapel in the cemetery grounds was consecrated by the Church of England; the other half was used by non-conformists. The example of their sister cemetery in Quebec City was always of interest to the Montreal trustees. Instead of naming specific denominations, Mount Hermon's 1849 charter simply restricted the cemetery's stock to "Protestants." The charter did, however, permit sections to be set aside in which particular groups would have "the exclusive right to burial" in ground consecrated for their use. Anglicans took advantage of this clause, and sections had been consecrated and set aside for their use. The burial of non-Protestants – described as "others" in the charter – was left to the discretion of the trustees.[23]

Given Montreal's history, the founders of Mount Royal Cemetery were understandably nervous about the issue of sectarianism. Instead of the term "Protestant," which was used throughout the Mount Hermon charter, specific groups – Anglicans, Presbyterians, Wesleyan Methodists, Congregationalists, Baptists, Unitarians, and Jews – were identified in the Montreal charter. Although a Protestant Montrealer might well not be a churchgoer, or even a member of a particular denomination, every purchaser of a cemetery lot was obliged to declare the denomination to which "he chooses to be deemed to belong."[24] Further, the 1847 charter provided that specific parts of the cemetery could be set aside for Jews and Anglicans; although these sections could not be fenced off or otherwise separated from the rest of the cemetery, they would be consecrated according to Jewish and Church of England rites and reserved for their members. Across the cemetery, denominations would be permitted to build churches or chapels, to consecrate them, and to appoint their own managers to supervise burials and the keeping of registers. Yet the laying out and landscaping of the cemetery as a whole was to be controlled by the superintendent.

These provisions would have resulted in a highly sectarian cemetery divided into exclusive sections, separate jurisdictions, and competing chapels. In the years between the original charter of the Montreal Cemetery Company in 1847 and the actual cemetery opening five years later, the trustees sought a compromise between the wishes of their Anglican "brethren" to be buried in consecrated ground and a general desire to avoid a cemetery in which members of the established Anglican Church would be physically segregated from other Protestants. In September 1852, the trustees petitioned the legislature to amend their charter, repealing clauses granting "exclusive powers of jurisdiction" to Anglicans and Jews.[25] As amended, the charter made no mention of burying Anglicans apart from other

Bishop Francis Fulford

Protestants; for their part, Jews might be assigned a section for their "exclusive use," but subject to conditions that the trustees might impose.

A solution to the issue of consecration was worked out at a trustees' meeting only two months before the first burial. Here, they approved a petition asking the Anglican bishop to consecrate the "entire ground" of the cemetery, adding the important proviso, that this "should not be construed to invest that Church with any exclusive privilege."[26] Enunciation of the policy did not result in imme-

diate consecration: this was delayed almost two years, by which time several hundred burials, including those of Anglicans, had occurred.

By the fall of 1852, four miles of roads had been built and the first lots surveyed and laid out. The cemetery was opened for business, and the first burial – that of William Squire, a Methodist minister and cholera victim – occurred on 19 October 1852 before the ground froze. Squire's status as minister and epidemic casualty was entirely appropriate, given the important role of Protestantism and public health in establishing the cemetery. The Reverend Squire was not alone in the cemetery for long: the receiving vault, completed in February 1853, contained fourteen bodies by spring. The attraction of the new cemetery to prominent families was clear from the rapidity with which they removed their loved ones from the Protestant Burial Ground. By April 1853, fifty-one bodies had been disinterred and reburied in new family lots on Mount Royal.[27]

Even as they conducted their first burials, Mount Royal officials worried that much of their original purchase was too rocky or otherwise unsuitable for burial, and over the next years they added substantially to their property. An important acquisition was made in 1855, when they bought the north part of John Redpath's estate, adding extensive burial space. Ten years later, sixty-three additional acres at the top northeast of the cemetery were purchased. These acquisitions were not simply about meeting future burial needs; rather, they spoke to the trustees' concern with controlling the development of the areas overlooking the cemetery. In 1864, a twenty-eight-acre plot north of the superintendent's house was purchased. Although not particularly well suited for burial, "the high ground covered with wood has a fine appearance from the Cemetery, and as it was apprehended that it might be acquired by parties who might cut down the trees and erect unseemly buildings,

Sentence of Consecration.

Wearing full canonical dress and accompanied by the cathedral choir and nine Anglican clergy, Bishop Fulford consecrated the cemetery on 15 June 1854. Held in the grounds, the consecration service, drawn from the Anglican Book of Common Prayer, included prayers, a reading from the burial service, a short litany, and a signing of the "Sentence of Consecration," which designated the cemetery as "a place set apart for the burial of the dead" and separated from "all profane and common uses."

Reverend William Squire (234S, Section A).

Squire was minister of the Methodist chapel that served workers in the industrial area along the Lachine Canal. On 15 October 1852, he sat with merchant Samuel Young as he died from cholera. The next day, after burying Young in the Protestant Burial Ground, he himself fell victim. On 19 October, after a service in his chapel, his funeral procession of seventy carriages wound up Mont Royal Avenue through the entrance and up Maple, Hawthorne, and Locust Avenues to his gravesite off Spruce Avenue.

Receiving vaults.

Opening graves was complicated enormously by winter, which froze the Montreal soil from early December until early May. Preparing winter trenches, as had been done in the Protestant Burial Ground and in which at least the poor could be deposited, was entirely out of keeping with the Romantic setting envisaged for the new cemetery. Instead, a large and discreet receiving vault was built into the side of a hill and opened for use on 3 February 1853. Bodies were deposited and frozen here until their removal for burial with the spring thaw. Given public fears of body snatching, Mount Royal authorities were proud to describe their vault as offering "convenience and perfect security." By the winter of 1859, the vault was crowded with 105 children and 100 adults and construction of a second, adjoining vault was undertaken. In the twentieth century the development of stronger tools and power machinery enabled the opening of graves in frozen ground. After 1919, the receiving vaults were relegated to their present use as an equipment storage area.

thereby injuring the picturesque view from the Cemetery … [we] considered it prudent to acquire the land."[28] The same attention to height and view led to the purchase of seventeen acres, including the peak of what they would rename Mount Murray. Although costly and unsuitable for burial, this site was a "very valuable addition" to the cemetery and showed how, as early as the 1870s, the trustees had an eye for commemoration and the potential use of national memory at the cemetery. Tombs in London's Westminster Abbey and the Pantheon in Paris, Napoleon's Tomb in the Invalides, the statute marking the glory of Horatio Nelson on Jacques Cartier Square in Montreal, and the monument to patriot Ludger Duvernay in the adjoining Roman Catholic cemetery were all examples of sites used to reinforce national memory. The summit of Mount Murray, the trustees noted "is the highest point in the island of Montreal, and will, in all probability, be one day deemed a fitting site on which to erect a memorial to the fame of some Canadian worthy, or as a record of some event in the history of our city or Dominion. Any structure erected on the spot would be a conspicuous beacon for many miles around."[29] The issues of national memory as well as the summit and its public uses, we will see below, would return to haunt the trustees in the twentieth century.

The physical work of burial, and indeed the day-to-day business of the cemetery, was the responsibility of the superintendent. At the old burial ground, such operations, including the supervision of the grounds and chapel, sales, and the direction of burials, had been handled for decades by two long-serving superintendents, a Mr. Prine and Joshua Pelton. For many years, Prine was paid a fee of 2s. 6d. for selling a grave site and registering the burial; in 1816, he complained and his fees were raised to 5s. In 1819, he was put on an annual salary of £12.10. On Prine's retirement in 1822, he was replaced by Pelton, sexton of

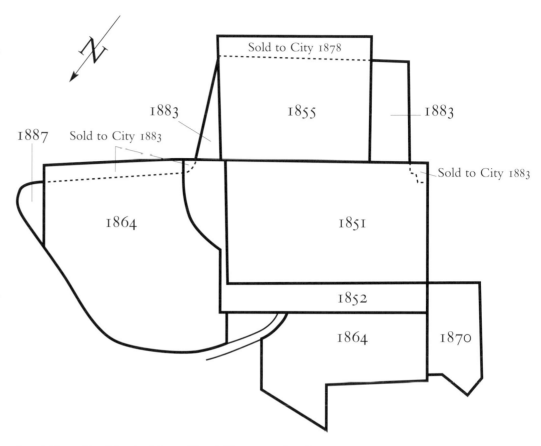

Acquisition of land by the Mount Royal Cemetery, 1851–83.

The original land purchased from Michael McCulloch in 1851 was enlarged by further purchases from the McCulloch estate in 1852 and 1864, from John Redpath in 1855, and by one from William Tait (consisting of much of Mount Murray) in 1870. During the 1870s and 1880s the cemetery exchanged several pieces of land with the City of Montreal for the making of Mount Royal Park. Parts of these lots were the subject of further exchanges with the city as the boundary of the park took shape. The results of these exchanges have been simplified for this map.

the Episcopal Church. Pelton managed both the Protestant Burial Ground and the Papineau Cemetery for the next thirty-six years, first as superintendent and treasurer and then as registrar, selling lots and arranging burials. With the opening of Mount Royal Cemetery in 1852, he acted as the cemetery's agent in the city, meeting the public at his office at the old burial ground, serving as registrar, and arranging lot sales and burials. His salary in 1848 was £75 a year, and on retirement in 1858 he was granted an annual pension of $200.[30] With Pelton's retirement, the cemetery's office at the Protestant Burial Ground was closed. Undertakers competing for Protestant business moved quickly to act as go-betweens offering their services so that bereaved would not be forced to travel out to the cemetery to arrange burials or to purchase lots. Joseph Wray, for example, proposed to distribute information on behalf of the cemetery from his establishment at St Lawrence and Dorchester Streets. Both he and his competitor George Armstrong offered to send mail up to the cemetery. In his *Montreal Gazette* advertisements, alongside offering mourning gloves, a child's hearse, and metal caskets, Armstrong stated that "Any communications or Message relating to Funerals left at his place would be taken to the Cemetery free of charge."[31]

The cemetery had in fact already opted for a resident superintendent. It had become clear that managing their large property, organizing its workforce, and ensuring burials on a large scale demanded skills beyond that of a church custodian, who had traditionally been in charge of the churchyard and burials. Cemetery manuals described the job as requiring "a man of intelligence, of cultivated feelings, with a taste for and some knowledge of gardening."[32] Gardeners were most sought after as superintendents of the new rural cemeteries and trustees often looked no further than their own estates.[33] In 1852, the cemetery placed newspaper advertisements for a "competent individual to fill the joint office of Gardener and Superintendent on the Grounds." Their choice was gardener Richard Sprigings. Born in St Albans, England in 1815, Sprigings immigrated to Montreal and was working as gardener on Henry Corse's estate. In his capacity as a director of the Montreal Horticultural Society, he would have sat alongside cemetery trustees like John Samuel McCord. Hired by the cemetery at an annual salary of £100, he moved immediately into the superintendent's house.[34] Cemetery by-laws devoted four pages to his duties: responsible for the entire cemetery, he was to ensure enforcement of all regulations; he was to lay out and sell graves, and to act as registrar, keeping the burial records and books; and his control over employees included the right to hire and fire.[35]

Cemetery superintendency was an occupation – a trade, one might say – that was passed from father to son. According to cemetery historian David Sloane, "fathers and grandfathers trained their sons and grandsons in the intricacies of the business."[36] In New York state, cemetery superintendencies in Auburn, Cortland, and Syracuse had family traditions. At Mount Royal, members of the Sprigings and then the Roy families, themselves related, have worked at the cemetery since 1852. Richard Sprigings's younger brother William, also a gardener, was hired at the cemetery in 1859 as sub-gardener, and for forty years he took charge of burials. A third brother, Edward, another gardener, was also hired in 1859, working as William's assistant in coordinating burials. Like his elder brother, William Sprigings lived on the cemetery grounds with his family, and the children of both men were born there. Two of William's sons, Duncan Charles and Edward Findlay, worked at the cemetery, the former as a gardener and the latter as foreman. Richard Sprigings's only daughter, Charlotte Ann, married Ormiston Roy. The son of Frank Roy, who had succeeded Sprigings as superintendent, Ormiston Roy was the dominant figure in the history of the cemetery in the twentieth century. As we shall see, a fourth generation of the Roy family, Andrew Roy, continues to work for the company.

The by-laws emphasized the superintendent's subordination to the trustees. He was to report "any matters of interest or importance" to them and was "at all times, and in all respects" to be "subject" to them. During the nineteenth century, all critical decisions relating to the cemetery were taken by the board of trustees, although their power declined as Ormiston Roy expanded the autonomy of his superintendency after 1898. Continuing the tradition of the Protestant Burial Ground, the Mount Royal Cemetery was led by men who came from the same social group, and indeed often the same families. Choosing among themselves, the trustees named the president, vice-president, secretary, and treasurer, as well as the members of the Finance and Grounds Committees. Under its 1847 charter, the board held its annual meeting on the first Monday of April and regular meetings on the first Wednesday of every month. The annual meeting of representatives of the denomina-

tions eligible to elect trustees was held four days after the cemetery's annual meeting.[37]

The charter gave proportional religious representation to its denominational constituents. The subscription to the company – that is, the total amount paid for lots – was divided by 21 and this number formed the base number. If a denomination had collectively purchased lots amounting to the base number, they would have the right to one trustee; if the amount were twice the base number, they were entitled to two trustees, and so on.[38] Fractions over one-half of the base numbers were to count as one trustee, while those under one-half did not; this latter proviso ultimately excluded the Jewish trustee who sat on the original board. In 1856, this formula resulted in nine trustees for the Presbyterians, six for the Church of England, two for the Methodists, two for the Congregationalists, and one each for the Unitarians and Baptists. Given the schism among Presbyterians, their nine trustees were divided among the St Andrew's congregation (three), the American Presbyterians (two), and the other Presbyterian churches. In 1925, the United Church was established from the union of the Methodist and Congregationalist churches and part of the Presbyterian Church. It was only in 1946, however, that the cemetery resolved the representation of Presbyterians, ceding five of their nine trustees to the United Church. By 1967, the United Church had the largest number of trustees, followed by the Church of England, the Presbyterians, and the Unitarians and Baptists.

Clearly the board of trustees was a self-perpetuating body emanating from the city's Protestant elite, confirming the fact that earlier attempts at uniting all religious groups in the creation of a new rural cemetery had come to naught. Historically, Jews had chosen to be buried separate from gentiles. In 1854, the Spanish and Portuguese Congregation (Shearith Israel) tried to purchase a small section of the

Table 2 Denomination breakdown of Mount Royal Cemetery's board of trustees

Denomination	1856	1865	1872	1917	1967
Church of England	6	7	8	7	7
Presbyterians	9	9	8	9	4
Methodists	2	2	2	2	–
Congregationalists	2	1	1	1	–
Unitarians	1	1	1	1	1
Baptists	1	1	1	1	1
United Church	–	–	–	–	8

cemetery from the Mount Royal trustees. Apparently un-satisfied with the section offered, they instead bought land from the McCulloch estate adjacent to the Protestant cemetery along Mount Royal Avenue.[39] Later, the German and Polish Congregations (Shaar Hashomayim) purchased a small strip of land right next to the Spanish and Portuguese lot. These two cemeteries would maintain a symbiotic relationship with their much larger Protestant counterpart over the next century and a half.

The same could not be said for the Catholic Notre-Dame-des-Neiges Cemetery, which opened in 1854. The Catholic and Protestant cemeteries shared a long fence – what the Mount Royal trustees called the "Catholic Fence" – but otherwise turned their backs to each other; whereas the two Jewish grounds lay next to the Mount Royal Cemetery's main gates, the entrance to Notre-Dame-des-Neiges stood some two kilometres away on Côte des Neiges Road. Having pulled out of the Protestant-backed scheme for a common cemetery, the churchwardens who ran the Roman Catholic cemetery applied historic rules as to who had the right to burial in consecrated ground: graves were reserved for those "professing the Roman Catholic Religion, interred with the honor of an ecclesiastical burial." Although the Catholic cemetery opened an unconsecrated section for the burial of stillborns, some unbaptised persons, or those "nominally belonging to the Catholic Church, but who shall be judged unworthy of an ecclesias-tical burial"– including, after 1902, those who had chosen cremation – were buried in Mount Royal Cemetery.[40] The latter's inclusiveness concerning the religion of those buried in their grounds would, on occasion, prove a point of contention between the two institutions.

Notre-Dame-des-Neiges Cemetery was designed by Henri-Maurice Perrault, a well-known Montreal architect and surveyor, later responsible for the City Hall and the Collège de Montréal, as well as the landscaping of the drive up to Mount Murray at the Mount Royal Cemetery. Although it shared some of the rural-cemetery features, Notre-Dame-des-Neiges presents a more monumental effect: the entrance gives way to a long straight avenue lined with trees, leading to a large cross. Other prominent symbols of Catholicism and French-Canadian nationalism include the cemetery's first memorial, commissioned by the Saint-Jean-Baptiste Society in honour of their founder, Ludger Duvernay, and the memorial to the Patriotes of the 1837–38 rebellions.

From their initial public discussions in 1845 to their first burial in 1852, the Mount Royal Cemetery founders chartered and laid out a cemetery that responded to Romantic impulses concerning Nature, Beauty, Christianity, and Death. Although it was soon joined on the north side of Mount Royal by Roman Catholic and Jewish communities, Mount Royal Cemetery was the most persistent in pursuing the spirit of the rural cemetery and in turning it into a reflection of Victorian society.

THREE

THE VICTORIAN CEMETERY

In terms of its geography, Mount Royal Cemetery was an integral part of the neighbourhood of English Montreal's elite, an extension onto the backside of Mount Royal of a coherent style of architecture and landscape found on neighbouring estates and on the McGill University campus. At the same time, the cemetery was part of a broader Protestant institutional fabric, with smaller lots and entire grave sections available to those of modest means – the family of the artisan, clerk, or worker. Yet a third Protestant constituency had to be accommodated in the cemetery: the poor who could not afford to pay for even the cheapest grave.

For those with means and not rushed by the urgency of a sudden death, the choice of family burial space was not unlike the preplanning arrangements encouraged by cemeteries today. The first plans for the cemetery spoke to these sensibilities, dividing the grounds between better sections with family lots and subdivisions with individual gravesites for the modest purchaser. Settling on a family gravesite had much in common with choosing a neighbourhood or home. Like a prominent church pew, a fine lot signalled status. As with the mountain estates they built in the vigour of life, families with means bought grave lots with height, view, good drainage, easy road access, and friends nearby. We have already observed that interests in architecture,

Visiting the cemetery, 1872

landscaping, and gardening were seen as positive attributes of Victorian manhood. Indeed, the greenery, fences, gates, and headstones of the cemetery lots owed by the most important merchants, judges, and manufacturers can be seen as an an extension of their estates. Shipper Robert Reford told a Toronto monument-maker that "My lot and the site for this monument is unique and the finest in Mount Royal the whole of which is overlooked from it besides which it has an almost unlimited view northwards and westwards."[1] Wealthy families sought out the architects who had designed their homes, warehouses, or factories to draw up plans for their monuments or mausoleums. Shipowner Hugh Allan commissioned three gates to his fenced family lot − each bearing the name of a different male relative.

This Victorian high culture, the interest in family memory, and the capital to invest in a lot and its development ensured that key sections of the cemetery would exhibit a coherent and attractive harmony of landscape, lot architecture, and monuments. Many important Montrealers were buried in section A, originally the highest point of the cemetery. Here, near the lot of cemetery president John Samuel McCord and his in-laws, the Rosses and Davidsons, were the plots of Peter McGill, brewer William Dow, of mayor and McGill chancellor James Ferrier, and of Benaiah Gibb, art philanthropist and merchant tailor to the wealthy. Section A is united by social affinity more than by religious denomination: while Lord Bishop Francis Fulford, Montreal's first Anglican bishop, is buried next to his proud parishioners the McCords, the nearby Ferriers were Methodist while the Gibbs were prominent Presbyterians. Further along, Methodist ministers are grouped around Reverend William Squire; it is here that Iroquois chief and Methodist minister Joseph Onesakenrat is buried as well. A number of trustees located their lots further down on the slopes of the cemetery's central sections. Here, in section E, for example, cemetery treasurer Hugh Allan developed his impressive lot; the influential Frothingham families are nearby in section G1. Across the valley, section C was a prestigious location: it attracted many of the mausoleums, including that of the Molsons, along with the lots of influential families like the Abbotts, the Bethunes, and Dawsons. Much closer to the main entrance but separated from it by a woods, section H was opened early. More modest in disposition, elevation, view, and price, it is here that patriot leader Thomas Storrow Brown is buried, as is cemetery superintendent Richard Sprigings.

When the cemetery later expanded dramatically up the slopes of the mountain with additional purchases, new sections (F, I, L) were opened up. Wealthy purchasers opted for these prestigious lots − indeed, some older families apparently opted to sell their original lots and move to higher ground. John Redpath, a contractor and industrialist of great wealth, moved from the older Section A to the

Opposite The McCord sarcophagus (A249, Section A).

A2, the first elite burial section, was constructed in the 1850s on what was then the highest part of the cemetery. It contains the lots of important Protestant families including those of jurist Charles Dewey Day, merchant David Torrance, tailor Benaiah Gibb, financier John Rose, and brewers William and Andrew Dow. The monuments here tend to be massive and, in Victorian tradition, boast lengthy epitaphs. In keeping with his status as a judge and first president of the cemetery, John Samuel McCord arranged his lot adjacent to those of his wife's family, the Rosses and Davidsons, as well as the lots of Francis Fulford, Anglican bishop of Montreal, and bank president Peter McGill. Twelve family members are buried here. Their epitaph emphasizes their role in the Conquest, the professions, and Canadian history. The wrought-iron fence, clearly visible in this 1918 photo, marked off private family space. Like most fences in the cemetery, it has since been removed.

Peter McGill (A248, Section A).

A merchant and president of the Bank of Montreal, the St Andrew's Society, and the Montreal Auxiliary Bible Society, McGill felt that working people should draw lessons from their betters.

Grave of Sir John Abbott (C395, Section C).

Sir John Abbott was a prominent Montreal lawyer and Canada's third prime minister. Here too are buried other members of the Abbott and Bethune families, including Sir John's father, Joseph Abbott, first registrar and vice-principal of McGill College, and his father-in-law, John Bethune, rector of Christ Church in Montreal and principal of McGill College.

John William Dawson (C100, Section C).

A geologist of international reputation, first president of the Royal Society of Canada, and principal of McGill University (1855–93), Dawson gave the university its character and its strong orientation to the sciences and commerce. A fundamentalist in his religious beliefs, Dawson was prominent in the campaign against Darwinism. The Dawson–Harrington lot where Dawson was buried in 1899 is one of the cemetery's most peaceful.

Joseph Onesakenrat – "Chief Joseph" (A233, Section A).

Joseph Onesakenrat is an exception to the virtual absence of Native people in the official records of the cemetery and from prominent gravesites. A Methodist minister as well as an Iroquois chief, Onesakenrat is buried in a section reserved for Methodist ministers. The grave has an usual iron marker. Like those of Thomas Hackett, Charles Chiniquy, and Joseph Guibord, Onesakenrat's grave emphasizes the centrality of religious struggle in nineteenth-century Canada – conflicts that marked the history of the cemetery. A full-blooded Iroquois born in 1845 at the Sulpician mission at Oka, Onesakenrat was raised a Catholic. Sent by the mission priests to their classical college in Montreal, he returned home and was elected chief in 1868. He was soon attacking his former mentors, questioning their claims to the seigneury. In the same year, Charles Chiniquy, a priest who had become a Protestant missionary, preached at Oka for three days. Following his visit and the subsequent arrival of Methodist missionaries, most Iroquois at Oka renounced Catholicism in favour of Methodism. Threatening violence, Chief Joseph told the priests to abandon their seigneury and to restore ownership to the Iroquois. In 1875, the Sulpicians dismantled the Methodist church that had been built at Oka; two years later, the Catholic church burned mysteriously. Accused of arson but ultimately freed, Onesakenrat received financial support from Protestant leaders in Montreal. Ordained a Methodist minister, he was working in 1881 as a missionary and translating the Bible into Iroquois when he died.

higher ground of Section L1, joining wealthy families like the Torrances and Birks; here, the grandeur of the Redpath obelisk competes with that of Mathew Gault, first managing director of what became the Sun Life Assurance Company. After 1885, the highest part of section M was developed, a site the trustees judged as having "some of the most eligible situations for vaults."[2]

Although the urns, obelisks, and celtic crosses of the wealthy are the most visible, these early sections are among the most eclectic in the cemetery, mixing style, religious denomination, and social class. Headstones here represent a variety of style and stone: granite, sandstone, and marble. One can see an occasional marker made of iron pipe, such as the one just outside the Allan family compound or the iron marker for the burial place of Joseph Onesakenrat. Unlike more uniform sections opened after 1900, monuments in these sections are unaligned, following the slopes of the valley or the loops of avenues like Spruce, Hawthorn, or Elm. Showing the influence of Romanticism, family lots give prominence to nature, emotion, and expressions of individual achievement, love, or religious devotion. Large headstones permit lengthy inscriptions, and their epitaphs recall birthplace, profession, civic contribution, and religious and human feelings. In exaggerated examples, such as the McCord sarcophagus, the family chronicled their place in Canadian history. While the headstones of men generally speak to work, church, club, and other public service, the epitaphs of women emphasize morality, family heirs, friendship, and faithful service.

Social and economic privilege could not insulate families from the deaths of infants and young children. In these Victorian sections, children were buried in family lots, their headstones of lambs and reclining babes still discernible. Jane Caldwell and Stephen Sewell, high-standing members of English Montreal, lost four children in the

Above Monument to a child in Mount Hermon Cemetery

Above right "Happy" monument of Alice Graham Oswald

1840s, burying them in the Protestant Burial Ground and then moving them to their new family lot in E5: W. Caldwell (eighteen months), Stephen (four years), Susan (six months), and Isabella (five years). High infant mortality continued throughout the Victorian period and into the First World War. In 1859, infants aged 0–2 years accounted for 33.1 per cent of all burials at the Mount Royal Cemetery. By 1915, this figure had declined slightly to 31.2 per cent. Only after 1916 did Protestant infant mortality, as reflected in cemetery figures, decline significantly; in 1924 it stood at 16.1 per cent. At the same time, the percentage of bodies over the age of forty increased dramatically. In 1859, only 21.6 per cent of the individuals received at the cemetery were forty or over; by 1924, this age group accounted for well over half the burials.

Edith Margaret Cleghorn (1900).

The skull, a common sculpture in graveyards before the rural-cemetery movement, is missing from the iconography of the Mount Royal Cemetery. The monument in the Quebec City Protestant cemetery, Mount Hermon, on page 45 is surprising by its association of skull and child. Mount Royal monuments to children commonly feature lambs or sleeping babes. Despite high rates of mortality across the nineteenth century and some historical claims that families with many children expected deaths and grieved less, the cemetery bears multiple witness to the intense emotional attachment of parents to their children. Alice Graham died of influenza at age ten. Their religious faith severely tested by the death of a child, parents looked to reunions beyond the grave as expressed in the frequently used epitaph: "She is not dead but sleeping." Loved ones had been traditionally remembered by painted portraits, lockets, or clippings of hair. With the commercialization of photography, bereaved parents, like those of infant Edith Margaret Cleghorn, coped with their loss by having their dead child photographed.

Above-ground entombment had long attracted the powerful: Europe is dotted with the mausoleums of aristocratic families and wealthy merchants. While mausoleums are often associated in the public imagination with Catholic burial, wealthy Protestants in Montreal, Quebec City, and Toronto built such tombs for their remains. At least twelve were built in Mount Royal Cemetery before 1883. Costing a minimum of $5,000, most were cut into the hillside, although several are free-standing. These landmarks brought immediate public attention to the cemetery, contributing to the myth that all of English Montreal was rich and powerful. Guide books described the Molson vaults, built between 1860 and 1863 for the three sons of John Molson, as the "handsomest" and "largest on this continent."[3]

Given public health concerns, the construction of mausoleums was tightly regulated in the cemetery's first set of regulations: if built of brick, their walls were to be at least sixteen inches thick; stone walls were to measure no less than twenty-four inches. For hillside vaults, double iron doors were to be provided, with at least eighteen inches between the inner and outer doors.[4] Quebec laws imposed further restrictions. Coffins placed in mausoleums had to be surrounded on all sides by a four-inch layer of cement. This was accomplished by building a brick casing with a four-inch leeway around the coffin. With the coffin resting on four-inch stone blocks, cement was poured in, filling the space on all sides.[5]

By the end of the century, leading families had turned away from mausoleums and the elaborate monuments of their parents' generation. Pine Hill Side, opened at the turn of the century, shows less flagrant statutary, more uniformity in building materials, and more frugality in its expression of religious or personal sentiment. Here are buried some of Canada's most important early-twentieth-century capitalists, including Sir Herbert Holt (d. 1941), president

of the Royal Bank, and Richard B. Angus (d. 1922), president of the Bank of Montreal and a founding director of the Canadian Pacific Railway. Although older sections of the cemetery often prominently memorialized the victims of ship- and train wrecks, Pine Hill pays tribute to victims of catastrophe more discreetly. It is here, for example, that Charles Melville Hays, president of the Grand Trunk Railway and victim of the *Titanic* sinking, 15 April 1912, is buried. Hays was one of the few victims whose body was found by searchers. His son-in-law Thornton Davidson also died in the disaster, but his body was not recovered, and he is just memorialized here. Both of their wives survived the sinking of the *Titanic* and were buried in the family lot years later.

In understanding the broader history of the cemetery and of Protestant Montreal, it is quite misleading to overemphasize Protestants of prominence and wealth. The cemetery remained a burial ground "common to all Protestants." By far the majority of the dead who came through the cemetery gates can be described as "modest" – workers, tradesmen, shopkeepers, clerks, and their families. Most funeral corteges emanated, not from Christ Church Cathedral or from the Golden Square Mile, but from non-conformist churches and chapels serving Point St Charles or the Quebec or St Laurent suburbs. These individuals buried family members in sections constructed specifically for single graves as opposed to the more expensive family-lot sections. Early maps show the laying out of attractive and central parts of the cemetery – Section B, the central part of Section C, and the lower parts of section M – for single graves.[6] Buying an individual grave implied that family members might not be buried together. The burial of infants and children by young families was particularly poignant, posing important logistical and commemorative considerations for cemetery officials. They had to

The Molson mausoleums (C61, 62, 63, Section C).

The cemetery's most impressive mausoleums were built between
1860 and 1863 for the families of the three sons of John Molson.
Designed by architect George Browne, aided by his son John James,
the three limestone vaults were built at a cost of $15,000. The elder
Browne had worked on several projects for the Molsons, including
their bank's head office, a suburban villa, and twelve workers' houses
near the family brewery. Between the two upper vaults on the
Molson lot is a 60-foot monument to John Molson, the elder, and
his wife, Sarah Vaughan, whose remains were moved there from the
old Protestant cemetery. In addition to Christian inspiration, the
mausoleums contain a mixture of heraldic, classical, and literary
allusions. The cast iron doors of the vaults with their crossed arrows,
bare-breasted female figures, and clover in the middle have been
described as "enigmatic" by one architectural historian.

Table 3 Bodies in Mount Royal Cemetery by age of death, 1859, 1915, 1924

1859		1915		1924	
stillborn	22	stillborn	185	stillborn	143
less than 2	154	less than 2	674	less than 2	278
2–4	51	2–4	71	2–4	52
5–9	16	5–9	39	5–9	35
10–19	13	10–19	83	10–19	58
20–29	48	20–29	186	20–29	94
30–39	46	30–39	181	30–39	126
40–49	30	40–49	153	40–49	186
50–59	23	50–59	182	50–59	192
60–69	27	60–69	163	60–69	236
70–79	14	70–79	157	70–79	207
80–89	6	80–89	71	80–89	101
90+	0	90+	12	90+	11
	14	unknown	0	unknown	4
total	464	total	2,157	total	1,723

Table 4 Mausoleums in Mount Royal Cemetery

Family	First burial	Total burials
Elizabeth Amelia Campbell Robertson (wife of Dr William Robertson)	1855	36
Stanley Clarke Bagg	1856	14
Frederick T. Judah	1858	18
Estate of John Molson	1860	32
Benjamin Hall	1861	16
Estate of Thomas Molson	1863	26
Estate of William Molson	1863	16
Estate of Thomas Kay	1863	9
Miss Barbara Scott	1870	7
Estate of William Workman	1878	1
Hiram Mills	1882	1
George A. Drummond	1883	21

William Workman's mausoleum (I-25, Section I).

While burial arrangements were usually not mentioned in Protestant wills of the period, William Workman was specific in his 1877 will that "my body not be buried under ground, but placed in a vault." He left $5,000 for construction of a "substantial cut-stone vault, strong and well built, with double iron doors." The mausoleum and lawn in front of it was to be modelled on that built by Mme Amable Prévost for her husband in Notre-Dame-des-Neiges Cemetery. Workman left capital that would generate interest of $24 a year to be used in perpetuity to keep his mausoleum repaired and "in perfect order": "the walls to be kept in good order, joints of the cut-stone neatly cemented, the top or roof (arched roof) to be kept water-proof, the doors well and freshly painted, the lawn well trimmed and the whole in a well cared-for condition, fresh and neat looking." Separated from his wife, he made no provision for her presence in the vault, requesting instead that his son and daughter be placed on shelves on either side of his coffin. In fact, he is alone in his mausoleum, which has been sealed.

Above left Giulio Lallo

Above right Lilian Pribyi

Above Gwendolin Evelyn Allan

Right Anna Allan (E198, Section E5).

The cemetery contains the bodies of hundreds of victims of disasters – boat, train, air – most of whom are little-known individuals. Wealthy Montrealers travelled for business, leisure, or education, and some were victims of famous ship disasters like those of the *Titanic* or *Lusitania*. The Allan family were perhaps Montreal's most prominent family: Sir Hugh Allan was the cemetery's first treasurer, and the Allan family lot is still among the most picturesque in the cemetery. Two granddaughters of Hugh Allan – and daughters of Sir Hugh Montagu Allan and his wife, Maguerite Ethel Mackenzie – Gwendolin and Anna Allan drowned in the sinking of the Cunard liner *Lusitania*, which was torpedoed by German submarine on 7 May 1915. "Saloon passengers" with their mother, the girls were en route to England to visit their sister, a war nurse in France. Anna Allan's body was not recovered, and she has a commemorative stone in the family plot. Gwen Allan's remains were found and she was buried 24 July 1915.

Wealthy families buried their children in family lots alongside other family members. The economic realities facing families of more modest means, along with ongoing high rates of infant mortality, led the trustees after 1888 to open separate children's sections in C3 and then G3. The physical separation from adult burial sections, the scale and themes of monuments, and the language of epitaphs emphasized the qualities of purity and innocence that our culture ascribes to children. This segregation was part of a larger specialization across society in the form of children's hospitals, libraries, and nurseries. Children's markers in this section feature hearts, open books, doves, cherubs, and especially lambs, all scaled to child size. George and Edna Ryan, who lost their thirteen-month-old son, Lawrence, on 24 July 1919, inscribed his marker "Sleep on Sweet Babe and Take Thy Rest. God Called You Home, He Thought it Best." Others chose to use the small space of a child's marker to simply list the child's name, date of death, and place of origin: "Born in England." Children buried in children's sections were normally under ten years of age, and usually under five. Also buried here in considerable number are what cemetery records describe as "New Born Child" – unnamed infants who died at birth or within a few days thereafter. While many stillborn babies were consigned to unmarked graves in the free ground, markers here make clear that these unnamed children were buried in graves purchased by their parents. Indeed, the cemetery permitted a few parents, years later, to be buried in G3 alongside these infants.

navigate between the financial realities of young parents and the profound emotions attached to the death of children. Cemetery records strongly suggest that the death of children was surrounded with the drama we associate with the death of the young today. Separating the young from the graves of their elders and burying them in new children's sections offered potential economies along with cultural visions of shared innocence and sleep. During the 1880s a small area in Section C3 was set aside as a special lot for children. A decade later, Section G3, a large area that had been intended for single graves but was found to be too shallow, was turned over to the burial of children. It remains the cemetery's main children's section.

Like infant death, the provision of grave markers touched nerves: popular feelings surrounding commemoration often clashed with the aesthetic and organizational principles of the cemetery fathers. To locate loved ones buried without benefit of a headstone, families, at least in the first years after burial, relied on the mound of dirt, normally eight inches, heaped on graves to compensate for later sinking. Mounds were of great importance in popular culture, serving in the absence of stone or epitaph as a physical reminder of the departed's presence. From the opening of the cemetery, the trustees faced debates over flattening these grass mounds as unsightly reminders of the presence of death or, at least, minimizing them by reducing the earth heaped on graves after burial. Sensitive to popular feeling, trustee William Murray called for the retention of mounds, arguing that "the people should be left to their own judgement … for though it might be but a question of taste, it was a very tender one to touch upon."[7] He was supported by trustee Benaiah Gibb, who aired complaints that, after the height of mounds had been reduced from the regulation size, "poor people, who could not afford to put up grave stones, could

not again recognise the place where their friends were buried. Was this so?"[8]

Strong voices opposed the mounds. Calling for their removal, Peter McGill spoke to the importance of harmony in the cemetery, a principle implying that the aesthetics of modest sections should imitate the more genteel. He saw the cemetery as a coherent instructional site where the poor and modest would draw moral lessons from their betters. President of the Bank of Montreal, the St Andrew's Society, and the Montreal Auxiliary Bible Society, McGill left instructions that he be buried in the presence of his domestic servants, each dressed in a mourning suit provided by his estate. To maintain the rural cemetery's essential character, he argued, mounds should be removed, leaving the single-grave areas and sections where families could not afford headstones as open, unmarked expanses that might accentuate the landscaping and architecture of the family-lot sections: "If they wished to make the Cemetery a beautiful one, and preserve it from what often made other burying places so unseemly, they must adopt one uniform rule."[9] While the opponents of mounds never succeeded in their abolition, their defendants were equally unhappy with a height limitation of eight inches. One compromise was to permit their natural disappearance over time in the older single-grave sections while banning them entirely from new sections. Sales contracts for graves in Section D, which opened in 1890, contained clauses forbidding mounds; lots would instead be "marked simply by small granite posts."[10]

The debate over mounds shows the trustees' complex involvement with the different constituencies they buried. The unique circumstances of some of these individuals prevented the trustees from falling back entirely on their own preference for the family as the defining social institution

Opposite Train wreck (1864).

Opposite Train wreck (1864).

On 29 June 1864, in what was described as the worst train wreck in Canadian history, a Grand Trunk train with 500 German immigrants on board went through an open drawbridge into the Richelieu River. Among the 100 victims, 52 Protestants were buried by the German Society in a special plot at Mount Royal Cemetery (C904).

and preferred client of the cemetery. In 1864, for example, a lot was granted to the Scots Fusilier Guards for the burial of guards who died in Montreal. That same year, the German Society buried fifty-two Protestants, victims of the crash of a train carrying immigrants. Important across this period was the work of the St Andrew's Society, established in 1834 to assist Scots immigrants. Its annual report of 1867 described one of the five individuals it buried that year:

An old man from Canada West, went to Scotland during mid-summer, to bring a brother and family out to Canada. On the passage out by the steamer "St. Andrew," his brother, a strong healthy man, caught a cold which ended in inflammation of the lungs. Notwithstanding all that could be done for him by Dr. Patton and Captain Scott of the ship he continued getting worse; on landing he was sent to the Montreal General Hospital on a Sunday and died the following day. The old man was in great distress being a stranger here and not having more money than was sufficient to pay the fare of himself and his brother's orphan children to their destination. His case was brought to the notice of your committee by Mr. Milloy, and orders were immediately given to have the body buried in the Society's lot, the Rev. Mr. Patton holding religious services. When told that the Committee would take charge of the Funeral arrangements, the poor old man was relieved of a weight that pressed heavily on his spirits, and on parting with him he could scarcely find words sufficiently strong with which to express his gratitude for the assistance thus extended to him.[11]

Ten years earlier, the trustees granted without charge a 750-foot lot in Section F5 to the St Andrew's Society, which had taken responsibility to bury sixteen Scots victims of the shipwreck of the steamer *Montreal*.

The trustees and their peers demonstrated their sense of Christian responsibility through benevolent activities in-volving cemetery, church, university, or associations such as the YMCA; working-class people expressed their social solidarity, patriotism, or Christianity through their unions, churches, the Salvation Army, militia units, or national societies. Among the most symbolic volunteer work was that of firemen. Synonymous with traditional masculine values of courage, strength, and the protection of life and property, the fire brigade consisted of volunteers until 1858 when a full-time, paid fireman was appointed to each of the city's twelve stations. As it professionalized, the brigade was structured as a military organization: men slept "booted and spurred" and, as one fire chief recalled, there were "a wild lot of young fellows around at all hours."[12] With uniforms, bands, sports, intercity tournaments, controlled drinking, and links to the national societies, the fire brigade was an important outlet for acceptable male behaviour. Like the Mount Royal Snowshoe Club and Montreal Amateur Athletic Association to which many trustees belonged, the brigade was a world of camaraderie and physical activity outside the home, and women came into the streets to watch their men showing their "steel." Fires, such as the great Montreal fire of 1852, were major catastrophes that destroyed whole neighbourhoods. They were also the city's largest spectator event, often occurring at night and including lights, explosions, screams, crashing walls, and half-frozen or burned men in uniforms and helmets. To civic and cemetery authorities, firemen's parades, like those of the militia, were much more acceptable forms of working-class identity than the marches of strikers, the Knights of Labor, the Orange Order, or the Salvation Army.[13]

Firemen, of course, died protecting lives and property. Civic pride surrounding the death of these heroes gave weight to requests for a dedicated cemetery lot and monument. An exception – but only one of many – to cemetery organizing principles based on the family, the

Firemen's Monument (G125-126, Section G1).

The most striking monument in the cemetery, the firemen's monument is a site of ongoing commemoration.

firemen's memorial commemorated civic values, community solidarity, and virtuous male behaviour. The issue of a separate firemen's lot in Mount Royal Cemetery was first raised with the death of William Sharpe (whose name is the first on the front of the firemen's memorial), who was crushed by a falling chimney on 17 September 1867 and buried in a purchased grave. In April 1868, just days after the death of two more volunteer firemen, including Hugh Scott, the trustees donated a five-hundred-foot lot for Protestant firemen who died in the discharge of their duty. In 1876 this lot was doubled in size; at that time despite the cemetery's financial difficulties, the trustees still offered the lot at a 50 per cent reduction.[14]

Another facet of Protestant responsibility was constantly tested by burial of the destitute. The indigent dead presented logistical problems in every urban centre. In Manhattan in 1848, for example, 2,897 bodies, or 18 per cent of the total dead, were buried in potter's fields.[15] Since the opening of their burial grounds in 1799, Protestant trustees in Montreal had struggled with similar problems. Providing a common winter pit and developing the cheaper Papineau cemetery site had been partial answers earlier in the century. In 1833 the trustees, faced with the filling up of the Papineau burial ground, resolved "to take immediate measures to procure a new lot of land for the internment of paupers only" and asked Protestant congregations to contribute to this end.[16] From the time of the opening of Mount Royal Cemetery, land was set aside as "pauper grounds" or "poor ground"; later, the class connotation was replaced by a monetary one and the area came to be known as the "Free Ground."[17] Although it does not appear on the 1852 map (which was intended to represent an ideal), the Free Ground lay on the western fringe of the cemetery, backing onto the fence separating Mount Royal from the Roman Catholic cemetery. Remindful of the persistence of poverty in Protestant Montreal, free burials represented a substantial part of the cemetery's activity. In 1896, for example, almost a quarter of that year's burials – 306 out of 1,204 – were provided in the Free Ground.[18]

It is important to linger on the meaning of the Free Ground, a concept that spoke to Protestant and class values of male responsibility to provide for one's old age, burial, and widow. These values were promoted by churches, the YMCA, and the expanding life insurance companies in which trustees such as Mathew Gault and cemetery president McCord held positions of power. At first, access to the Free Ground was relatively liberal and could be granted by written certification provided by a clergyman or physician of the inability of the deceased's family or friends to pay for burial. By the 1890s, in an attempt to control free burials, certification was limited to members of the cemetery board. The price for burial in the Free Ground, was anonymity.

Grave markers were not permitted and, at least after 1900, the cemetery limited to five years its responsibility to identify burial places in the Free Ground.[19] Such a practice stood in marked contrast to the superb record keeping for other sections of the cemetery. The equation was direct: in contrast to the perpetual care and granite provided to the paying, the destitute would not have the right to commemoration in either physical or written form.

Even if the grave were provided free, the cemetery tried to have the destitute pay at least something. In 1853, the cemetery charged 5s. for digging a poor grave in "ordinary," frost-free ground, with an additional 2s. 6d. charged if the body had to be transported from the winter vault.[20] The grave rate for burying children was two-thirds of the adult rate. This was cheaper than in Kingston, where the government paid 7s. 6p. to dig graves for prisoners who died in the penitentiary.[21] By 1865, the Mount Royal Cemetery was charging $1 to dig graves for the poor, but "a deduction is always made to parties not able to pay if they ask for it."[22] Storage of the poor in the winter vaults left the cemetery to assume vaultage fees as well as the costs of the spring transfer of their bodies to the Free Ground. All bodies stored in the vault were assessed a charge of 10s. for the first month and 2s. 1d. a month thereafter; children under eight were assessed half price. In 1857, however, relatives of thirteen of the sixty-two bodies in the winter vault paid no storage fees, presumably because they were "deserving" cases.

Cemetery archives, contemporary newspapers, and other documents permit some interpretation of the thousands buried in the Free Ground. In just three years – 1882, 1885, and 1888 – 737 burials were made in the Free Ground. John Robinson's card in the cemetery archives gives no address or country of birth, stating simply that he cut his own throat and was buried on 31 July 1866. At least seven

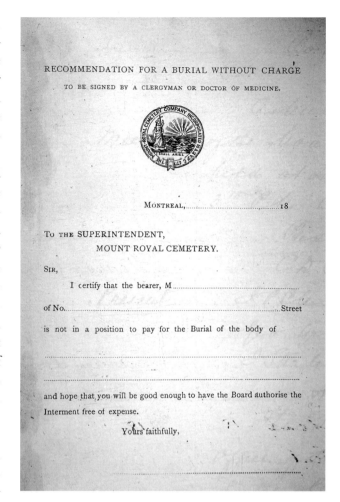

Recommendation for a Burial without Charge.

In the Old Burial Ground, access to a free burial could be granted only on demand from a Protestant minister. This petition for free burial in Mount Royal Cemetery provides evidence of the growing power of the medical profession in the late nineteenth century and the power of the doctor, alongside the clergy, to evaluate matters outside the sickroom such as religion and economic condition.

Malones were buried in the Free Ground between 1860 and 1895 and, although not buried together as family, several seem related. Catherine Malone, daughter of William Malone, died of diarrhea at eight months and was buried on 28 July 1862. An Irish-born victim of tuberculosis, Catherine Montgomery Malone, wife of William Malone and probable mother of Catherine, was buried on 25 July 1865. Thirty years later, on 9 January 1895, seventy-five-year-old William Malone, also an Irish-born tuberculosis victim,

died in the Protestant House of Industry and Refuge, and his body joined other Malones in the Free Ground.[23]

Like the Malones, one's status as an immigrant was critical in determining one's destiny towards the Free Ground, as can be seen in an examination of the backgrounds of sixteen individuals who died exceptional deaths in 1882, 1885, or 1888 – suicide, murder, accident – and who were buried in the Free Ground. The death of thirteen of these individuals was reported in the *Montreal Daily Witness*. Of these, nine were employed and several were married with families in Britain, but all thirteen were immigrants.[24] Even more important, the Free Ground was the ultimate destination of stillborn babies and many other infants: these two categories formed the majority of free burials. In 1882, 19 per cent of burials in the Free Ground were stillborn babies and 43 per cent were infants aged under one year.[25] The three most important addresses listed in cemetery records for these unfortunates were the University Lying-in Hospital (Montreal Maternity Hospital after 1885), the Hôtel-Dieu Hospital, and the Protestant Infants' Home.

While the most helpless cases such as the stillborn, infants, and destitute immigrants found their way to the Free Ground, the costs of burial of other paupers had historically been assumed by the various Protestant denominations. As Montreal industrialized, the major Protestant denominations competed to bring skilled workers and their families into their churches. At the same time, they found themselves increasingly distanced from the Protestant sailors, domestics, canal workers, and factory labourers, who made up an important part of the city's workforce. These workers might be single and transient without family or institutional affiliation; many died in boarding houses, on the streets, or at the Montreal General Hospital. Some of these dead were buried by institutions like the Montreal General Hospital or the jail both of which bought

Table 5 Major lots conceded or sold to ethnic and charitable groups to 1903

Group	Lot	Date	Square footage	Price
Protestant Orphan Asylum (1)		1853		free grant
Ladies Benevolent Society (1)		1853		free grant
St Andrew's Society	F28★	1857	750	free grant
Firemen's Benevolent Association (1)	G125★	1868	500	free grant
Protestant House of Industry and Refuge	G400	1868	1000	free grant
Protestant Orphan Asylum (2)	G401	1868	500	free grant
Ladies Benevolent Society (2)	G402	1868	1000	free grant
Firemen's Benevolent Association (2)	G126★	1876	500	$100
YMCA	G398	1882	1600	$400
Boy's Home	G397	1886	500	$125
Irish Protestant Benevolent Society	G399	1886	1000	$250
Montreal Sailors' Institute	G396	1890	740	$225
Firemen's Benevolent Association (3)	G126★	1895	1000	$500
St George's Society	G394	1895	500	$300
St Margaret's Home	G403	1896	400	$200
Irish Protestant Benevolent Society	G399-A	1897	240	$60
Independant Order of Oddfellows	G1198★	1900	600	$420
Protestant House of Industry and Refuge	G1197★	1901	500	$225
Chinese Colony of the Province of Quebec	N500★	1903	1500	$1200

★outside charity section
Source: based on chart drawn from Minutes by Darcy Ingram

single graves as the need arose. The Old Brewery Mission, still active in Montreal, owns grave sites scattered through the cemetery in which it buries men who die with the resources for a minimal funeral and grave.

The cost of burying the mounting number of unaffiliated poor, where they were presumed to be Protestants – a 'native of Glasgow,' an 'Ulster servant girl,' an 'English labourer,' a 'former British soldier,' a British or German immigrant victim of epidemic or accident – was often assumed by one of the Protestant benevolent societies. In 1868 large lots near the Free Ground were granted without charge to the Ladies Benevolent Society, the Protestant Orphan Asylum, and the Protestant House of Industry and Refuge.[26] The latter institution arose from the decision not to establish public poorhouses; it was chartered in 1863 to provide refuge for the homeless, or what its annual report described as "the dregs of society," "the very lowest in the social scale."[27] In 1865, it buried two people who died at the refuge, an aged female and an infant, at a total cost of $9.50; in 1868 at a cost of $19.50, it buried five adults who died in the refuge and three who died at the Montreal General Hospital.[28] A total of 192 people are buried in its lot. By 1903, fourteen benevolent, national, or friendly societies had been granted or had purchased lots, almost always located along the fence at the cemetery's western extreme. Among the most important of these was the Montreal Sailors' Institute, which was organized with strong support from the Allan shipping family and which buried in its lot some five hundred sailors who died in the Montreal area.

Protestant responsibility to provide burial was further shaped in the late nineteenth century by the social gospel movement. Strongest in the Salvation Army and Methodism but present in Presbyterianism and even high-church Anglicanism, the social gospel emphasized the broad responsibility of Christians towards others. Alongside the YMCA, missions, and temperance, the provision of a decent burial can be seen as part of this movement.[29]

Perhaps benevolence in the cemetery was simply an elite tactic to deter class resistance. Certainly, the trustees included many of Montreal's most important industrial employers, with the Redpath, Ogilvie, Allan, and Molson families owning the city's most important sugar, milling, shipping, and brewing enterprises. The interest of Protestant employers in the growth of the YMCA, the Montreal Sailors' Institute, the Protestant House of Industry and Refuge, and the Scots, English, and Irish national societies undoubtedly spoke to their motives of controlling Protestant workers.

The poor never easily accepted anonymity in death or charity from the elite. To force authorities to grant the boarder, the sailor, or the immigrant worker a visible place in the cemetery, the poorer classes used ethnicity, military service, fraternal associations, and new religious movements like the Salvation Army. To be buried without a coffin, religious rites, or funeral ceremony, without a grave marker or even a grass mound to mark one's passage through life, has been described as the pauper's "final stamp of failure."[30] Into the 1930s, it was a matter of public rebuke that the destitute who died in Montreal's Protestant hospitals were buried without a religious service.[31] Even worse in the popular imagination was to lose ownership of one's own body, ending ignominiously on the medical school's anatomy slab.

A better scenario for the poor was burial in a benevolent association lot. On the Catholic side and helped by their clergy, working men organized self-help societies like the Union des Prières, which assumed the costs of burial for its members and provided some help to widows. In 1907, with the Archbishop of Montreal as patron, a literary and musical benefit was held to raise money for a statue of

The Ladies Benevolent
Society (1909)
(G402, Section G6).

Prominent Protestant women,
including many of the wives
of cemetery trustees, ran the
Ladies Benevolent Society,
which began caring for children and widows in 1832.
In 1853, along with the
Protestant Orphan Asylum,
it obtained a cemetery lot for
burial of its charges. Of the
59 people buried in its lot
between 1870 and 1921, the
overwhelming majority were
women. However, two adult
males were buried. Of the
fifteen children buried in
the period, six are boys.

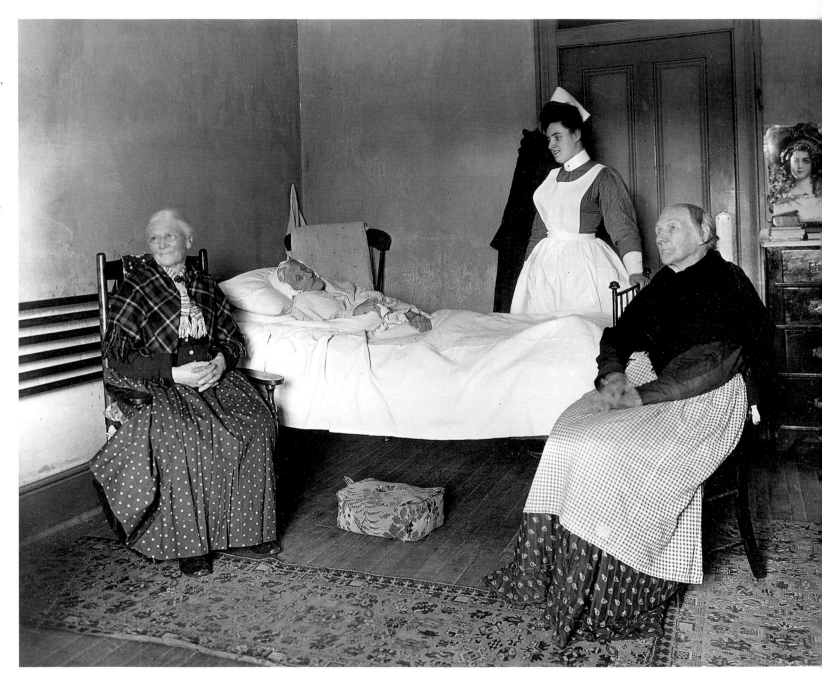

the Virgin that might serve as a common monument for those buried in the pauper ground of Notre-Dame-des-Neiges Cemetery.[32] Among Protestants, friendly and ethnic societies like the St Andrew's Society assumed the mission of providing decent burials. The Irish Protestant Benevolent Society can be taken as a case study. At first, it paid the costs of burying destitute Protestant Irish in the Free Ground, and it would have seemed an ideal candidate for a free lot similar to those granted in the 1850s and 1860s to societies like the Protestant Orphan Asylum. Cemetery minutes, however, show a certain ethnic and class distrust between the trustees and the Irish Protestant Benevolent Society. In addition, the cemetery by the 1870s was caught between financial stringencies and its mission of burying all deceased Protestants. In 1871, the trustees offered the society a lot at "half price"; over the next years, the trustees struggled with the society over location of its lot, forcing them to locate in the charity section.[33] Finally, in 1886, the society agreed to pay $250 for a thousand square-foot lot, and this was enlarged again in 1897. As part of the sales, the cemetery agreed to provide free interments and perpetual care of the site. The lot was subsequently graded, levelled, sodded, and marked by stone copings. Responding to protests concerning unmarked graves, the society began providing identical headstones for all graves. In a typical year such as 1888, the society provided the funeral and burial expenses for seven people.[34]

Individuals from minority groups such as the Jews, have always been present in the cemetery's registers, and, as we have seen, the Jews had their own section. Before 1885, however, the cemetery buried only the occasional ex-slave, Aboriginal, or individual born in "Madras," "Calcutta," "Hindostan," or the "East Indies." Some of these might, in fact, have been members of British colonial families. Growth of construction work on transportation projects

Monument of Montreal Protestant Homes (G400, Section G6).

Typical of many monuments in the charity section, this monument emphasizes the solidity of philanthropic institutions and the anonymity of the poor they buried.

Monument of the Montreal Sailors' Institute (G393, G393a, G396, Section G6).

In contrast to most monuments in this section, individual sailors are named on this memorial.

such as the Canadian Pacific Railway brought large numbers of Chinese to Canada. By 1901, Montreal's Chinese population, almost entirely male, had grown to over 1,000 and the city counted 228 Chinese laundries. This Chinese presence elicited conflicting attitudes. Eugenics, with its notions of race betterment, restrictions on immigration, and breeding of the fit, was a strong force at McGill University and among Montreal Protestants.[35] While a scientific theory at one level, eugenics also contributed to racism against the Chinese and fears about the sexual fate of European women who might work for Chinese employers. In 1900 the head tax for bringing a Chinese family member into Canada was doubled to $100, in 1903 it was raised again to $500, and in 1923, the Chinese Immigration Act stopped Chinese immigration entirely.[36] On the other

Temple Emanu-el.

Montreal's first Reform Congregation was formed in 1882. By the turn of the century this Jewish congregation had acquired a burial plot on Mount Royal. Although the site was near the Shearith Israel and Shaar Hashomayim cemeteries, it was, in keeping with the Reform character of the congregation, within the boundaries of the Protestant cemetery. In 1917, Mortimer Davis, one of its leading members, approached the trustees with an unusual scheme whereby the congregation would buy an additional piece of land, which the Mount Royal Cemetery would then subdivide into family or single lots much as in any other section. The trustees retained complete authority over the sale and maintenance of lots, but the congregation remained the owner. The trustees agreed to landscape the area (D3) and to provide paths.

hand, the Protestant churches were involved in Asian missionary work, and progressive Protestants were increasingly positive in their attitudes to eastern religious and burial practices. An 1873 article published in Montreal, "Chinese Burial Places," described their gravesites as "objects of pleasing, perhaps profitable, contemplation."[37] The Presbyterian Church was particularly active in the Cantonese community of Montreal. In 1897, a Chinese mission was established by Knox Church, and Cantonese Christians began recording their births, marriages, and deaths in the Knox registers. It was a group from this church that, early in the twentieth century, bought a burial lot (N500). Ostensibly for Christians, the concession was apparently used to bury Cantonese of all religious persuasions. While cemetery archives do not permit confirmation, some may have been exhumed and sent for burial in family graves in China.[38]

The out-of-the-way location of the Chinese concession in a hollow at the back of the cemetery, adjacent to the Free Ground and the Roman Catholic cemetery, emphasized the trustees' uneasiness with a definition of pluralism that would give space and formal recognition to a non-white, albeit Protestant, group. In 1903, Chinese elders asked for permission to hold ceremonies in which their dead would be honoured "according to their custom."[39] Unsympathetic to Chinese cultural manifestations on their grounds, the trustees refused. Nonplussed, the Chinese responded with a petition signed by 450 and the assurance that the request was "unanimous." Another petition asked the trustees to show the same tolerance for their "harmless" practices as shown in cities like New York and Vancouver, themselves "governed by Christian Anglo Saxons." Again, the trustees declined, this time arguing that "exceptional privileges" could not be granted to a particular community.[40] Cemetery minutes do not make clear when Chinese burial rites were finally permitted.

Chinese ceremony in Ross Bay Cemetery.

The Chinese community of Victoria, British Columbia, owned "the Chinese Corner" in Ross Bay Cemetery and held ceremonies similar to those requested at Mount Royal Cemetery. This late-nineteenth-century photograph shows the community offering a funeral sacrifice of a roast pig to the deceased. Other traditional customs included bell ringing and the placing of fruit and flowers on the grave to accompany the soul of the deceased.

Signatures on letter from the Chinese colony, 7 December 1903 (N500 to 504, Section N1).

Literate, insistent, and well-aware of appeals that might strike chords of Christian charity with the cemetery trustees, leaders of Montreal's Chinese community addressed several requests for the right to hold traditional commemorative ceremonies on the lot they purchased in Section N. While the Chinese signatures of these seven men apparently struck the trustees in 1903 as foreign and possibly threatening, Chinese script is evident today in many parts of the cemetery, indication of a different approach to Montreal's pluralism.

FOUR

CONTESTED DECORUM:
THE CEMETERY AS PUBLIC SPACE

True to their prescription that the new cemetery should be a "natural laboratory to instruct the public" and be "admired as much for its retired position as for its beauty," the trustees strove to make the Mount Royal Cemetery a place that was well worth visiting – albeit on carefully controlled terms. Its distance from the city presented challenges not only to casual visitors, but to funeral processions themselves, which were conducted on very different terms than had been the case in the Protestant Burial Ground. The trustees constantly had to walk a fine line between encouraging and limiting visits, between promoting the cemetery as a place of moral instruction and protecting it as a site with perennial security problems, between supporting large symbolic burial processions that commemorated mayors, war heroes, and university principals, and avoiding the disturbances possible in the ethnically charged processions of a Joseph Guibord or Thomas Hackett.

Fences, gates, and buildings were essential components in defining cemetery space and in separating it from the civic world outside. The trustees moved quickly to enclose their property with a fence; as the cemetery expanded over the first decade or so the original fencing was periodically moved and replaced. The trustees were also conscious of the visual impact of a formal entranceway. Confronting visitors and mourners as they arrived at the top of Mount Royal Avenue, an impressive gate would demarcate the passage from the domain of the living to that of the dead – a reverent and private space where different codes prevailed. In 1856 the trustees turned again to landscaper James Sidney, asking him to design an entrance and gate – "something substantial and ornamental … a Carriage Way and side entrances with Railing to enclose the remainder of the front."[1] Sidney's plan, at a projected cost of $1,600, which included demolition of the superintendent's house so that the gates could "front a lawn or ornamental piece of ground," was not undertaken.[2] Temporarily shelving their plans for a grandiose entrance, the trustees opted instead to construct a greenhouse just inside the entrance. As well as providing cemetery flowers, the greenhouse would, in the horticultural tradition of rural cemeteries like Mount Auburn, serve an educational purpose, being both "ornamental" and "an object of interest for the inspection of visitors." Practicality also ruled on the other side of the entrance, where a stable and kitchen garden were built for the superintendent's use, although the garden was fenced off "so that now anything out of keeping with the character of the grounds is screened from view."[3]

Five years later, the trustees came back to the idea of

Entrance gate to the cemetery c. 1880–90.

Forty-eight feet high and constructed of cut stone in Gothic style, the gates demarcate cemetery space from the secular. This Notman photo shows the stylization of the entrance area in the late nineteenth century. At the right the waiting room is evident while the woman and girl identify the cemetery as acceptable space for respectable women. As automobiles replaced horses as the principal means of transport to the cemetery, the walks and cobbled driveway were replaced by pavement.

The gate house or waiting room.

This is the cemetery's oldest surviving building. The annual report of 1862 described it as being "convenient for parties attending funerals … to warm themselves in the severity of winter, or as a shelter from the rain."

Superintendent's residence.

Richard Sprigings's first residence at Mount Royal stood immediately in front of the original gate and was demolished when the wrought-iron gates were built in the 1860s. The new and imposing superintendent's house, evident in this photo, stood to the west side of the gates: In 1901 the house was destroyed by fire and rebuilt. The present main offices of the cemetery now occupy the site.

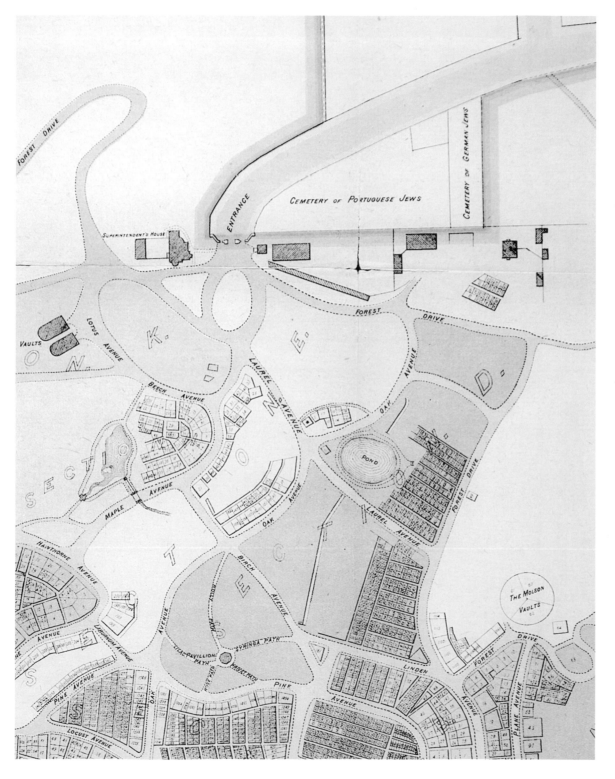

The entrance area, 1885.

Joseph Rielle's map of the Mount Royal Cemetery, drawn in 1885 (with a reprint in 1891), is the only detailed map of the nineteenth-century cemetery that indicates individual lots, buildings, and landscape features. This detail from that map shows the entrance area at the head of Mount Royal Avenue leading up to the city. The Jewish section of the cemetery is clearly visible ("Cemetery of Portuguese Jews") as is the "Cemetery of German Jews," which is not part of the Mount Royal Cemetery. On one side of the entrance gates, the superintendent's house is marked, and its garden is visible behind. On the other side of the gates is the 'gate house' or waiting room, with the greenhouse behind and sheds alongside. At middle left, on Lotus Avenue, can be seen the two receiving vaults.

Mount Royal, 1866.

This detail from a map of Montreal in 1866 shows the concentration of forest on the northern slopes of the mountain. Except for a large clearing in the centre and a small one near the entrance, Mount Royal Cemetery (its boundaries in 1866 outlined in black) was still heavily forested. Similarly, the high ground to the northwest of the cemetery (later called Mount Murray) and the slopes of Westmount at centre-left were (and for the most part still are) thickly covered in trees. Côte des Neiges Road can been seen at left, snaking northwards and dividing Mount Royal from Westmount. Off this road, at centre-left, can be seen the entrance to Notre-Dame-des-Neiges Cemetery, then a relatively narrow strip of land stretching to the boundaries with Mount Royal Cemetery. Mount Royal Avenue can be seen at centre-right, curving up to the cemetery gates.

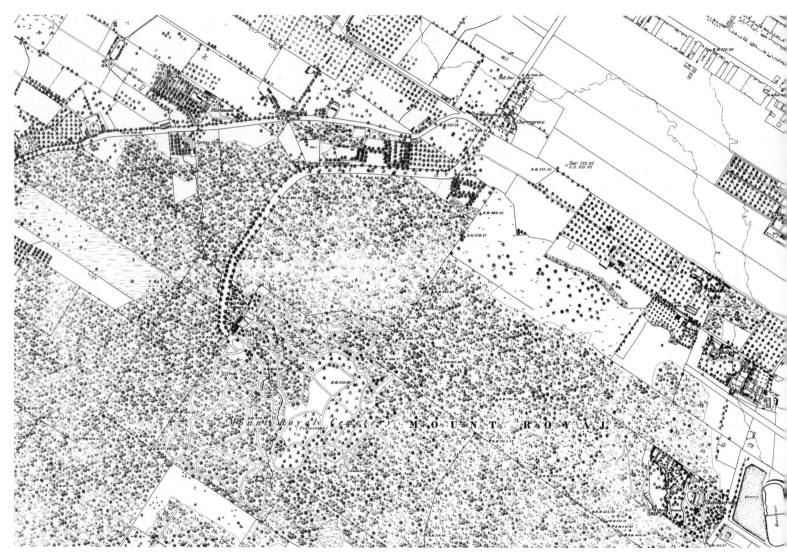

reconstructing a fitting entrance area. Abandoning Sidney's plan, they announced a local competition with a $100 prize for a gate design which might be built for less than $6,000. The contract attracted entries from well-known Montreal architects J.J. Browne, Fowler and Roy, Lawford and Nelson, William Footner, and John William Hopkins. The latter's design, which included a new house and reception room as well as gates, was accepted and completed in 1862 at a cost of between $9,000 and $10,000. The superintendent's house was subsequently razed and the entrance grounds planted with flower beds: the result was "a fine view of the grounds from the entrance" – what the 1875 annual report described as "an uninterrupted vista."[4]

Early photographs illustrate that, in the first years, the cemetery grounds remained heavily forested. It was only in the 1870s that the Victorian landscape, still evident in much of the cemetery today, was created with a thinning of the forest, which transformed "impervious, tangled thickets into park-like glades and vistas."[5] In the early 1870s a prominent rocky area was set aside as a "Rustic Alcove" for visitors to rest, a "Rustic Bridge" was built over the ravine between Hawthorne and Oak Avenues, and a "lakelet" replaced a swampy part of section D. Sheds and workshops behind the superintendent's house were removed, lawns were extended, and waterways "embanked and turfed." The repeated use of expressions such as "vista," "pleasantness of the view," "attractive," and "hidden beauties" in the cemetery board's minutes throughout the 1870s emphasizes the trustees' preoccupation with landscape. Plans for drives to the summit of what became known as Mount Murray were commissioned from surveyor Henri-Maurice Perrault, and by 1877 three circuits led to its summit: "This fine spot will be accessible, as well as for carriages as for pedestrians: the approaches to it will, when finished, afford unrivalled sites for tombs and monuments, which cannot

fail to prove attractive." Visiting was further encouraged by construction at its crest of a 50-foot-high wooden observatory crowned with a "carved winged figure."[6]

The effort taken to landscape the grounds and to improve the entrance to the cemetery was matched by a concern that standards be maintained on individual lots. Regulating the appearance of lots and the materials to be used in building monuments and mausoleums was a means to enforce a uniform aesthetic within cemetery space. In drawing up cemetery regulations, John Samuel McCord relied directly on the rules of Mount Auburn, a copy of which remains in his papers. Mount Auburn regulations – hours of opening, the ban on refreshments, rules for horses, and the prohibition on gathering wild or cultivated flowers – were copied verbatim into Mount Royal rules.[7] Both cemeteries printed pamphlets introducing visitors to their vistas, drives, and mausoleums.

The efforts of trustees, superintendent, and lot owners made the Mount Royal Cemetery a Protestant showcase in which language, landscape, horticulture, and sculpture united into a powerful public display of beauty and morality. The cemetery, it was noted, "is becoming a place of great interest and attraction, not only on account of the natural beauty of the grounds, but also … the great number of superior and costly monuments and vaults that have been erected in such a short time."[8] In 1869, the new Anglican bishop of Montreal was surprised to be taken to the cemetery as a first order of business: "On the very day of our arrival in Montreal a very kind and wealthy member of our Church took us for a drive in her carriage and proposed a visit to the Cemetery. This was not a very cheerful pilgrimage to select; but it was – quite unconsciously on her part – a somewhat suggestive one, especially as she was careful to show me the burial-place of the late Bishop, and a space to which some of his successors might wish to

Advertising postcard for photographer J.G. Parks.

This stereoscopic photograph of the cemetery was used in the advertising of Montreal photographer J.G. Parks. The popularity of such images and their use commercially emphasizes how the cemetery was a source of civic pride.

apply."[9] By this time, the cemetery was considered a tourist destination, with guides to the city drawing attention to its "picturesque position in the valley," its monuments "shining through the foliage," and its "perfect maintenance," as well as to the "judgement and taste" of its management.[10]

As a final consideration in making the cemetery an attractive place for visitors, the trustees also monitored the appearance of Mount Royal Avenue, the road leading up to the gates. In 1869, the avenue was graded, trees were planted, and "unsightly and superfluous trees" were removed. Several of the cemetery's charter churches, particularly the Methodists, were at the core of moral reform, Sunday observance, and the temperance movement. It was therefore not surprising that the trustees, having constructed what they called "the solemn associations" of the north side of the mountain, would react strongly to the announcement of plans for a tavern "for the alleged accommodation of

visitors to the Cemetery" on Mount Royal Avenue near Côte Ste Catherine Road. Indignantly refusing the tavern owner's somewhat surprising request to erect a sign on Mount Royal Avenue to attract homeward-bound mourners to the tavern, the trustees convinced municipal authorities in Outremont to withdraw his liquor licence. When the discouraged proprietor offered to sell, they apparently promptly bought his property. To further emphasize the private and controlled nature of their side of the mountain, the trustees erected a gate on Mount Royal Avenue near the bottom of the mountain, despite protests from the McCulloch family that the original deed stated that the avenue was to be a public thoroughfare.[11]

Their opposition to the proposed tavern and their attempt to install gated access not just to the cemetery but to Mount Royal Avenue underscored the trustees' determination to construct Mount Royal Cemetery as a model of Protestant respectability. On this score, the old burial ground had failed to measure up, as was particularly evident in the absence of genteel women from its premises. A Glasgow observer noted that, in Scotland, as late as the 1920s only men went to burials: "the women stayed behind to prepare the funeral tea."[12] In Montreal, as a local newspaper noted, men visited the old burial ground only to attend a funeral; women never visited at all: "No Lady is ever seen there … It must be a disgusting place, which a mother cannot visit, to console her feelings over the grave of an only child, which a wife cannot enter, to shed a tear on the last resting place of a beloved husband; and we are satisfied that it is because ladies cannot go there, that the ground remains in its present condition."[13]

The Mount Royal Cemetery was to be everything the old ground was not, solemn instead of "disgusting," a place where ladies could go: indeed, its suitability for women visitors would be the yardstick of respectability. To this end, the cemetery was gated, fenced, and supervised to ensure what the regulations called "quiet and good order."[14] To avoid the "detrimental, dangerous, or inconvenient," it was open only from sunrise to sunset and was closed at all times to unaccompanied children and dogs and to parties "carrying refreshments" – the cemetery's preferred term for alcohol. Sunday observance was a critical part of the moral reform movement, a means of regulating the behaviour of men on their day off. To this end, Sundays were officially reserved for lot holders "on foot with their tickets" and members of their families and friends. Along with attendance at church, the Sunday afternoon visit to family gravesites in Mount Royal was another badge of Protestant respectability. The carriage drive up the mountain, a visit to the Observatory, the tending of graves, and the late Sunday tea with family elders both reflected and encouraged propriety in leisure pursuits, dress, and language as well as in gender roles and the observances of family obligations.

While they had a clear vision of how the middle-class family would relate to the cemetery, the trustees were always more ambivalent about how to deal with the popular classes, their "riotous and improper manner," and their tendency towards "wounding the feelings" of more circumspect visitors. Should those not owning lots be excluded from the cemetery entirely, or would introducing them to its controlled moral environment encourage "refining influences"? Certainly, cemetery regulations for those with family in the better sections differed from those wishing to visit the Free Ground. According to the printed rules, visitors with "a relative interred in the Public Lot" could be admitted on Sundays only if they had been issued a "special pass" by a trustee or the cemetery secretary.[15] In practice, tickets were not issued, and the cemetery gates remained open on Sundays through the cemetery's first decade of operation. In 1862, however, the trustees were

The Michael Family Lot.

Purchased in 1894 for $115.20 by William Michael, this family lot of 144 square feet – its copings and entrance with family name inscribed – contained one headstone set off to one side in August 1895 when this photo was taken. The woman arrived for her visit to the family lot by buggy. The tended grave is clearly evident at her feet while the rough background gives a good sense of the development of new sections.

Louisa Goddard Frothingham in mourning (c. 1899)
(G24, Section G1).

Although renowned for her independence, Louisa Frothingham,
following the death of her husband, J.H.R. Molson, adhered to the
mourning code, which was much stricter for women than men.
Professionals and businessmen who lost their wives had only to
add black gloves, hatband, and tie to their customary public attire
of dark suits. Women's full mourning-dress – "widow's weeds"
made of full black paramatta and crepe – was de rigueur for two
years, after which the widow could wear the greys, lavender, and
white of half mourning.

warned of "crowds of visitors" and behaviour "not becoming the character of the place." With its new gates symbolically in place, the cemetery in 1863 applied Sunday
closing, and admission tickets for "proprietors" were prepared: "It was with great regret that such a course was
deemed necessary in consequence of too many of the visitors on Sunday having been discovered conducting themselves in a very riotous and improper manner, disturbing
and wounding the feelings of those visiting the resting
place of their dead."[16] This restriction on visitors angered
some lot owners who, as one letter writer to the *Gazette*
put it, saw the cemetery visit as uplifting: "Montreal is
destitute of parks, gardens or pleasure grounds. Our peace-
able and respectable mechanics and operative classes have
no time to visit these grounds on week days, and if shut out
during our short summer Sundays their whole beauty and
refining influence is lost to them. This loss is a direct injury
to the whole community, for I defy any man to leave these
grounds, after a visit with his wife or family, without carrying with him or with this family more hallowed and
refining influences."[17]

Sunday funerals, with their suggestion of open gates,
noise, and distraught crowds, were another challenge to
advocates of a strict Sunday observance. In 1876, the trustees banned Sunday funerals despite protests that this
would cause hardship for working people who would lose
a day's pay attending a weekday funeral.[18]

Location of the cemetery on a mountain site five kilometres from the city imposed dramatic change on the form
and logistics of Protestant burial. At the Protestant Burial
Ground just outside the old city, coffins had arrived in carts
and sometimes on the shoulders of friends. With its on-site
chapel and handy location, the old burial ground accepted
mourners of all social strata. Sunday burials were convenient for working people, less so for cemetery authorities

and the clergy. The funeral might be held in the chapel, after which mourners could easily accompany the body to its grave. In its first half century, no chapel existed on the grounds of the Mount Royal Cemetery, thus physically separating funeral and burial. A hearse and carriage were theoretically necessary to transport the coffin and principal mourners to the new cemetery, although in 1856 Montreal City Council discussed "the fact of dead and dying bodies being carried in the public cabs." For all, the procession to the cemetery was taxing: "a dreadful scene, and drive to Mount Royal and the conversation on the way – *frightful* rain from 3 pm," was how one mourner put it.[19] Distance and cost discouraged the frail, the poor, the lame, and the boisterous from making the trip; except for the corteges of the prominent, large processions or crowds in the cemetery were also discouraged. In 1855, the chapel at the old burial ground was reopened for funerals: the service over, "it would be understood that none but the relatives and immediate friends would form part of the procession" to Mount Royal.[20]

Military funerals were an exception to the rules concerning Sunday burials, closing hours, and discreet burial parties. Many of the trustees were themselves militia officers, part of a male culture in which it was important to salute a dead comrade with a burial that included military honours. However, the Union Jack–draped casket transported on a gun carriage drawn by four horses, the accompaniment of a firing party, a marching band with drum rolls and the Dead March, and hundreds of tramping men tested the cemetery's emphasis on private decorum and on family and female-friendly public space. The cemetery trustees were always concerned by nighttime activities in their grounds. The superintendent was under strict orders not to permit volleys at funerals without special authorization from the cemetery president.[21] Whatever the rules,

Skating party on Mount Royal by the girls of Misses McIntosh Bute House (1873).

Before the construction of the cemeteries, the mountain was essentially male space reserved for activities like snowshoeing. The cemeteries brought respectability and a female presence to the mountain, at least in daytime. Whether skating on the mountain's lake or visiting a family plot, proper dress was important.

military processions regularly arrived late in the day after the long march up from the city. The burial service might be read with "the lantern dimly burning," and volleys, often in the dark, would signal the end of the ceremony.[22] A gun salute was permitted at the 1912 funeral of Colonel Edward Ashworth Whitehead, Boy Scout leader and commanding officer of the 3rd Victoria Rifles. Borne on a gun carriage through a drizzling September rain, his coffin was accompanied by 200 regimental comrades on foot, 500 Boy Scouts with "sloped staves," and officials from the St Paul's masonic lodge, the Grand Trunk Railway, and the Rose and Thistle Football Club: "Just as the first long shadows of the evening were stealing across Mount Royal, the body of the soldier-citizen reached the crematorium. The committal service concluded, three volleys were fired, then the Rifles swung round, formed in line of quarter column, and marched away, leaving its dead to rest until the morning break."[23]

Richard Choules.

Choules, commemorated on the firemen's monument, was a salvage fireman whose job was to remove books, furniture, and other valuable property from burning buildings. At the 1877 Oil Cabinet and Novelty Works fire, Choules survived collapse of part of the building, jumping from a second-storey window. He went to his nearby home, woke his wife, brought her to see the fire, and then re-entered the burning building to his death.

Equally large and even more emotionally charged were the funerals of firemen killed in the line of duty. Funerals of the Protestant firemen killed in a factory fire in 1877 were held in their respective homes and their coffins brought afterwards to the central fire station for a joint funeral procession to Mount Royal. The Church of England burial service was read in Richard Choules's house and his hearse was followed by the Royal Lodge of Oddfellows. At the central fire station, the bodies were placed on a catafalque erected on a fire-station wagon; the helmets, belts, and hose keys of the victims were laid on the coffins.[24] The procession included the mayor and city officials, eighty police, the grand director of the Masons, the marshall in chief of the Oddfellows, and the deputy master of the Loyal Orange Lodge as well as firemen marching alongside the catafalque as pallbearers. From Place d'Armes the procession moved into St James Street, through Victoria Square and up Beaver Hall Hill to Phillip's Square, Union Street and along Sherbrooke to the corner of Bleury, where many of the mourners entered carriages for the long ride to Mount Royal. Outside the city, people stood in the fields to pay tribute. At the cemetery, the bodies, while awaiting completion of the firemen's lot, were placed in the vault, accompanied by volleys from a firing party and burial rites from the Masons, Oddfellows, and the chaplain.

Though large manifestations of male culture that included a range of social classes, these military and para-military funerals represented a respectable, working-class face of Protestant Montreal. The trustees were much less willing to accommodate controversial figures whose funeral processions – or even whose presence in the cemetery – might be a cause of unruly behaviour. This was certainly the case with Joseph Guibord, whose body lay in the Mount Royal Cemetery's receiving vaults for several years and provoked violence upon being transferred to Notre-Dame-des-Neiges in 1875. Somewhat later, the burial of the highly controversial renegade priest Charles Chiniquy also prompted the trustees' fears that the cemetery would become the scene of violence.

The most problematic burial was that of Thomas Hackett, a member of the Boyne Loyal Orange Lodge, whose death in a street brawl on 12 July 1877 ignited religious tensions throughout the city and placed the trustees in a delicate political position. With thirteen lodges in Montreal in 1862, the Orange Order was a major force of violent opposition to the city's Catholic majority. The most important Protestant fraternal order, its lodges with their male club rooms, their drinking, parades, and recurring violence, had strong attraction for Irish Protestant workers.[25] Above all, the order was united in opposition to what it saw as Catholic tyranny. Armed with a Colt revolver and reputedly defending Protestant girls from Catholic toughs, Thomas Hackett was shot dead in a melee on Victoria Square. Victim of what one newspaper headlined as "Meditated Wholesale Murder," Hackett was laid out in the Prince of Wales Rifles Reading Room in the St James Street Orange Hall.[26] Among the Union Jacks, black drapes, and masses of flowers that decorated the hall, the Orange lily dominated. Hackett had three bullet wounds to the face, making full exposure difficult, but his coffin was fitted with a glass cover through which his mutilation could be viewed. On a black-covered table near the head of his coffin was a simple notice: "Thomas Lett Hackett, 'No Surrender.'" In this setting, emotions ran high. As a local paper recorded, "All the morning, an immense crowd of people, including many ladies and young girls pressed forward to view the remains of the late Thomas Lett Hackett … The spectacle presented by the body was deeply affecting; the women sobbed as they peered through the

The burial of Joseph Guibord.

Ostensibly about family, Protestant views of nature, and commemoration, the cemetery was often political theatre. Guibord had belonged to the Institut canadien, a liberal reading and discussion society condemned by the Roman Catholic Bishop of Montreal, Ignace Bourget. On his death in 1869, Guibord was refused burial in his plot in Notre-Dame-des-Neiges Cemetery. While court challenges were undertaken, Guibord was placed in the Mount Royal holding vault. With appeals that ended in London in 1875, the case was finally decided in his favour by the Judicial Committee of the Privy Council. Yet, having a judgment did not ensure an orderly burial. The first attempt to bury him in the Roman Catholic cemetery was blocked by a mob, forcing the return of his body to the Protestant vault. In November, both cemeteries became armed camps. A thousand militia were dispatched up St Lawrence Boulevard and Mount Royal Avenue, marshalling a mile from the Mount Royal burial vault. With mayor William Hingston present, the body, surrounded by 40 armed police and followed discreetly by the militia, was taken into the Catholic cemetery. Bishop Bourget having deconsecrated his grave, Guibord's burial occurred without disturbance. To protect the body from vandalism, an unusual stone coffin was created. Although this cumbersome coffin was eventually rejected in favour of the simpler solution of filling Guibord's grave with concrete, it proved an object of curiosity with respectable Montrealers, visible in this engraving, visiting the stoneworks to view the work in progress.

Charles Chiniquy
(D2018, Section D1).

Like Joseph Guibord and
Thomas Hackett, Charles
Chiniquy emphasizes the centrality of religion, much more
than ethnicity or language, in
strife in nineteenth-century
Montreal. He began his career
as a Roman Catholic priest. A
passionate advocate of temperance, he was always a difficult
subordinate for his episcopal
superiors. Sent as a colonization priest to Illinois in 1851,
he was soon in conflict with
the Irish bishop of Chicago.
Excommunicated in 1858, he
ultimately joined the Presbyterian Church. In 1875 he
came to Montreal on behalf of
the Société franco-canadienne,
the goal of which was the conversion of Catholics. Attacking
papal infallibility, the imperial-
ism of Roman Catholicism,
and its intolerance of
Protestants, Chiniquy preached
the importance of the Bible to
large crowds across Quebec.
With his armed guards, aggressive style, and volatile message,
his meetings were often punc-
tuated by riots. He died in
Montreal, 16 January 1899, and
his funeral cortège to Mount
Royal was accompanied by
1,000 mourners.

glass plate of the coffin at the mutilated features, and even strong men were moved to tears."[27] In all, 20,000 people trooped through the hall to view his body, all of them giv-en orange and scarlet ribbons for the funeral procession. Delegations totalling over 1,200 men arrived from Buf-falo, Toronto, Kingston, and Ottawa to broaden the Orange Order's statement of Protestantism and Britishness: "We have come to protect the Orangemen of Montreal," the grand master of Kingston proclaimed, "and woe betide this city if we have to come again."[28]

Whatever their distaste for popular violence and ethnic hatred, the trustees, in the face of the intensity of feeling among English Canadians, had to show solidarity and pro-vide a suitable grave. The St Andrew's Society, on a motion from cemetery trustee Senator Alexander Walker Ogilvie, agreed to attend the funeral in a body; the St George's Society, "as a society of Englishmen," agreed to do the same. Accompanied by a squadron of cavalry, a battery of artillery, the infantry of the 5th and 6th military districts, city police, and marching bands, the procession, which extended for blocks, was led by the Grand Marshall of the Orange Order and included the Protestant working men from Point St Charles, the Orange Young Britains, and groups of boy apprentices. While Hackett's body was being received at Christ Church Cathedral by the rector of Mon-treal, the dean, and three canons, the Prince of Wales Reg-iment marched directly to the cemetery to ensure order when the procession arrived. At the cemetery, Reverend Charles A. Doudiet pronounced a long oration over Hack-ett's body, announcing that the grave memorial would be a "mark of the value set by true Britons upon religious and civil liberty": "let the occurrences of the last few days be written on the granite obelisk that will mark his last rest-ing place, that in days to come our children may clearly understand the origin of the coming struggle for the equal rights it is our glory to claim, to fight for, and to die for, under the glorious constitution of the British Empire, and which a certain dangerous class of men in this Province at-tempt to assail."[29] As the procession wound back to the city, marching bands abandoned the "Dead March" in favour of popular songs like "The Protestant Boys."

Establishment of a fund to erect a monument to Hackett's memory ensured ongoing controversy for the trustees. Ceme-tery bylaws gave them the right to remove any "offensive or improper" monument or epitaph, a right they exercised in the case of Hackett. As a condition of the sale of Hackett's lot, the trustees specifically insisted on approving the monu-ment's design and inscription. But when the monument was raised, the trustees were shocked to find that its inscription violated their agreement. Although an inquest into his death had concluded that Hackett had fired his own pistol and that he had died with sixty bullets in his pocket, the epitaph read that he was "barbarously murdered" while "quietly returning from divine service." While permitting these words to remain, the trustees, in March 1881, unanimously agreed that the words "by an Irish Roman Catholic mob" be removed.[30] Hence, the monument now reads:

In Memory of
Brother
Thos. Lett Hackett, LOA
Who was Barbarously Murdered
[line removed here]
On Victoria Square
When Quietly Returning from
Divine Service
12 July 1877
This Monument was Erected by
Orangemen and Protestants of
The Dominion, as a Tribute to his Memory
And to Mark Their Detestation of His Murderers

The trustees also resisted the efforts of the Hackett Memorial Fund to locate his monument on a prestigious site. While these negotiations dragged on, Hackett's body, like that of Guibord several years earlier, remained in the cemetery vault. In the end, the Orange Order had to content itself with a site that was near the entrance, but not in plain view. A spot close to the cemetery gates but far from the major grave sites suited the trustees perfectly: if Hackett's legacy continued to be inflammatory, violence would not take place in the heart of the cemetery and could be more easily stopped. This was very much by way of contrast to the prestigious site granted to the Firemen's Benevolent

Hackett's death on Victoria Square.

Newspapers with large Protestant readerships turned the site of the Hackett shooting into a virtual shrine. Despite the presence of William of Orange on his monument, the cemetery avoided popular demonstrations at his gravesite.

Thomas Hackett (E1)

Detail of King William on Hackett Monument

Masons group, Montreal 1877.

There were two worlds of Freemasonry in nineteenth-century Quebec. Eminently respectable in Protestant Quebec, where it was seen as a unifying and benevolent institution, the Masons attracted many of the Mount Royal Cemetery trustees. Conversely, it was associated by Roman Catholic authorities with secret societies, the French Revolution, and anti-clericalism. Although generally cautious in their dealing with Roman Catholic Montreal, the trustees accorded prestigious space near the Firemen's Monument to French-speaking lodges, the Denecheau Lodge (E434 a, b, c, Section E6) and the Coeurs-Unis Masonic Lodge (A135M, Section A1). While some of the Masons buried in these lots were Belgian, Swiss, or French Protestants, others were French Canadians married to Protestants and members of Protestant churches; many of the Masons buried here between 1902 and 1964 had been cremated, which until 1964 precluded burial in consecrated Roman Catholic soil.

Society. Funerals to the Firemen's Memorial went deep into the cemetery, up Hawthorne Avenue past the lots of powerful Montrealers like Hugh Allan to a hillock in section G125 where heroes of the Fire Brigade lie surrounded by mayors and bank presidents. Also near the firemen are the graves of several French-Canadian Masons, forbidden burial in the Catholic cemetery, and therefore buried in Mount Royal in lots purchased by their lodges. The history of the Masonic lodges is quite different from that of the Orange Order. The Masons were more inclusive of a broad range of social classes; indeed, many of the trustees were themselves Masons. Masonic lodges served as benevolent societies helping less fortunate members and emphasizing social solidarity. In a *Montreal Gazette* ad entitled "Funeral Emergency," the brethren of Montreal Kilwinning Lodge were called out on 24 December 1866 for the funeral and burial on Mount Royal Cemetery of Quarter-Master Sergeant John Brewster, who died of lung disease in the military hospital: "Deceased was universally esteemed, not less by his brothers in arms than by all with whom he had become associated since his residence in this city."[31]

The most sensational, and potentially explosive, interment at Mount Royal was that of Charles McKiernan — better known as Joe Beef — who may have been Irish and Catholic but was, above all, a symbol of working-class culture. After British service in the Crimean War, McKiernan was posted to Canada and, following his discharge, he opened a tavern near the Montreal docks in 1868. Joe Beef's Canteen, advertised as the "Great House of the Vulgar People," featured dancing bears, music, and billiards. Besides drink and companionship, his tavern offered food and beds to boys, transients, and dockworkers, and without the moral qualifications of reform institutions like the YMCA or Montreal Sailors' Institute. His tavern was also a regular focal point of worker resistance in dock and canal strikes against prominent employers and cemetery trustees like Hugh Allan.

These politics inevitably spilled into the cemetery, where Joe Beef's rough-and-ready sense of "the vulgar people" and his legitimization of leisure drinking and gambling clashed with trustee notions of respectability. Violating the cemetery's emphasis on lots as commemorative of family, McKiernan provided a grave and headstone in his lot to an unrelated individual who had committed suicide by jumping into the St Lawrence River. As if this were not bad enough, in a speech to 2,000 Lachine Canal strikers, he connected worker demands for a just wage of a dollar a day to the culture of the Mount Royal Cemetery, to the indignities of dissection in an anatomy laboratory, and to pauper burial without a shave or a proper laying out: "if you die in the hospital," he told the workers, "they want the almighty dollar to shave you and keep you from the students."[32] McKiernan again clashed with trustees' notions of propriety following the death of his first wife, Margaret McRae, in September 1871 four days after giving birth. Despite cemetery authorities' disapproval of large processions, she and her dead infant were accompanied to their graves by a marching band. The crowd, ignoring cemetery rules, became boisterous as the graves were filled in. Inviting the funeral party back to his tavern, McKiernan told the band to pass through the cemetery gates playing "The Girl I Left behind Me."[33]

Joe Beef's own burial in January 1889 gave Montrealers an occasion to show solidarity and to control the streets with a large procession that included sailors, "wharf rats," "professional idlers," and many women. In contrast to the decorum of the silent house and drawn curtains favoured by respectable society, the bedroom above his tavern was transformed by white drapery and a black band into a *chapelle ardente*. Here, Joe Beef was laid out in full evening

Joe Beef's Canteen, Montreal.
Take away the Beef and Beer from the British Army, and England is no more!
—o—
JOE BEEF'S ORIGINAL GENIOUSES

Citizens, we eat and drink in moderation ;
Our head, our toes, and our noses are our own,
And all we want is to be left alone !
We eat and drink what we like,
And let alone what we dislike !

JOE BEEF, OF MONTREAL.

Who will feed a Poorman, if is hungry,
Cure him if he is sick,—He does not give a damn
Whether he is an Indian a Nigger, a Cripple a
Billy or a Mich—He never let a poorman die on
The floor and never went back on the Poor !

Above
Life in Joe Beef's Canteen.

Joe Beef's emphasis on the popular classes – in this case, a Black man – on male conviviality, on rough leisure as represented by the drinking bear, on the desire of working men to be "left alone" in their taverns, and on the centrality of meat and beer to the might of the British army, were direct challenges to Protestant respectability as symbolized by the cemetery.

Left Joe Beef
(B991-E, Section B2)

dress, and thousands, it was reported, climbed the stairs, to pay their respects.[34] Despite Joe Beef's ambiguous religious past, the rector of St Thomas Church came to his bedroom and read parts of the Church of England burial service. Drawn by four black horses, his hearse was followed by representatives from fifty labour societies and the cortege, which wound its way along Common, McGill, and Bleury Streets en route to the mountain, was reputed to be Montreal's largest since the funeral of the assassinated Thomas D'Arcy McGee. His epitaph, commissioned by his second wife, was a blunt comparison of Joe Beef's generosity with the selfishness of Montreal's rich:

… Full many a man of wealth & power
Has Died and Gone Before
Who Scorned to Give a Poor Man Bread
When he Stood at his Door
But Joe took in the Great Unwashed
Who Shared his Humble Fare
He Made their Life a Merry One
Without a Thought or Care …

One concern that these sensational funerals raised was the appropriate place of women in the procession and, indeed, at the cemetery. Women were, of course, primary caregivers at death and traditionally had prepared bodies for burial. Although they were present for laying outs and funerals held in the home, their participation in church funerals and burials was increasingly problematic. Etiquette books published in England in mid-century condemned female participation in funeral processions. In the 1870s, many widows attended the church funeral service of their husbands but left for home as the cortege departed for the cemetery. The same situation was evident in South Africa, where women were discouraged from attending Calvanist

funerals. Describing the funeral of the wife of the Dutch governor of the Cape Colony in 1789, Robert Ross remarked that, of the forty-three people in the funeral procession, the only woman present was in the coffin.[35] Protestant practice in Canada seems to have duplicated the conservatism evident elsewhere in the empire. Some men felt that funerals were too emotionally draining for women. Cemetery president McCord may have been typical: particularly wrenching moments such as disinterring his parents from the old burial grounds for re-interment in the new cemetery, or removing his brother' body from the winter vault, were male duties in which he was accompanied by his sons. At Joe Beef's laying out – a scene "full of pathos," as one journalist put it – men expressed their condolences "in somewhat rugged phraseology" despite the presence of a number of women who had mounted the tavern stairs to view the body.[36] The same concern applied to the "many ladies and young girls" attending Hackett's funeral.

These issues of drinking, processions into the grounds, female decorum, and the presence in the cemetery of what Joe Beef's epitaph called the "great unwashed" again raised issues of respectability and even of the personal safety of people visiting the grounds. The latter was brought home in September 1877, when Superintendent Richard Sprigings was attacked in broad daylight near the cemetery entrance. Pulled from his carriage and knocked unconscious in an apparent robbery, Sprigings was rescued by a passerby. Just a year later, the trustees called in the police to investigate the systematic theft of the decorative chains that enclosed many of the better lots. Traced through a nearby junk-dealer, two of the cemetery's employees – carpenter David Vaillancourt and blacksmith Magloire Labelle – were convicted and sentenced to two months imprisonment at hard labour.[37] In the wake of these incidents, the trustees hired a constable to oversee the grounds. By 1887 four employees had been uniformed and sworn in as special constables to ensure that "due order and decorum" were preserved. The constables patrolled the grounds on Sundays, watching for dogs and speeding horses. They were to prevent "littering by basket parties" and to investigate complaints of the theft of flowers or the desecration of graves.[38] In 1880, constable Pierre Gauthier stopped Mrs Benjamin White and her children as they left the grounds with baskets of flowers. In the resulting altercation, Gauthier took hold of White, "dragging her about." In his defence on an assault charge, the cemetery constable testified that White had provoked him, telling him, as the newspaper report put it, that "when a French Canadian was invested with a 'little brief authority' he generally made himself disagreeable."[39] Stealing wood from cemetery forests led to other court cases.[40] Further down the list of disrespectful behaviour was the issue of urinating on cemetery grounds. While women, at least in the discourse of the minutes, did not apparently share this activity, urinating men joined stray dogs, galloping horses, and flower thieves as matters for trustee consideration. At least one of these problems was alleviated in 1899 when "a convenience for gentlemen, in the shape of closets," was erected near the main entrance.[41]

Many of these issues revolved around contradictions between Protestant norms and the popular use of the cemetery as public space. This conflict undoubtedly contributed to the enthusiasm with which the trustees welcomed construction of Mount Royal Park in the 1870s as an alternative site for leisure activities on the mountain. In 1870, the city proposed expropriating the top of the mountain as a public park, and called upon the cemetery to relinquish some of its land. After some negotiation, the trustees agreed to exchange some of the rocky terrain on higher ground for several acres to the southeast that would lend themselves much better to burial.[42] This transaction also brought the trustees a strip of land adjacent to Notre-Dame-des-Neiges Cemetery that was to serve as a "road or means of communication" with the Catholic institution.[43] This strip of land eventually became a rear entrance to both grounds. Though a public space, Mount Royal Park, at least as designed, was no threat to the cemetery. Designed by Frederick Law Olmsted, the heir to Andrew Jackson Downing as North America's leading landscape architect, the park was to emulate Mount Royal Cemetery as an oasis of natural beauty entirely in keeping with nineteenth-century Romanticism. Olmsted's prescription against the popular use of the mountain must surely have reassured the cemetery trustees: "If [the mountain] is to be cut up with roads and walks, spotted with shelters, and streaked with staircases; if it is to be strewn with lunch papers, beer bottles, sardine cans and paper collars; and if thousands of people are to seek their recreation upon it unrestrainedly, each according to his special tastes, it is likely to lose whatever of natural charm you first saw in it."[44] There was also, at least initially, little fear that the park would be more than an extension of the gardens of genteel families already living on the mountain, as access was limited to one or two meandering carriage drives.

Expansion of the Montreal working class and its need for leisure activities and the democratization in attitudes towards public spaces such as the mountain soon brought transformation to both park and cemetery. In 1891, the Montreal Island Railway proposed running tracks up Mount Royal Avenue, presumably to the cemetery gates. When the trustees refused permission, the railway tried unsuccessfully to obtain provincial legislation enabling the project. Three years later, the Montreal Park and Island Railway promoted a trolley line up Mount Royal to the park: this would have given the general public access to the park and to both the

Right Inauguration of Mount Royal Park.

Montrealers took advantage of Queen Victoria's birthday, 24 May 1876, to inaugurate the new Mount Royal Park. The event consisted largely of a mock-battle staged, with canon and cavalry, for the benefit of well-dressed ladies and gentlemen.

Opposite Funicular railway to Mount Royal Park.

From construction of Mount Royal Park in 1876, and more so with the opening of the funicular railway in 1886, the mountain became increasingly mixed in its uses. The two cemeteries remained apart from popular leisure activities on the mountain, and, as private corporations, remained under the control of Protestant and Catholic authorities. The funicular railway, and later the streetcar, brought Montrealers to the top of Mount Royal for the view, fresh air, or a picnic.

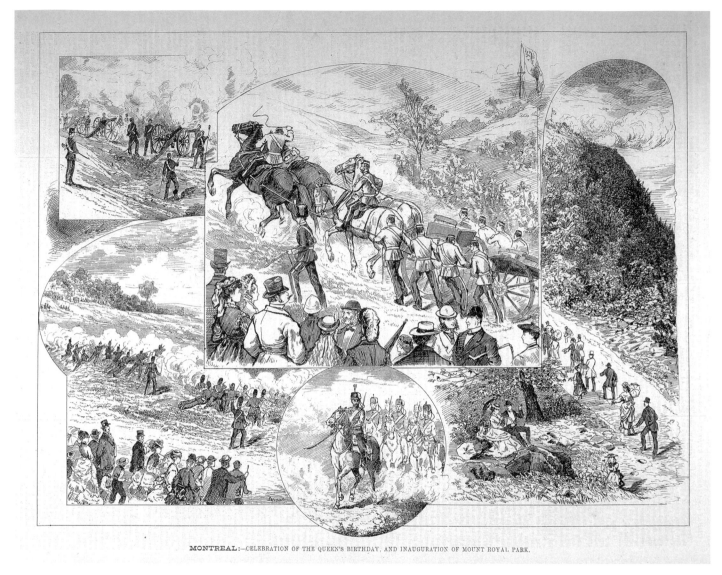

MONTREAL:—CELEBRATION OF THE QUEEN'S BIRTHDAY, AND INAUGURATION OF MOUNT ROYAL PARK.

Catholic and Protestant cemeteries through their back entrances. Supported the Knights of Labor as a means of giving working people access to the mountain, the plan provoked stiff opposition from the cemetery. Defending "natural beauty and seclusion," "solemnity," "unique charms," and "quiet," the trustees protested to Montreal City Council against any intrusion of the trolley "within sight and hearing of those attending funerals or visiting the graves of relatives."[45] In 1896, the project for a trolley was shelved; three decades would pass before it would be realized.

FIVE

RUNNING A BUSINESS
1852-1924

Although the Mount Royal Cemetery trustees concerned themselves with a wide range of social issues surrounding death, notions of beauty, moral regulation, and the like, the cemetery was also a business, and they were charged with its operation. And it was quite a concern – hundreds of acres of mountain property, miles of roads, buildings, horses, a residence for its superintendent and a dormitory for its labourers, a greenhouse and forests, an office, and investments. Sales of real estate, the tasteful and efficient burial of its property holders, management of a large and seasonal labour force, and meticulous record keeping were the essential components of the business.

While the purchase of gravesites by bereaved families occurred daily, it was the advance purchase of lots by well-off individuals seeking a family burial site that provided the cemetery company with essential up-front capital. As in any real-estate subdivision, the developer, if the property's prestige and value was to be maintained, had to work out delicate issues of location, gating, views, site usage, and the compatibility of neighbours. Advance sales to affluent families depended on the attractiveness of the cemetery's property and the integration of gates, buildings, roads, landscaping, and vistas into an architectural and natural ensem-

ble that spoke to profound Protestant cultural aspirations. These purchasers were undoubtedly reassured by the fact that, in the Mount Royal Cemetery, a lot became a permanent possession, a family estate in miniature. Unlike other cemeteries, where concessions were "temporary," ranging for terms up to ninety-nine years, Mount Royal sold its lots as immovable property.[1] Paid-up lots could be freely conveyed or willed to heirs. Following British common-law tradition rather than the civil law, lot transfers did not need to be notarized; a written conveyance, signed by two witnesses, and registered in the cemetery's books, was valid. An important difference between a lot at Mount Royal Cemetery and most other forms of immovable property was that cemetery lots could not be encumbered by mortgages or other assignments; this was a protection against undignified situations such as the seizure of a grave lot for bankruptcy. Graves of the endebted were sometimes restored years later by family or benefactors.

Although cemetery regulations did place certain limits on the appearance of lots, proprietors, like home owners, enjoyed important rights concerning monuments, fences, greenery, and the upkeep of their property. They were permitted to "cultivate trees, shrubs, and plants" in their lots, although the trustees had the right to enter lots to remove "detrimental," "dangerous," or "inconvenient" trees, branches, or roots. In keeping with liberal principles, general maintenance of the lot was the responsibility of the owner.[2] Many proprietors were assiduous in planting, pruning, and mowing, and the purchase of ornamental plants grown at the cemetery itself was an important source of company revenue. Demand for ornamental plants was such that in 1893 a second large greenhouse was built. The trustees rarely interfered in the lot owner's design for the monument or enclosure, although they reserved the right "to prevent the erection of large improvements which might interfere with the general effect, or obstruct any principal view."[3] Lots could be enclosed with iron or stone railings; impermanent and subject to rot, wood was not permitted for either fences or grave markers. Stone enclosures were not to exceed a height of eighteen inches, while iron railings were to be "light, neat, and symmetrical" and not over

four and a half feet high.[4] Lots with stone enclosures and fences were equipped with stairs and gates that permitted access to private, family space.

Given the richness of the masonry, ironwork, and mausoleum buildings decorating the better lots, owners turned to a network of artisans, entrepreneurs, and architects who catered to their tastes. Manufacturers of cast-iron products – extremely popular in the fences, gates, and fireplace grates of Victorian homes – enjoyed a substantial trade in cemetery railings: William Clendinneng & Co. was responsible for a number of impressive enclosures, some still visible, throughout Mount Royal Cemetery. Stone enclosures called for master masons, with owners of the more prominent lots often turning to the same artisans they had employed to construct their homes.

Another specialized trade was that of sculpting the often massive headstones favoured by many. Urns were a favourite

Deed to Hance Alderdice's lot.

As implied by this 1854 deed, lots in Mount Royal Cemetery were acquired as pieces of property and could even be subdivided.

The Lovell's gravesite (F154, Section F1).

John Lovell (1810–93) was Montreal's foremost printer of books and newspapers, as well as the publisher of the *Montreal Directory*. Sarah Kurczyn, whom Lovell married in 1849, operated a girls' school. The motif of an open book is an apt monument decoration.

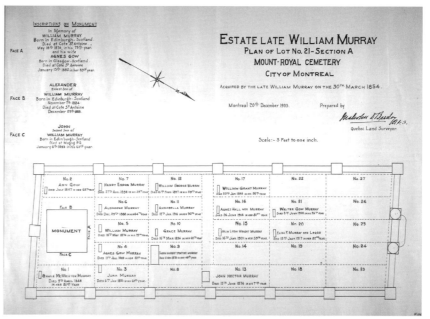

The Murray family lot (A21, Section A1).

David Thompson in the Athabasca Pass (C507, Section C5).

Among the most influential individuals buried in the cemetery is explorer David Thompson (1770–1857). He "discovered" the source of the Mississippi River and, in 1811, reached the Pacific Ocean. After a life spent exploring and mapping the Northwest, Thompson died deeply in debt and was buried in an unmarked grave. Seven decades later, the Canadian Historical Association paid for a suitable monument. At the unveiling in 1926, Thompson's evaluation of his own achievement was recalled: "I have fully completed the survey of this part of North America from sea to sea; and by almost innumerable astronomical observations have determined the position of the mountains, lakes and rivers, and other remarkable places on this continent; the maps of all of which have been drawn, and laid down in geographical position, being now the work of twenty-seven years."

Passers-by can only guess at the world below their feet. This plan, preserved in the cemetery's archives, gives a sense of the layout and use of a large cemetery lot – in this case, that of William Murray, long-time trustee and president of the cemetery company. The lot, bought by Murray in 1854, is set off from its neighbours by a low stone wall with regular buttresses, an opening at one end forming a "door." The lot is dominated by a large monument with Murray's epitaph and that of his wife, Agnes Gow, on the front, and those of his eldest and second sons, Alexander and John respectively, on each side. Who is eligible for burial in a lot can be compared to the distribution of bedrooms in a large house. Here in the Murray plot, family patriarch William, his wife Agnes, and eldest son Alexander lie in front of the monument, with the other siblings, spouses, and children further to the side and to the front; the couple's two mothers are buried on either side of the monument.

Hannah Lyman (G213, Section G).

A New England family prominent in the drug-wholesaling trade in Montreal, the Lymans played an important role in the early years of Mount Royal Cemetery. Benjamin Lyman was a founder of the cemetery and president, 1875–7. Hannah Lyman opened a girls school in Montreal in 1839. A devout Congregationalist, she held Bible classes in her home for soldiers from the British garrison. In 1865, she became principal of Vassar College in Poughkeepsie, New York. She died of tuberculosis in 1871. Her monument, unusual in a Protestant cemetery for its female sensuality and its use of the cross, testifies to her influence on women:

Her Noble Work most worthily done
Was the moulding by her instruction and influence
The minds and hearts of many of her own sex
By whom her memory will ever be tenderly
And gratefully cherished.

motif. In their last declarations to the living, these Victorians favoured lengthy epitaphs that gave weight to words, morality, and life achievement. Men, not surprisingly, gave priority to public achievement, although their role as fathers, husbands, and good Christians was often mentioned. The epitaphs of women emphasized domesticity, although there were important exceptions. For example, the unmarried Hannah Lyman is remembered on her epitaph for her "moulding by her instruction and influence" of both "the minds and hearts of many of her own sex." More traditional is that of Jane Davidson Ross, mother-in-law of cemetery president John Samuel McCord. Her lengthy epitaph, dating from 1866 is a litany of moral, religious, and family responsibility:

Here is laid in the Grave
Beside her Father, her Mother and her husband
Jane Davidson Ross
An humble Christian woman
through life instant in prayer
whose pilgrimages it pleased HIM to prolong
beyond the allotted term of four score years
that she might be a bright example
to her Children's Children
At length her accomplished and her journey over
she on the 25th of March 1866 fell
asleep in Jesus
Nor was she startled by the cry
Behold the Bridegroom cometh
For the lamp was always full of oil
and she shall hear the joyful words:
Come ye blessed of my Father
receive the kingdom prepared for you
from the foundation of the World

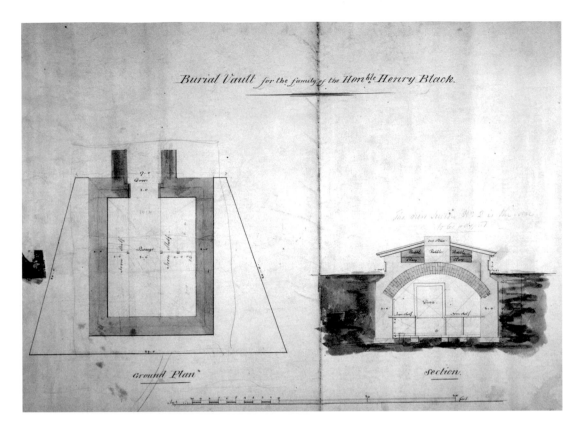

Burial Vault *for the family of the Hon.ble Henry Black.*

Ground Plan

Section.

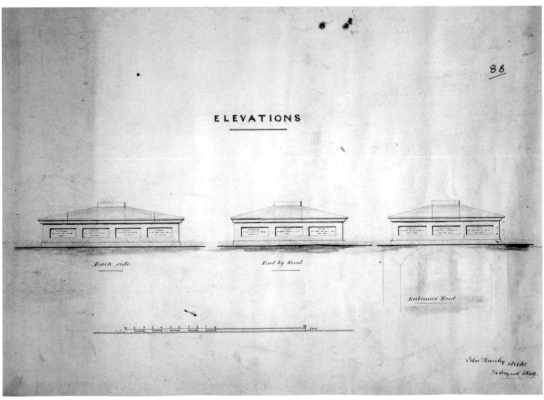

ELEVATIONS

88

Each side

End by Head

Entrance End

Architect's designs for burial vault of the Hon. Henry Black (1849).

While simpler headstones were copied from pattern books, local architects offered the carriage-trade business custom designs for both monuments and mausoleums. In Quebec City, judge Henry Black built his mausoleum in Mount Hermon Cemetery using plans drawn up by architect Edward Stavely.

Grave of Isabella Smith, wife of Andrew Allan (1881) (E169, Section E5).

The lot belonging to Hugh Allan, Canada's most important capitalist in the post-Confederation period, is the best surviving example of a Victorian enclosure, with its wrought-iron fence and gates cast by the Clendinneng foundry, its diversity of monuments, and its garden atmosphere giving a strong sense of private space and public power.

In the nineteenth century, several companies produced headstones as part of a wide range of products: the Montreal Manufactury in Marble advertised "imposing" tombstones in addition to table tops and hearth stones. A competitor, William Cunningham's Marble Factory, manufactured chimney pieces, baptismal fonts, and "at the Shortest Notice," monuments, tombs, and grave stones.[5]

The grandiose displays of the better lots were matched by increasingly elaborate funerals and burial ceremonies. At mid-century, a gamut of small entrepreneurs – coffin makers, engravers of coffin plates, upholsterers of coffin interiors, livery men with hearses, florists, milliners, and printers of funeral cards – offered services to bereaved families. For most of these, funeral products and services formed only part of larger, diverse businesses. John Hoggard, a bill collector and, in a period of a rudimentary postal system, a distributer of bills and circulars, developed a promising sideline delivering funeral invitations. Shopkeeper Henry Morgan advertised "mourning goods" as a specialty at his St James Street store. Before the opening of Mount Royal Cemetery in 1852, undertakers were not prominent in Montreal. Rather, tradesmen such as "cabinet-maker and upholster" C. Robertson advertised that he furnished funerals "on the shortest notice" and that he kept coffins of "various qualities and sizes always on hand."[6]

Construction of Protestant and Catholic cemeteries distant from the city gave new visibility to the funeral procession, to the provision of transportation, and to what undertaker Robertson called "style and taste." Whereas in 1851 Robertson had used the phrase "hearses and crepes at very low prices," his 1864 ads promised a "first class glass hearse" and a "first class glass child's hearse" "unsurpassed in this city." Well aware that the grim reaper was a democrat, Seale and Tees advertised in 1860 that they had "first

J. Brunet's shops, c. 1901.

Responding to the needs of those who couldn't aspire to the wrought iron or elaborate marble sought by established families, entrepreneurs like Thompson and Kinch offered "practical marble workers and sculptors" in addition to "monuments, tombs, tablets" and "all kinds of cemetery decorations." By the 1890s, location near the mountain cemeteries had become important for several industries serving their clientele. While a florist would open near the Mount Royal gates and monument producers along St Lawrence Boulevard, J. Brunet, proprietor of the Laurentian Granite Quarries, established his Marble and Granite Works on Côte-des-Neiges Road near the entrance of Notre-Dame-des-Neiges Cemetery. As well as importing monuments for the well-to-do and offering a repair service for monuments, his shop and stonemasons produced headstones, vaults, and posts.

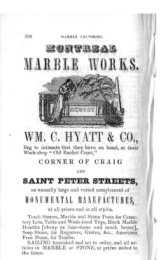

Right Hyatt Marble Works advertisement, 1857.

The rise of the funeral director as a burial professional and the presence of Sunday visitors and tourists at the cemetery contributed to a greater emphasis on public display and spurred a wide range of specialized manufacture, such as the headstone manufacturers pictured here. Much more than simple grave markers, monuments and their surrounding lots were markers of social place conveying symbols of family status and moral and spiritual messages. Construction of the more elaborate sites required artisans, artists, and often architects to produce the desired effect.

and second class" hearses that could be fitted with glass or, for the more discreet, cloth panels. Given the distance, isolation, and strangeness of the two new cemeteries on the mountain, many citizens accepted the service of undertakers as intermediaries between family and cemetery officials. Undertaker Robertson, for example, offered to relieve the bereaved of the administrative worry of dealing with burial details: "all directions relating to funerals will be promptly forwarded to the Cemetery without charge, thereby saving relatives all the trouble."[7]

Organizing the digging of graves and the orderly passage of burial parties – to say nothing of the relentless seasonal tasks of maintaining the cemetery's appearance – rested on the shoulders of the superintendent and his assistants. The reorganization of the cemetery workforce reflected notions of professionalization and the application of new principles of management from the business world to a non-profit service company. While the staff grew more specialized, stability was ensured by the employment of sons and other family members. In 1875, departments were established and the job descriptions of five permanent employees approved by the trustees. Just below Richard Sprigings in the hierarchy was head gardener and forester Peter Turner, who was responsible for "the ornamental condition of the entire domain," laying out new sections and roadways, supervising landscaping, and directing horticultural tasks like maintaining greenhouses and pruning vegetation. Sprigings's brother William, who was given the title sub-gardener and sexton, was in charge of digging the graves, mowing the lawns, maintaining flower beds, and overseeing the "ornamentation of lots." Head labourer and horse keeper Charles Wilson was responsible for keeping the drives in good order, for the horses and stables, and for the critical seasonal task of removing bodies from the vault.

Above Cast iron posts and iron gates, Clendinneng design.

An Irish Protestant, William Clendinneng (1833–1907) built his Montreal foundry into a major enterprise. By 1891 his 450 workers were producing up to 55,000 stoves a year. His wrought-iron fences were purchased for the governor general's residence in Ottawa and for the mansions of the Molsons and Allans. Railings, gates, and posts designed and cast by the foundry can still be seen in the cemetery at the Allan, Phillips, Oxley, and Lauder family lots as well as in the main gates. Rendered deaf by foundry noise, Clendinneng was struck and killed by a train in 1907. He and his wife are buried in the cemetery.

Opposite
Interior of foundry, 1891

William Clendinneng

Exterior of Clendinneng Foundry, 1891

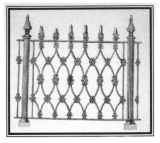

Railing No. 19, with Iron Posts and Gate included. Source: Wm. Clendinneng & Son Co., Ltd. 1894 Trade Catalogue

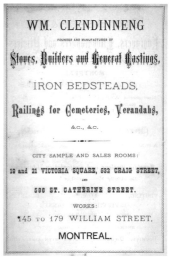

Clendinneng advertisement

Children's hearse.

The glass window in Joseph Wray's hearse illustrates the importance of public display in funeral transport to the mountain cemeteries. By the end of the century, death increasingly occurred in hospital; by 1889, Wray operated his service from the Montreal General Hospital. Wray's ad cleverly used the mountain as a backdrop. Undertakers offered elaborate white hearses for the transport of children.

Right Advertisement for undertaker Joseph C. Wray, 1889

ESTABLISHED 1840.
JOSEPH C. WRAY,
UNDERTAKER AND PRACTICAL EMBALMER,
123 St. Dominique Street, - MONTREAL,
Telephone 1503.
Caskets, Coffins, and First-Class Hearses. Every Essential
Personal Supervision. Moderate Charges.
MONTREAL GENERAL HOSPITAL AMBULANCE STATION.

Gate porter John McCuaig was in charge of cleaning the lodge, of cemetery security, and of opening the gates at 7:00 A.M. and closing them at sunset.[8] Since Richard Sprigings's wife was Ann McCuaig and William Sprigings's wife was Christina McCuaig, John presumably was related to them. In addition to these specialists, the cemetery employed a large seasonal workforce to handle the heaviest manual labour – gravedigging, roadwork, forest maintenance, beautification of the grounds in the high season, and pulling bodies out from the winter mortuary for burial in the critical days as frost came out of the ground.

To get a sense of the superintendent's responsibilities in the late nineteenth century, think of the cemetery as a series of layered work spaces. Clearing forests, blasting gravesites, quarrying rock for roadways, burning stumps, grading lots, landscaping and planting, laying stairs and headstone foundations, digging graves, positioning headstones, chiselling epitaphs, and installing wrought-iron fences produced multiple sites for noise, dust, smoke, trash, traffic, horses, and sweating men. A look at its charter reminds us of the breadth of the physical at the cemetery: alongside burial, its clauses specifically mention sewers, fences, chapels, horses, hearses, roads, parkways, streets, lanes, squares, ditches, drains, water courses, trees, shrubs, and plants. By their charter, the trustees were authorized to hire surveyors, architects, gardeners, superintendents, clerks, and "other officers and servants."[9] Among tools common to large cemeteries like Mount Royal – and all evocative of their physicality – were

Cemetery work crew.

The differentiation among types of outdoor work in the cemetery is clearly visible in this undated photo from the cemetery archives. Five of the men have shovels and one has a saw; ropes used to lower coffins are evident in the foreground. Three of the men have ties and no tools; the man with bowler, vest, and watch chain may well be the superintendent.

axes, picks, spades, shovels, levers, rakes, scrapers, brooms, buckets, wheelbarrows, pumps, ropes and pulleys, planks, ladders, graveboards, graveplatforms, graveboxes, gravecovers, frames, and shelters of many sorts.[10] Within the grounds was an expanding world of work, of family homes, of accounting, registering, transporting, storing, growing, and fixing – a virtual village that included houses, office, bank vault, receiving vault for bodies, stable, greenhouse, pump-house, blacksmith and carriage shops, tool houses, sheds, storage yards, pastures, quarry, seedbeds, and dump. The children of residential cemetery staff grew up on the mountain, played among the graves, and learned trades and cemetery mores by working alongside their elders. Officials were increasingly concerned to separate these behind-the-scene worksites with their muscle, noise, dirt, and visible death from the respectable norms of neatness, order, peace, and beauty expected in the burial zones.

These work and domestic activities required sophisticated transport to provision work and life on the mountain: food for the staff, hay for the horses, and flowers for the departed, along with heavier and slower loads of chain, iron fence, and granite. Moreover, every corpse was accompanied by paperwork, as contracts, doctors' certificates, and pastoral declarations gave the obligatory civil legitimacy to registration and burial, and provided administrative staff and record keepers with employment. Humans, living and dead, joined the transport of materials on the long incline up Mount Royal Avenue from the base of the mountain and busy St Lawrence Boulevard further in the distance. The most visible human traffic consisted of

Grave box.

Grave boxes were used to hold the soil dug out of a grave so that it did not soil the grass; one to four boxes were required per grave. Some boxes were equipped with wheels higher on one side than the other so that gravediggers could wheel them away, leaving the gravesite free of planks or dirt during the service. At Mount Royal, superintendent Ormiston Roy found grave-boxes conducive to a tidy, efficient, and silent work-site. "These boxes," he reported in 1899, "are manipulated by two men, and besides answering the purpose of keeping the lot clean, by their use a grave can be filled in with much less noise and in one-quarter the time that is required to do the same work with shovels."

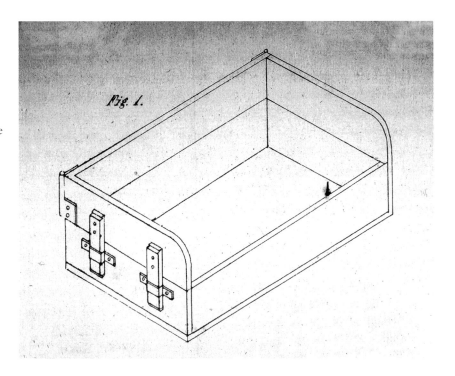

Fig. 1.

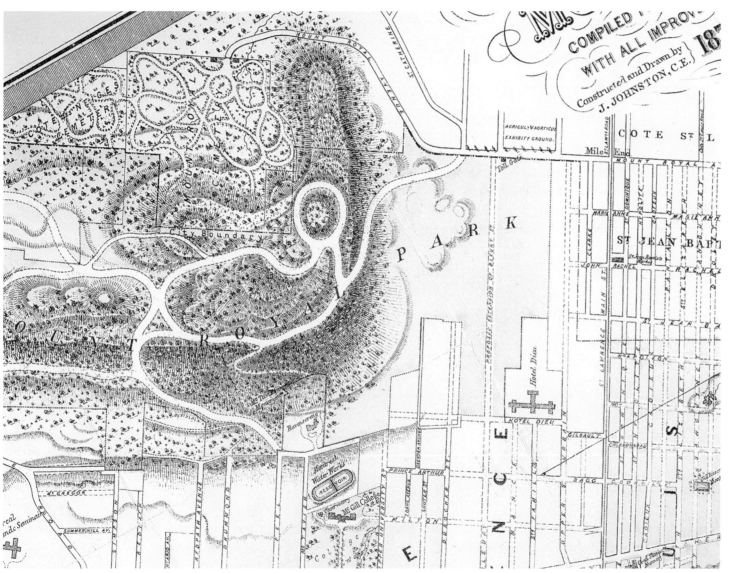

The mountain and Mile End, 1872.

By the early 1870s the trustees were campaigning to have Bleury Street extended north from beside Hôtel-Dieu Hospital to the tollgate on Mount Royal Avenue. This would be advantageous to people attending funerals from central and western parts of the city while permitting people to avoid "the heavy traffic and turmoil" of St Lawrence Bouvelard (MRC, *Annual Report*, April 1873). The roads shown within Mount Royal Cemetery are somewhat fanciful, and the design of Mount Royal Park – drawn some years before park designer Frederick Olmsted came to Montreal – purely invented. Nevertheless, the prominence of the mountain is very much in evidence here.

A. 250

Phillips Martha Anderson
Portland Maine
205 Mansfield St.
27 Oct.1881
31 Oct.1881
94 years 6 months
Bronchitis & Senility
Wid.of Thomas Phillips

Registration card for
Martha Anderson Phillips.

The card-indexing system still
provides an efficient means of
finding out who is buried in
what lot.

burial processions, the bereaved, and visitors, but workers and clergy for the cemetery's multiple constituents had daily business at the cemetery.

As in any smooth-running business, unexpected events could test standard operating procedures. In the particularly disastrous year of 1880, Mount Royal Cemetery had two fires, one in the greenhouse and a second that wiped out the stables, killing five horses and destroying sleighs and harnesses.[11] Events outside the cemetery, like epidemics and natural disasters, also taxed its systems. Yet throughout these periodic crises, the cemetery was obliged to maintain the rhythm of burials. Cholera, typhoid, and smallpox visited Montreal regularly, and burying contagious bodies could be dangerous. Despite the distance from the city, superintendent Sprigings often found bodies left overnight on his doorstep.[12] Smallpox was highly contagious among the unvaccinated, with the airborne virus living for several days on the clothing, shroud, or coffin of the victim. Public health laws were strict concerning burial of smallpox victims; funerals were to be "strictly private" and corpses were to be buried within twenty-four hours in the municipality in which they died. By law, smallpox victims could not be deposited in a receiving vault, and in 1872, Mount Royal Cemetery built a temporary wooden shed to hold such corpses over the winter. Two years later, the trustees chastised Sprigings, who, despite the existence of the separate smallpox shed, had placed victims in the regular vault. Apologizing, the superintendent explained that he had weakened "through regard for the sentiments of private individuals."[13]

Except for crises such as epidemics, cemeteries like Mount Royal were strict in their regulations that graves could be opened only with eight hours daylight notice to the superintendent.[14] Gravediggers at Mount Royal

Cemetery formed a skilled workforce that worked under the direct supervision of the sub-gardener and sexton. They practised a range of techniques to minimize distress and convenience for mourners and clergy around open graves. In churchyards, gravediggers traditionally threw out the soil in random fashion, forcing pallbearers to clamber over piles of dirt to reach the grave. Cemeteries worked hard to reduce mud and disquieting mounds of dirt. In large cemeteries like Mount Royal, wheelbarrows or graveboxes were used to move the soil away, leaving the gravesite surrounded by clean grass. Grave covers equipped with wheelbarrow handles were used to protect newly opened graves from rain and snow as well as to guard "against the danger of persons approaching too near its edge." Among cemetery professionals, Mount Royal's gravediggers were known for their particular expertise in softening the starkness of opened graves by lining them with cedar boughs.[15] During the burial service itself, planks were placed as ground cover alongside the grave. Although some cemeteries provided a clergyman's shelter, which might include a black canvass roof and a raised flooring from which the minister could address the mourners, the practice at Mount Royal is not known.

The issue of grave maintenance – what Mount Royal Cemetery minutes described as "securing a desirable uniformity of order in keeping the grounds" – was a perennial problem.[16] All cemetery superintendents apparently fussed with what was described in one manual as the "want of perpendicularity" of gravestones.[17] The "leaning" problem called for strict enforcement of regulations concerning the construction of monument foundations below the frost line. Things were bad enough at well-maintained graves, but unkempt sites, particularly larger lots with substantial embellishments, were a scourge. With their dilapidated fences, leaning monuments, and overgrown greenery, these abandoned lots represented a flagrant eyesore. Always concerned with the overall attractiveness of the grounds, the trustees ordered the superintendent to report neglected lots. By 1887, a total of 524 proprietors were paying an annual fee for maintenance of their lots by cemetery workers, but many other owners neither paid this fee nor undertook upkeep of their sites.

The issue of maintenance was part of a larger paradox in which the stability of lots as immovable property and the timelessness projected in the rural cemetery contrasted sharply with the impermanence of the Protestant family in Montreal. While the cemetery's reputation was built on constancy and a discourse of "eternal sleep," grave owners were subject to the vagaries of urban life: migration, infertility, epidemic, catastrophe, decadence, or lack of interest might jeopardize a family's capacity to ensure upkeep of their plot. Owners who moved away from Montreal were a particular problem. To resolve this troubling contradiction between the permanence of the dead and ongoing costs to maintain their gravesites, the cemetery, within a decade of its opening, moved towards "perpetual care," a policy in which a lot's sale price included its maintenance in perpetuity. No doubt there was a certain coincidence between the opening of the Grand Trunk line through to both southeastern Ontario and Maine in 1859 and the trustees' discussion in 1860 of the problem of proprietors "who may be leaving the City either permanently or temporarily."[18] In 1861, they announced a perpetual-care option and over the next decades the plan was adjusted several times. In 1869, lot owners received letters describing the rise in "public favour" of this option and inviting them to convert their lots to perpetual care. An extract from the 1879 bylaws provides an idea of the costs:

The Trustees will assume the charge of Lots, and of the preservation and repair of Enclosures,
Tombs and Monuments in perpetuity, on the terms and conditions following:

For the Charge of Lots Only
For every 100 feet superficial up to 400 feet, a payment in Cash of $10.00
For every 100 feet superficial above 400 feet, a like payment of $5.00
If it be required to include the providing, planting, pruning and replacing from time to time, of Perennial Flowering Shrubs, 50 per cent extra on the above charges.

For the Preservation and Repair of Monuments, Tombs and Enclosures.
If the structure be
Of Granite, a cash payment on the cost … of 10%
Of Marble, Limestone, or Sandstone, a cash payment on the cost … of 15%
Or such special price as may be agreed upon by the Trustees

And for Enclosures on the same principle:
The age and condition of the Structure at the time of assuming the charge being
considered, and subject in all cases to the approval of the trustees.[19]

In 1883, faced with the alternative of ignoring neglected graves across its landscape or of assuming their maintenance costs, the cemetery initiated an endowment fund, with revenues from the invested capital to be used to beautify the grounds.

The increasing use of grass as the characteristic cover of graves – what the minutes called keeping the lots in "lawn-like order" – and the efficiency of mowing large open sections with horse-drawn mowers brought another twist to perpetual care. In 1887 a resolution was proposed that all lots should be sold with the condition "of the care of the grass in perpetuity." It was however, still not obligatory to purchase perpetual care, and only a minority of proprietors opted for it. In 1893, only a quarter of the purchased lots were maintained by either annual fee or perpetual care.[20]

The implementation of perpetual care and the rising concern for the maintenance of graves led to the gradual adoption of more scientific attitudes towards cemetery management. Under Sprigings's, successor Frank Roy, and especially under his son Ormiston Roy, modern business theories were applied to the upkeep of the grounds and to the running of the company. In the interests of maintaining standards of appearance, the cemetery imposed its right to regulate run-down lots. Proprietors would be notified by registered letter at their last known address, and, if repairs were not made within ninety days, the superintendent, theoretically at the lot owner's expense, could remove fences and lower boundary posts to ground level, which facilitated access by large mowers. In 1902, Ormiston Roy was able to report to the trustees that many of the older shareholders had acquiesced, removing "high fences, hedges, posts or copings from their lots." Owners who could not be traced and whose lots had "fallen into decay and become an eyesore" had their copings and tombstones removed to storage. A careful record of these removals was kept in case owners or their descendants turned up.[21]

In this spirit of efficient management, lots under perpetual care increased dramatically, rising from 59 in 1887 to 2,750 in 1904. There were difficulties, however, with the principle of perpetual care. At meetings of cemetery superintendents, Ormiston Roy learned of the dangers of overly broad definitions of the care provided to perpetual lots and the assumption by owners that their grass would be watered in dry weather and re-sodded if damaged by grubs.[22] When he had a chance to impose his own vision at the new Hawthorn-Dale cemetery in 1910, he ensured that perpetual care was tightly defined as the "permanent reasonable care of grass." Mausoleums presented another maintenance problem. Although owners left funds for their maintenance, their upkeep required a substantial investment. As the model of the lawn-plan cemetery predominated after 1900, mausoleums fell out of favour with cemetery officials, despite their importance as architectural attractions. In 1908, after discussion of their "present condition," the trustees refused a Molson family request to convert their mausoleums to perpetual care.[23]

Clearly evident by 1875 in its outdoor operations, the principles of scientific management were applied somewhat later to the cemetery's business operations. With the rise of late-nineteenth-century corporate structures associated in particular with transcontinental railways and industries, the office became synonymous with the modern enterprise. Introduction of the typewriter, new forms of records management, and the presence of female administrative staff brought new bureaucratic forms. Like tracking inventory in a commercial operation, record keeping and knowing exactly where people were buried was a critical management function in a business where burials mounted into the tens of thousands. By 1875, the cemetery had become more assiduous in recording information about burials in the free ground, and in the 1880s record keeping was improved again to include the religious affiliation of the poor. In 1890, when Ormiston Roy began work at the cemetery, there were 1,170 interments; in 1958, the year of his death, the company registered 1,734 burials and 636 cremations.[24] At a meeting of superintendents, Roy learned that most cemeteries used a card-indexing system, such as that used in public libraries, in preference to the book indexes used at Mount Royal. By 1904, a card index of all lot owners and graves had been installed; cross indexing permitted quick retrieval of information on burial sites as well as the status of all lots.

In 1885 the trustees appointed the first secretary-treasurer who was not also a trustee. The appointment went to George Durnford, a chartered accountant who would work part-time for the cemetery organizing finances, advising on policy, and selling lots. Durnford was not an employee in the strict sense of the term. His family and benevolent activities linked him to the Protestant gentility. A member of the Sewell family and resident of the estate

Green Hythe on Sherbrooke Street West, he was a justice of the peace, an Anglican, a Freemason, president of the United Empire Loyalist Association, captain in the 68th Durham Light Infantry, and an officer of the Homeopathic Hospital, the Numismatic and Antiquarian Society, and the Society for the Prevention of Cruelty to Animals. Although he received remuneration and was not on the board, he was clearly of the trustees' social rank. He wrote the company's important pamphlet on cremation and, a clear sign of status, co-signed the company's annual reports with the cemetery president.

Neither the Protestant Burial Ground nor the Mount Royal Cemetery in the first half century of its operations had had permanent business offices. In the 1850s, registrar Joshua Pelton had received grave purchasers in the chapel at

Canon F.G. Scott reading the burial service.

Rector of Holy Trinity Cathedral in Quebec City and Canada's best-known chaplain during the First World War, Canon Frederick George Scott presides here over the burial in 1912 of Augustus Kilgore, a bellboy at the Chateau Frontenac Hotel. The scene is Mount Hermon Cemetery in Quebec, but the procedure at Mount Royal would have been similar. Father of poet Frank Scott, Canon Scott is himself buried in Mount Royal Cemetery (394, Section C).

the old cemetery. Later, the company rented offices in the Lancashire Life Building on St James Street, which served the trustees as a venue for meetings and a place to keep records. This office was apparently kept open at irregular hours, depending on Durnford's availability. Purchasers, having made financial arrangements downtown, would proceed to the cemetery, where, accompanied by the superintendent, they would choose their grave site or lot.

In 1913, George Durnford retired as secretary-treasurer, and within a year the company's business operations were reorganized and centralized under the superintendent. Despite opposition from some trustees, Ormiston Roy convinced the board to move its office from downtown to a building at the Papineau Road cemetery: "a home of our own will more than compensate for the little inconvenience that some people will be put to in having to ride at most 10 minutes extra in a street car to reach us." Located at the tramway terminus for the company's recently opened Hawthorn-Dale Cemetery (see chapter 6) and replete with fireproof vaults, the new office was completed at a cost of between $3,000 and $4,000. By 1919, Roy was forced to admit that his experiment had failed. While he had expected the public to use the streetcar to visit the Papineau cemetery offices, where they would purchase lots, funeral directors had intervened with their offer of services. "Prospective buyers," Roy told the trustees, "instead of coming to the Company, bought their Lots from the Undertakers whose interest naturally lay in selling a high-priced coffin and a low priced Lot."[25] As with any other business in the service sector, location and customer convenience were crucial. The move back to the central business district into the Standard Life Building on St James Street improved the cemetery's access to the public. When fire destroyed that building in 1922, the company bought an office building at 1207 Drummond Street, opening its cemetery office there a year later.

Durnford's departure also coincided with further bureaucratization of the office and the naming of new administrative employees. These included Ormiston Roy's brother, John F. Roy, who in 1914 was named assistant superintendent; a new secretary-treasurer, J.A. Ryan; and a chief office clerk, Mrs A.W. McEwen. At Hawthorn-Dale, Henry Gwilliam was appointed superintendent under Ormiston Roy's supervision. This "reorganization of the Company's work in the different departments," Roy reported, "has been a marked benefit and has relieved me of certain detail and enables me to devote more time to the general planning and management of the Company's affairs."[26] During the First World War, cemetery management was reorganized again, with John Roy becoming general superintendent and Ormiston Roy being given the title of landscape architect. Six years later, John Roy became the cemetery's manager, a position he held until his retirement forty years later. In recommending his brother to the trustees, Ormiston Roy neatly combined traditional company values like honesty and respect with qualities expected in a professional – a university education, knowledge of new technologies, and a capacity for efficiency and cost-cutting: "He is faithful, honest, trustworthy, sympathetic and respectful in his dealings with the public. He is young, energetic, a graduate of Macdonald College, and already his idea of shoring the sides of graves as they are quarried (held together by a simple means of tying with wires) has saved the Company many hundreds of dollars in grave digging."[27]

Despite this bureaucratization, the cemetery remained a paternal employer, giving first hiring to sons, providing housing for some, a modest pension for most, and a gravesite for all. Henry Gwilliam served as superintendent at

Hawthorn-Dale from its opening in 1910 until his death forty years later. He emigrated from Shropshire, England, working first at Raeburn Farm in Pointe Claire and then as manager of Elmwood Farm in Longue Pointe near the site of Hawthorn-Dale. William Duffield worked at Mount Royal from its opening in 1852, was pensioned in 1915, and was buried in the cemetery in 1917. Alfred Nall worked as a foreman for sixty years. When he retired in ill health in 1924, he continued living in one of the cemetery's cottages, receiving a pension until his death in 1932. Louis Laviolette worked as a gravedigger at the cemetery for almost sixty years, retiring in 1924. John Short, worked as a clerk in the cemetery office from 1907 until his death in 1934. The deaths of long-time employees were marked in the trustees' annual report. "I report with regret," Manager John F. Roy told the trustees in 1930,

the death during the year of two of the company's faithful workers. Joseph Allaire, who for over fifty years rarely missed a day, regardless of weather. He was insured with the Sun Life Assurance Col, under the Group Insurance Policy, for the amount of $1,000 which has been paid to his widow. Benjamin Paquet, who died last November, after a long illness, could also, for over forty years, be depended upon at any hour of the day or night. Unfortunately, he was not included in the Company's insurance scheme, as he took sick just before the policy came into force, but during his illness he received a small weekly pension, and his son, who replaced him, gives promise of being as devoted as his father."[28]

Like superintendents everywhere, Ormiston Roy's daily concerns centred on the orderly routine of burials and the efficient organization of cemetery work. To alleviate the discomfort of mourners and ministers coping with rain and mud, he experimented with easily erected shelter tents and tarpaulins that kept gravesites clean. Mourners were discouraged from lingering at the gravesite and observing its filling in. Roy's preference was that mourners leave as soon as the body was lowered in the grave; this allowed workers to fill the grave "at their leisure" later in the day and to undertake the graceless and heavy labour of pounding the soil to reduce later sinking of the grave.[29] His larger sense of orderly operations extended to the problem of watering containers that were brought by families to water flowers planted on graves and were apparently abandoned or left for later use. To end this confusion, "and after all their bother, having them stolen," he proposed to place twenty-five stamped cans at the entrance.[30]

Burial parties traditionally advanced to the cemetery at various speeds, their progress dependent on grief, the inevitable delays of funerals, and the capacity of horse and hearse under unpredictable road conditions. Cemetery and church officials had long struggled to keep funerals and processions on time. In 1841, while burials still occurred at the Protestant Burial Ground, officials of St Paul's Church sent a resolution to city newspapers calling for the punctuality of funerals:

The Kirk Session of St Paul's are of opinion that no longer space of time should elapse than ten minutes after the hour specified in the circulars of invitation, before the funeral procession should begin to move. They conceive that the time at present wasted through the dilatoriness of many in coming forward is not to be measured by the loss sustained by one but by the aggregate loss of time sustained by all who are punctual, and the inconvenience and danger resulting to those who may have to remain standing exposed to the vicissitudes of the weather for perhaps three quarters of an hour.[31]

With schedules always approximate, the bell at the entrance of Mount Royal Cemetery had traditionally served to alert gravediggers and cemetery workers to the arrival of a burial party. In 1903, imitating "a handy and inexpensive" system he had seen in operation at Mount Auburn Cemetery, Roy set up telephones throughout the grounds. This enabled foremen to be given instructions "without having to come down to the office, thus affecting a great saving of their time." In 1907, he reported on other methods instituted to improve efficiency:

During the year a change has been made in the organization of the working staff. Heretofore, it has been the custom to have different works, such as grave digging, grass cutting, etc., in charge of separate foremen, but under the new arrangement, foremen oversee all work in their respective divisions including interments, repairs to avenues, grass cutting etc. The experience has so far been quite satisfactory, giving the Public by reference to the foremen, easy means of information, and enabling the carrying on of the work in the different branches more efficiently and economically.[32]

The timing of burials and the organization of work were particularly critical on those spring days when bodies, usually in the hundreds, were brought out of the winter vault for burial. Provincial health laws obliged burial by 20 May of all bodies stored in winter vaults. However, opening the ground, frozen in Montreal to a depth of at least a metre, depended more on weather than government regulation and could be undertaken only when frost was entirely out of the ground. In 1907, a late thaw left the cemetery just twenty-one days to bury over six hundred bodies; excluding Sundays, this meant that an average of over thirty-three bodies had to be buried each day. In such years, up to two hundred men might be employed digging graves across the cemetery. Many families attended these burial ceremonies and their preference for afternoon burials meant that funerals in peak periods had to held at ten-minute intervals, all of which gave weight to the superintendent's insistence that appointments be "punctually" kept.[33] The development of equipment for breaking frozen ground permitted the gradual introduction of winter burials during the First World War. In 1918, only thirty-nine bodies were stored in the winter vaults compared to up to seven hundred in earlier years.[34] Despite the costs of keeping roads across the cemetery open in winter, this was a major transformation in the organization of work, lessening the dependence on seasonal labour and permitting the employment of a more permanent labour force. By avoiding the need for a second service, it also reduced the anguish of families.

Managing seasonal labour was a critical responsibility of the superintendent. During the busy season, labourers were kept on the grounds by converting the upper part of the carpentry shop into a dormitory. During the Spanish influenza epidemic of October and November 1918, the cemetery buried 667 more bodies than in the same months the previous year:

We took the precaution at the outset of having the staff … wear masks – as prescribed by the Montreal General Hospital for their nurses, and I am thankful to say, not one of our employees, as far as I am aware, contracted the disease. At any hour of the day or night all were at their post, when needed, and burials in the moonlight were made in Mount Royal, when all the workmen had gone home and the Superintendent had to call out foremen to fill in the graves.[35]

Roy proudly reported that although some labourers "afraid of contracting the disease" had refused to work, he had, by "encouraging in various ways the men we had, to work harder," succeeded in burying all victims without having to store any remains in the burial vaults.

Ormiston Roy's long career across the first half of the twentieth century coincided with major transformations in North American cemetery practices. The model rural cemetery where he began work in 1890 was essentially a one-product company dispensing its services with a view to Victorian respectability and, where necessary, Christian charity. Its focus was the Protestant family, and burial – be it in a family lot, single grave, charity lot, or Free Ground – was carried out in partnership with the city's Protestant ministers and leaders of the benevolent societies. The coherence and practices of this rural cemetery were challenged throughout Roy's career. Principles of the lawn-plan cemetery became increasingly important. The religious demography of Montreal changed and the death rate of infants declined dramatically. Cremation emerged as an alternative to in-ground burial, while new technologies in communication, transportation, and construction changed the organization of burial and work. Professionalization made the funeral director an increasingly important figure in cemetery operations. At the same time, the emergence of new professions such as that of landscape architect and cemetery superintendent challenged the authority of the trustees and their traditional view of the cemetery.

SIX

THE LAWN PLAN VERSUS
"WIDOWED STONE"

In its first half century, Mount Royal Cemetery – as a visit to some of its oldest sections still confirms – had developed as one of the continent's most attractive rural cemeteries. Users of John Langford's popular 1868 guidebook to Montreal discovered a setting he described as "pretty," "picturesque," "handsome," "pleasant," and "sheltered."[1] Once past the imposing gates and attractive residence of the superintendent, a drive around the grounds in the 1870s and 1880s brought a profusion of images that were nonetheless coherent: mausoleums built by the wealthy as family shrines; large lots whose fences and gates imitated the privacy and intimacy of a comfortable home; monuments of different sizes, shapes, and building materials that testified to lives well lived, to love cut off; and memorials marking the communal graves of orphans, Freemasons, firemen, and train-wreck victims. Much of the cemetery grounds remained under forest, what Langford called "the luxuriant foliage of the trees." In their drives, visitors might savour the lengthy epitaphs on the finer monuments, short essays that spoke of family origin, individual achievement, religious feeling, public service, and female rectitude.

The cemetery's tone was set in large part by prominent Montrealers intent on having their religious and aesthetic sensibilities reflected in a natural space established for the educational, domestic, leisure, and commemorative activities of their community. Even in the second and third generations – for example, four generations of Hodgsons served as trustees, from 1880 to 1954[2] – the board remained a coherent social group linked by interests, class, neighbourhood, and a sense of Protestant responsibility. Yet, over the years the superintendent became increasingly important in influencing the shape and functions of the cemetery.

Superintendents employed in the cemetery's first decades came from a social class distinct from that of the trustees and had honed their skills within the craft tradition of gardening. Horticulture and the creation of a romantic landscape

Postcard commemorating Sarah Maxwell (G200M, Section G2)

The Burning School, Hochelaga, Scene of Miss Maxwell's Sacrifice.

Funeral procession of Sarah Maxwell.

By the twentieth century, mass-circulation newspapers increased readership by the sensational reporting of disasters such as the 1907 fire that burned Hochelaga School and cost the lives of a teacher and several pupils. Reports praised teacher Sarah Maxwell, who helped many children to safety and died attempting to rescue more. Postcards, such as the one on page 105, were produced commemorating the event. Her Mount Royal epitaph reads: "In Loving Memory of Sarah Maxwell, aged 31 yrs, who lost her life whilst endeavouring to save the lives of the pupils at the Hochelaga school fire, Feb 26th 1907, also the little ones who perished with her."

were, as we have seen, fundamental to the concept of the rural cemetery. At Glasgow's Necropolis, for example, officials from the Royal Botanical Garden advised cemetery authorities as to the choice of weeping elm, cypress, cedar, ivy, and other plants suitable for the new burial environment.[3] The relationship of cemetery presidents John Samuel McCord, George Moffatt, or William Murray with superintendent Richard Sprigings was an extension of the attitudes they had with gardeners on their own estates. Usually British-born, gardeners in Montreal were craftsmen, knowledgeable about plants and landscaping and capable managers of work around estate properties. To augment their primary skills in horticulture, landscaping, and surveying, cemetery superintendents acquired the graveyard sexton's knowledge of burial practices as well as the sensi-

tive public relations involved in arranging committals.

The tenure of Richard Springings as gardener and superintendent at Mount Royal ended with his death in 1890, almost four decades after he was engaged by the cemetery. He was replaced by Frank Roy. Born in Scotland, Roy had worked as a gardener at several estates and as head gardener at the Royal Botanic Gardens in Edinburgh. He came to Canada as manager of the Montreal Floral Nurseries and added to his reputation as a landscape gardener by laying out the Forest and Stream Club in Dorval.[4] Like Sprigings, he was active in the Montreal Horticultural Society, serving as its president. He was one of the rare Canadian members of the Royal Horticultural Society in Britain and wrote frequently in the *Canadian Horticultural Magazine*. In 1890, the year Frank Roy was named superintendent, his teenaged son W. Ormiston Roy was hired as a clerk at the cemetery. Roy senior was soon afflicted with rheumatic fever, and during his illness his son assumed many of the functions of superintendent. On his father's death in 1898, Ormiston succeeded to the position of superintendent. In marrying Charlotte, the daughter of former superintendent Richard Sprigings, Ormiston Roy took a wife used to the particular life of the cemetery environment. Charlotte Sprigings grew up, married, and raised her children on Mount Royal.

Ormiston Roy, as we have seen, entered a company dominated by its trustees' Romanticism, ethic of benevolence, and particular vision of nature. Photographs taken in the period by William Notman and others depict the cemetery as highly rustic, with burial sections and the buildings, gate, fountain, and gardens around the entrance representing only manicured pockets within a larger forested and steep, rocky terrain. As American lawn-plan concepts came to the fore in his thinking, Ormiston Roy turned against the unkempt nature, the stark, massive stone and mausoleums that dominated the rural cemetery. His generation was uncomfortable with Victorian exaggerations of Death, Classicism, Religion, and the Individual. Seeing the large monuments, iron fences, elaborate urns, and lengthy epitaphs as invasive and narcissistic, he used blasting, forest-clearing, and construction technology to create a more secular and park-like setting, one whose vistas would emphasize "spreading lawns" broken only by well-maintained shrubs and perennial plants and flowers. Upright headstones were to lose their centrality: they would become smaller, might be placed flat on the ground, or might be replaced by bronze plaques that did not obstruct lawn maintenance or the terraced perspectives. Rust, burial mounds, tipped stones, iron fences, and stone copings

Table 6 Presidents of the Cemetery, 1851–2002

Name	Years of tenure	Name	Years of tenure
John Samuel McCord	1851–4	Douglas G. Macpherson	1956–8
George Moffat	1855–7	Ernest C. Koch	1959
William Murray	1858–74	Roy L. Campbell	1960–1
Benjamin Lyman	1875–7	J.C. Hope	1962–3
Robert Esdaile	1878–9	R.H. Dean	1964–6
Henry Bulmer	1880–1	Dudley S. Thomas	1967–8
Henry Lyman	1882–3	Frank E.H. Gates	1969–71
M.H. Gault	1884	John de M. Marler	1972–80
James McDougall	1885	Joseph S. Connolly	1981–92
C.D. Proctor	1886–92	Robert M. Everson	1993–6
John Stirling	1893	John W. Durnford	1996–9
Richard White	1894–5	Donald B. Wilkie	1999–
J.P. Cleghorn	1896–7		
A.W. Ogilvie	1898–1900		
Alex Macpherson	1901–2		
James Tasker	1903–4		
G.F.C. Smith	1905–6		
Seargent P. Stearns	1907–8		
S.O. Shorey	1909–10		
John Beattie	1910–12		
C.J. Fleet	1913–14		
E. Goff Penny	1915–16		
William Hanson	1917–18		
Farquhar Robertson	1919–20		
John Patterson	1921–3		
Dr. Milton L. Hersey	1946–7		
W. Gordon Hanson	1948–9		
H.P. Thornhill	1950–1		
C.G. Mussell	1952–3		
Prof. C.M. McKergow	1954–5		

View in Mount Royal Cemetery, c. 1915

Founder of Montreal's most important photographic studio and himself buried in the cemetery, William Notman had a keen entrepreneurial sense of the cemetery's commercial value, taking multiple landscape photos that might serve for souvenir albums, postcards, or for his collections of Canadian views. Taken above the Drummond mausoleum, this view combines the subtle presence of Drummond family power with landscape beauty. The core of Notman's business was portraits – the individual, family, or group photos that responded to Victorian demands for commemoration that silhouettes or painted portraits could not satisfy. With the stark realism of photography and understanding his customers' desire to remember, his studio accepted commissions from the bereaved to photograph chapelles ardentes, gravesites, or the deceased themselves. The growth of the cut-flower industry brought florists to centre stage in decorating funeral and burials, as is evidenced by the photo of Miss McDougall.

Flowers for Miss McDougall, 1910

William Notman (F-2C, Section F3)

Ormiston Roy's patent (1909).

As superintendent, Roy contended daily with the practicalities of preparing graves in the rocky ground of much of Mount Royal. His patent, granted in 1909 as the "Hollow Block Burying Ground," was intended to minimize the expense of quarrying and removing rock by the use of hollow concrete blocks that would be placed vertically and then covered with topsoil to create an artificial surface. Graves, placed in any direction, could be easily prepared by simply removing the topsoil and the required blocks. A test of his patent was proposed to the trustees, with Roy agreeing to renounce royalties until the method had been tested. The results of the test are not clear.

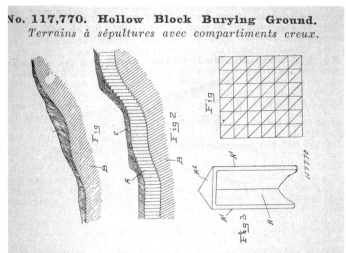

No. 117,770. Hollow Block Burying Ground.
Terrains à sépultures avec compartiments creux.

William Ormiston Roy, Montreal, Quebec, Canada, 13th April, 1909 ; 6 years. Filed 11th December, 1908. Receipt No. 164,948.

Claim.—1. The method of preparing ground for burial purposes consisting of constructing a bed of hollow vertical blocks on the surface and covering the surface of the blocks with a layer of earth as described.

2. The method of preparing rocky ground for burial purposes consisting of removing the surface earth, constructing a bed of hollow vertical triangular blocks on the rock surface and then spreading earth on the surface of the blocks, as described.

represented blight that should be removed wherever possible. Perpetual care was an effective means of imposing the coherence of the lawn-plan model since it transferred control of gravesites from families to cemetery management. The lawn plan would depend less on individual lot owners or the craft of poets, stone masons, or iron workers and more on professionals skilled in horticulture, construction, engineering, and landscape architecture. Roy himself obtained a patent on the utilization of hollow cement blocks that could be used to terrace rocky slopes and then be converted into easily opened graves. With the trustees' permission, he also began designing and charging

for monuments in the better sections; he experimented with "chaste, classic designs" that featured a bronze plate on the table or base stone.[5]

Autocratic and proud of his initiatives, Roy described the lawn cemetery as "the greatest American creation of Art-Out-of-Doors, and as original with the American people as their skyscrapers."[6] At Mount Royal Cemetery, he wrote: "we have made bird sanctuaries of our grounds; we have demolished some very unsightly vaults and thousands of posts, bars, copings, iron fences and enclosures of all kinds inherited from the past; we have exerted a very large influence in getting smaller and more artistic monuments than in most places, and have made it fashionable to have a background of shrubs and planting on our best lots."[7]

Roy's fascination for the lawn plan came through his contacts with American cemetery professionals. The trustees had always encouraged the participation of their superintendents in conferences: in 1864, "anxious to add to the embellishment of the cemetery," the trustees sponsored the visit of Roy's father-in-law Richard Sprigings to horticultural displays in Boston, New York, Philadelphia, Baltimore, and Cincinnati, while Roy's father was sent to Philadelphia in 1894. In his first year as superintendent, Ormiston Roy attended meetings of the Association of American Cemetery Superintendents. Established in 1887, this professional association, which had 360 members by 1921, promoted an expanding place for superintendents in the administration of cemeteries, and through meetings and publications informed members of technological and landscape innovations.[8] At his first meeting, Ormiston Roy met Ossian Cole Simonds, superintendent of Chicago's Graceland Cemetery. Simonds had enormous influence on North American cemeteries: as well as laying out Graceland, he designed arboretums and parks, was the innovator of university programs in landscape architecture, and was the author of the classic *Landscape Gardening* (1920). He was founder of the American Park and Outdoor Art Association (1897). Roy quickly came under Simonds's influence, describing him as his "mentor" and a "born artist."[9] Simonds would visit Montreal several times, advising Roy on how to implement his lawn plan on the grounds of Mount Royal and on the soon-to-be-established Hawthorn-Dale Cemetery.

At their first meeting in 1899, Simonds took Roy to the Hartford Cemetery in Connecticut and pointed out his distaste for its headstones, monuments, and posts. Promoting the lawn plan, he urged substitution of "natural beauty in the form of trees and shrubs and hardy flowers for the cold, bare effects produced by too much stonework."[10] One way of reducing the effect of stone was to restrict construction to one monument per lot. Other superintendents agreed with Simonds, condemning "all unnecessary stonework" and insisting that lot owners be obliged to submit their architectural plans for approval by cemetery officials. Mounds, – familiar markers of graves without headstones and a long source of debate in Mount Royal Cemetery – were considered an eyesore in the lawn-plan landscape. Simonds proposed to ban them in favour of ground-level markers denoting the corners of lots. Monuments themselves would be diminished, serving more as a foretaste to a powerful backdrop of trees, shrubbery, and perennial plants. Roy, back from the 1899 convention, reported his ideas to the trustees. Grass, he suggested, would become the predominant natural feature, even replacing gravel in the construction of paths.[11] Annual flowers, carpet beds, tender plants like geraniums, and "monstrosities" like flower sundials, clocks, and calendars had little place in this grassy landscape, while tropical vegetation like palms and banana

trees were dismissed as "abnormal" and entirely out of place in a North American cemetery.

To criticisms that cemeteries were tax-exempt institutions that blocked urban needs for industrial and leisure space, Simonds emphasized the cemetery as "a real asset" and a "work of art," a place that did "something for the living." Simonds saw their contribution to leisure as essentially one of observing, giving to the urbanite "the pleasure that comes from looking," "from watching," "from listening": "in short, the pleasure that comes from the charm of nature." These priorities separated the cemetery from most parks of the period, with their emphasis on movement, diverse activities, and artificial landscapes that might include playgrounds or playing fields.[12] In his philosophy Simonds anticipated later environmental concerns. Cemetery grounds protected not only the bodies of the deceased but served as a "a safe place for trees, shrubs, flower, ferns, mosses, turf and all the smaller plants that make an attractive ground-covering, the whole arranged in a way to provide beautiful landscapes, its perpetuity … assured, … in fact, … demanded by future generations."[13]

The young Ormiston Roy's enthusiastic conversion to the lawn plan was quickly reflected in cemetery rules. Lot owners intending to "enclose their lots, construct vaults, or to have their boundaries more fully defined" were obliged to apply to the superintendent. The cemetery's campaign against neglected lots, and the demolition of ironwork and stone enclosures by owners unwilling to pay for their upkeep – or by the cemetery itself in the case of owners who could not be traced – dates from the first years of Ormiston Roy's superintendancy.

Although Ormiston Roy's ideas represented a highly visible rupture with the rural-cemetery principles on which Mount Royal Cemetery had been founded, his father had already moved to introduce certain lawn-plan concepts. Frank Roy undertook several major landscaping projects designed to improve the cemetery's beauty and to diminish its overly rustic atmosphere. In 1891, he directed construction of "a handsome fountain" near the main entrance, which added "to the general appearance and attractiveness of the flower beds." Alongside the superintendent's residence, he constructed an English garden, known long after his death as the Frank Roy Garden.[14] He groomed areas around the main gate that had previously been left in hay, forming them into "the beauty of a nice surrounding lawn." In 1893, rocky areas in Section M were excavated to produce new burial areas and to give a gentler, less rugged appearance; the quarried rock was hauled off to grade cemetery roadways. In the summer of 1896, Frank Roy supervised the draining of a large area in Section E, uncovering a spring that was thereafter used to supply water to the greenhouse.[15] He also implemented a tightened policy on mounds, opening Section D as an area in which mounds and fences were banned in favour of posts installed by the cemetery. He opened a children's section in G3. Its small monuments or flush stones represented a powerful psychological addition to the idea of cemetery as lawn. Development of this inexpensive area, along with moderately priced graves developed in Section G, encouraged all but the destitute to buy a gravesite and, by extending lawn towards the back of the cemetery, reduced the Free Ground's "isolated appearance."[16]

In the 1890s, sprucing up the unkempt charity and Free Ground areas became an important issue. For two decades, the trustees had discussed placing them "in as respectable order" as other sections, but little improvement had occurred. These areas were increasingly visible with growing public use of Mount Royal Park and of the cemetery's parkside entrance, which brought visitors close to these unattractive areas. The easiest solution was to open a new Free Ground further north and out of sight of the entrance. The old site was graded, cleaned up, and virtually forgotten. The trustees also discussed acquiring land at the rear of the cemetery near the park. This would enable them to close the existing southern gate in favour of a new entrance from the park opening onto an area "where the improvements and expenditure for monuments, etc. have been the greatest."[17]

Opening the new Free Ground may have alleviated the aesthetic problem, but it did not solve the practical one of burying large numbers of paupers without charge. Mount Royal officials were not only concerned about the number of pauper burials; they felt that those denominations strongly affected by the reformist social gospel movement were far too inclined to grant free burials. Free burial, they were convinced, was a privilege that should be reserved for the deserving poor, as opposed to malingerers. The trustees were particularly bothered by reports that some beneficiaries of free burial had been given "expensive funerals."[18] Annulling the right of clergymen to authorize access to the Free Ground, the trustees limited "the privilege of free interment to cases where the necessity is vouched for by a member of the trust or other responsible person."[19] Ormiston Roy was still not satisfied and, a few years later, complained that "under the conditions of our charter we are forced to bury the poor of the several Protestant denominations of the City, free of charge." He calculated in 1906 that, since opening the new Free Ground in 1891, over 4,000 bodies had been buried free of charge. The cost to the cemetery had been some $10,000 "when we consider that it furnishes the land, vault accommodation in winter, transportation from vault in spring, grave digging, and a lead number for each coffin, besides the time involved for registration and keeping a record for five years of the exact

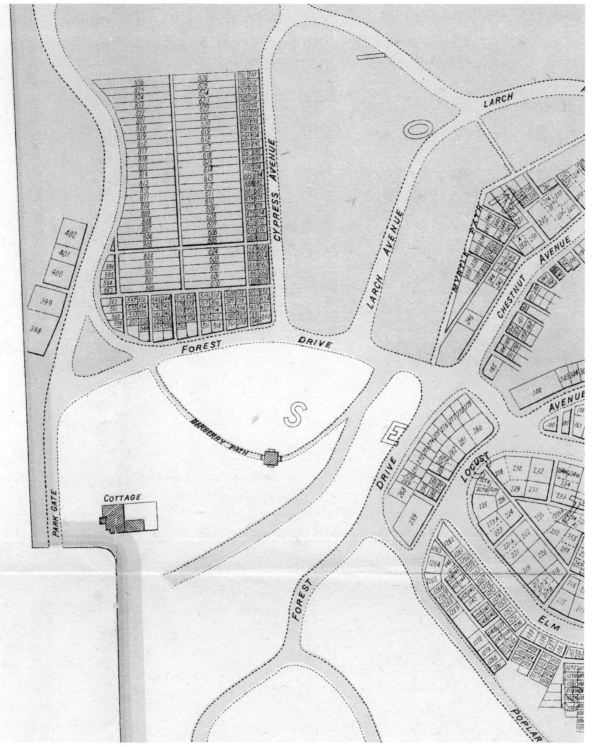

The park entrance, 1885.

With the opening of Mount Royal Park in 1876, a strip of land straddling Mount Royal and Notre-Dame-des-Neiges provided access to both cemeteries. The road, which can be seen at the lower left, led to two gates: left into Notre-Dame-des-Neiges, and ahead into Mount Royal. Entrance by the "Park Gate" led visitors to the Protestant cemetery past the cottage that served as a gatehouse (home for many years to William Sprigings, brother to the superintendent) and straight into the charity section (398–402). This area belonged to various Protestant Charities and beyond it was the Free Ground (top left). Just across the road from the charity lots and free ground and bounded on two sides by Forest Drive and Cypress Avenue is a section laid out in part as single graves and intended for Protestants of modest means. Further east, on the other side of Cypress Avenue, the cemetery would create its main children's grave section.

location of each grave to enable relatives to reclaim the bodies."[20] In 1905, there were 255 burials in the Free Ground, an average of about one a day during the burial season, as well as ongoing burials in the charity lots.[21]

Ormiston Roy was also concerned by the increasing expense of opening free and inexpensive graves as usable land became increasingly rocky and hard to work: "We have been forced within the last few years," he reported,

to devise the present process of making burial places, by filling about four feet of broken stone in the bottom of each lot. On top of this is placed about six inches of smaller stones or screenings, and the lot is finished off with about a foot and half of soil, just sufficient to grow grass. When lots are sold in such sections the purchaser is informed that the bottom of the lot is filled with broken stone. The stone found in each grave is carted away as the grave is dug and sufficient earth brought back to make the interment.[22]

This method, feasible for expensive family lots in Pine Hill Side, which was being developed, was impractical for sections in which single graves were dug close together. Dirt and stones tended to cave in on these graves and plank sidings were required. "The day is not distant," the trustees were told in 1906, "when every foot of burial ground will have to be converted from almost solid rock."[23]

Construction of a suburban satellite cemetery on a site with suitable soil, good drainage, and easy public access was one means to provide affordable graves. In 1906, after a considerable search, the trustees paid $23,000 for George Irving's 142-acre farm at Bout de l'Isle, at the eastern end of the island of Montreal.[24] They described it as "beautifully situated, having a frontage on the St Lawrence River of a little over five arpents and running back to a depth of twenty eight arpents. The ground is well situated for drainage, being rolling and undulating, and when laid out and planted with trees and shrubs, – arrangements for which are in contemplation, – it will be in every way an attractive location."[25] In addition, its workable soil would reduce the labour of opening graves, while undeveloped sections could serve as a shrub and plant nursery or as a working farm producing feed for cemetery horses.[26]

The final consideration in terms of a site designed to attract working people was accessibility of public transportation. It was anticipated that the new cemetery would follow many cemeteries in American and British cities in its use of trams. Since two lines operated adjacent to the property, the trustees expected to benefit from competition as these companies reached out for "business in any direction in which it may be offered."[27] Negotiations to organize stations, a spur line, and reduced fares for funeral parties resulted in a 1908 contract with the Montreal Tramways Company to run a special cemetery tram three days a week. At the new Hawthorn-Dale Cemetery terminus, a station, waiting room, and receiving vault capable of holding 300 bodies were built. At the city terminus, located near the Papineau Cemetery, the company built a special station. Arriving here by horse-drawn hearses and accompanied by funeral processions, coffins were loaded onto the "Funeral Car." At first, space was not provided for mourners in the Funeral Car, leaving the bereaved to travel to the cemetery in a regular tram alongside other passengers. In 1915, a new funeral tram was introduced with special side openings for the loading of coffins and with seating for mourners: "the car was divided into sections. Of course there was a space for the motorman and conductor in the front. Immediately next was a space for the undertaker and his assistants, the middle section being devoted to the holding the coffin, and floral arrangements. The back part of the car

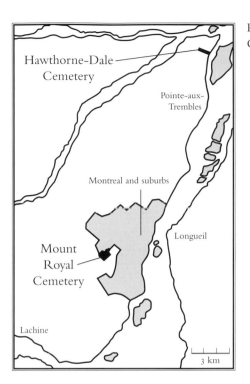

Relation of Hawthorn-Dale
Cemetery to Montreal

Hawthorne-Dale
Cemetery

Pointe-aux-
Trembles

Montreal and suburbs

Longueil

Mount
Royal
Cemetery

Lachine

3 km

Plan of Hawthorn-Dale Cemetery.

The long narrow farm extending back from the
St Lawrence River became Hawthorn-Dale Cemetery,
but not without being subjected to the eastward
extension of transport links. Already traversed by the
CN Railway, the site was cut in half in the 1930s by
the extension of Sherbrooke Street. This map shows
a cluster of buildings near the original entrance off
Notre-Dame Street.

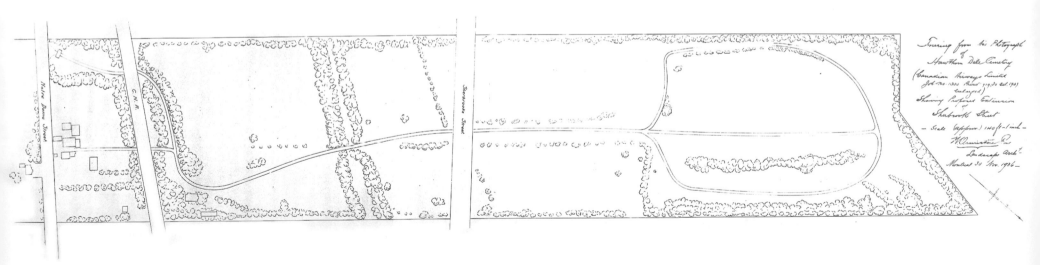

Funeral car.

In 1915, a tram coach was altered for service to the cemetery. The interior was stripped and a raised shelf built along each wall for storage of two rows of coffins. Frosted windows were installed and hinged doors built into the right wall for the loading of coffins. Painted black, the car was marked "Funeral Car" in gold lettering on the front and "Hawthorn-Dale Cemetery" on both sides.

The Buick of the Armstrong Funeral Home, 1927.

The versatility, privacy, and prestige offered by motorized hearses doomed the use of public transit for burial parties travelling to Hawthorn-Dale Cemetery.

was arranged a little like a parlour car for the immediate family and mourners."[28] The Funeral Car remained in service until rendered obsolete in September 1927 by the growing use of motorized hearses.[29]

For Ormiston Roy, the Hawthorn-Dale site represented a fresh slate on which principles of professional landscaping and modern cemetery management could be applied free from the regulations, property rights, and battles over mounds and fences that had bedevilled Mount Royal Cemetery. Hawthorn-Dale's plan was drawn up by Roy

after a site visit with his friend Ossian Cole Simonds. The burial area was reached by a paved circular road. Other driveways were to be graded, rolled hard, and planted in grass, thus reducing maintenance and enhancing a park-like atmosphere. Regulations at the new cemetery were copied from those published by Simonds in a landscaping encyclopedia. The trustees were told that these had been endorsed unanimously by the Association of American Cemetery Superintendents.[30]

Hawthorn-Dale's rules imposed strict control over all visual aspects of the cemetery. With a twentieth-century tone of egalitarianism and what was called "justice to all," the cemetery reserved the right "to exclude or remove" headstones, structures, or trees "injurious to the general appearance of the grounds." The planting of shrubs and trees was restricted "to protect the rights of all and to secure the best possible results." All plantings were subject to approval by the superintendent. With estimates of the costs of maintaining fenced lots at four times that of a lawn-plan cemetery, Hawthorn-Dale refused all iron or wire work, seats, and vases unless specific permission was accorded. And, in the new aesthetics of the automobile age, corroded iron denoted decay rather than vintage. Any object showing rust was liable to removal. Coping and enclosures were forbidden, with lot boundaries marked instead by standard cement posts installed by the cemetery – but at the owner's expense. Burial mounds, which blocked lawnmowers and drew attention to the presence of death and away from park views, were discouraged. Mounds represented a simple form of physical commemoration and, like headstones, that privilege was determined by one's ability to pay. Mounds were not permitted on the cheapest graves – that is, on the $5 children's gravesites or on adult graves sold for less than $15. On higher-priced graves, mounds were limited to a height of four inches.

Headstones could be constructed only of cut stone or real bronze: "no artificial material will be permitted." They were not to exceed 5 per cent of the area of any lot and, to discourage their tipping, any stone over a foot in height was to be placed on a concrete foundation poured by the cemetery. On children's graves and on the cheaper adult graves that sold for between $12.50 and $15.00, stones were restricted to a height of eight inches; on all other single graves they were to be no higher than one foot. Mausoleums had no place in the new cemetery, with the trustees concurring with the " best landscape gardeners of the day" that they are "generally injurious to the appearance of the grounds … are apt to leak … and to become unsightly ruins."[31]

At Mount Royal, efficient management of the labour force had been hindered by the presence of outside workers who entered the grounds to tend lots, to garden, or to repair stone or ironwork. At Hawthorn-Dale, except for stone work, all work was to be performed by cemetery employees. All regulations were to be enforced by the resident superintendent Henry Gwilliam; he, in turn, answered to company superintendent Ormiston Roy.[32]

While the visitor's attention in Mount Royal Cemetery is drawn to monuments and mausoleums, Hawthorn-Dale's mission was to provide an accessible, attractive site for modest burials. For its opening in 1910, four acres were laid out, "drained, graded, top-dressed with a covering of loam, fertilized, and made ready for burials." Prices of all graves at Hawthorn-Dale included gravedigging, transport of the body from Montreal, and perpetual care. Children's graves were advertised at half the $10 to $16 charged in Mount Royal, as were the adult sites, priced at $12.50, $15, $17.50, and $20.[33] The key solution to having to provide Free Ground burials was to keep graves at a cost that all but the most destitute could afford: "we have made the prices at

Hawthorn-Dale so low," Ormiston Roy reported in 1918, that "only people in the direst straits of poverty have to resort to asking for free burial."[34] In the mid-1930s – the worst years of the Great Depression – the cemetery insisted that its "land" prices were among the cheapest in urban North America, ranging at Hawthorn-Dale "from 41 cents to a little over a dollar a foot," while Mount Royal graves "on the rural lawn plan, with bronze markers allowed level with the grass are provided at $1.75 a foot."[35]

Although the Hawthorn-Dale grounds were purchased in 1906 and the cemetery was opened for burial in 1910, it was not dedicated until October 1911. The careful compromise surrounding the Protestant partnerships at Mount Royal and the incidents surrounding the burial of controversial figures such as Joseph Guibord and Thomas Hackett had sensitized trustees to the repercussions of religious politics on cemetery grounds. Thus, at Hawthorn-Dale, the term "dedication" was used in preference to "consecration." In answer to a petition from the cemetery president John Beattie to seperate the new burial ground "from all profane and common uses," Anglican Bishop John Cragg Farthing agreed to dedicate the cemetery. After reading Psalms 90 and 103, he declared Hawthorn-Dale a cemetery, in which "the bodies of the faithful may therein rest in peace."[36]

The impact of Hawthorn-Dale on Mount Royal was immediate, with the transfer to its grounds of much of the clientele for modest graves, of virtually all free Protestant burials, and of an increasing percentage of charity burials. In 1905, Mount Royal granted 255 free burials; in 1912, none. In its first year of operation, 89 free burials occurred in Hawthorn-Dale's Free Ground, and of the 348 paid burials, 47 were listed as "cheap."[37] In 1914, there were 673 burials at Hawthorn-Dale, including 80 free burials, as compared to 1,647 interments at Mount Royal.[38] Newer groups like the Salvation Army, which worked with the Protestant poor, did not follow the nineteenth-century middle-class model of benevolent institutions with their communal charity lots and large institutional memorials. They instead bought single graves as need arose, and their social service remained anonymous. In 1908, the Salvation Army paid $3.50 for a grave at Mount Royal Cemetery and over the next decades they bought nineteen graves at Hawthorn-Dale. These were entered in cemetery records as "8 feet" or "24 square feet" and were sold at prices ranging from $3.50 in 1908 to $72 in 1973. These graves were used to bury men, women, and children from the Salvation Army's Maternity and Rescue Home, Men's Hostel, Industrial Department, the Men's Social Department, the Eventide Home, and the Salvation Army French Corps. Other burial entries at Hawthorn-Dale are marked "City of Montreal burial," speaking to the city's role in burying the unclaimed and sometimes unidentified. Non-identified bodies in Montreal were assumed to be Roman Catholic and were delivered by a contract undertaker to the Cimetière de l'Est for burial without religious ceremony in its common grave; in 1948 the city paid $3 to bury an adult and $1 for a child (designated, in a unique definition of childhood, as an individual with a coffin under four feet in length).[39] Corpses identified as Protestant but unclaimed by family were delivered to Hawthorn-Dale. Buried at city expense, these individuals did not normally receive a religious service, although in 1936 the Montreal Protestant Ministerial Association expressed willingness to provide free services.[40]

The combination of cheap graves with the sale of individual gravesites to the city and to charities resulted in a steady decline of the Free Ground burials assumed by the Mount Royal Cemetery group. In 1919, Hawthorn-Dale's fifteen free burials – there were none at the main cemetery – were the fewest since the company had begun operations in 1852. This decline continued to four free burials in 1954 and the same number in 1955.[41] Assumption of burial costs by a provincial welfare program after 1969 relieved the burden of the destitute entirely from the cemetery company. In 2002, families on welfare or charity organizations who buried a destitute individual received $2,500 to cover burial expenses. This was the equivalent of the death benefit paid to the heirs of individuals who had contributed to the Quebec Pension Plan.

In keeping with its mandate to provide affordable gravesites, Hawthorn-Dale's overall impression is one of egalitarianism and orderliness. No stones are visible from the entrance, and, except for the paved avenue that loops through the cemetery, grass dominates. To maintain perspective, all graves bordering the avenue feature flat stones level to the ground; graves with above-ground stones are set back near the trees. There are distinct children's, military, and free-ground sections. The diminutiveness of monuments – even those commemorating disasters – is striking. Given the smallness of stones, epitaphs are necessarily limited and their language is often popular or colloquial – "Pop," "Little Smiler," "It is finished," "May we meet in Heaven."

In contrast to its sister cemetery, Mount Royal continued to expand as a showcase of the Protestant elite, especially with the development of Pine Hill Side and then Rose Hill. Where he could, Ormiston Roy encouraged the removal of dilapidated enclosures and the opening of sections intended for low monuments. Having designed and opened Hawthorn-Dale, Roy devoted more time to what he saw as his role as a naturalist and guardian of beauty. In 1914, he negotiated a new contract by which the company secured his services as landscape architect and general superintendent; as part of the contract, the trustees recognized Roy's right to "greater liberty to devote himself to the profession of Landscape Architect" and to accept "outside work as a landscape gardener."[42] In addition to his annual salary of $1,800, he continued to have free lodging in a company house on the periphery of the cemetery grounds in which his lighting, taxes, and heating were paid. Under his new contract, Roy would no longer be provided with a company horse and rig, but an automobile, purchased at his expense, could be parked in a cemetery garage and washed by a stable man.

We have seen Roy's distaste for the cemetery clutter evoked by what poet Stéphane Mallarmé called "widowed stone."[43] One of his landscape models was New York's Central Park; its open spaces, "a perfect imitation of country and nature," Roy wrote in 1899, "would make an ideal cemetery."[44] He continued to work at giving the cemetery a new and coherent landscape, what he called a "finished and harmonious effect to a whole section" that would predominate over individual "tastes." He discouraged the haphazard placement of annual flowers planted according to the "varied tastes of individual lot-owners." In their place, he preferred "the natural grace" of trees like the lilac or crabapple or perennial flowers like the rose and peony.[45] In 1916, the cemetery announced its intention to cease greenhouse production of flowering plants; henceforth, lot owners wanting to lay or plant flowers would have to buy them from local florists. This announcement was apparently not carried out since in 1918 a new cemetery greenhouse, devoted to flowers, was built near the park entrance.[46] While it is not clear if he participated in the founding of the Montreal Botanical Garden in 1931, Roy collaborated with internationally known botanists drawn to its employ. He and Henry Teuscher developed dwarf species, like the Siberian Flowering Crabapple, that might replace the old evergreens and diseased apple trees that characterized much of the Montreal landscape. While many of the shrubs and trees were grown in the Hawthorn-Dale nursery, imported stock before the Second World War came particularly from nurseries in Orléans, France, and Boskoop, Holland.[47] Although there is an Ormiston Roy shrub rose and an Ormiston Roy flowering crabapple, his particular passion was the peony and he saw to its planting around the grounds. If the headstone urn was the symbol of the nineteenth-century cemetery, he made the peony synonymous with the lawn-plan look. He organized distribution committees in every province to introduce the Wembley peony rose to gardens. Part of his dream of making the peony Canada's national flower, these would be grown in private peony nurseries organized with his son.

Peonies near the crematorium.

This undated photo of the crematorium shows the importance given by Ormiston Roy to an overall horticultural plan. Large shrubs hide the furnace area while climbing vines outline the chapel doors. The winding driveways are accentuated by the massive use of perennial flowers.

Streetcars up the mountain.

One of the most spectacular journeys in the Montreal area was a tram ride up the east side of the mountain. From its departure loop on Park Avenue, the streetcar wound through tunnels and rock cuts to the summit, offering impressive views of city and cemetery. The tracks, in place by 1930, were torn up in the 1950s to make way for the Camillien Houde Parkway, today Montreal's most popular drive.

Especially after the opening of Mount Royal Park, which drew large numbers of Montrealers to the mountain, a greatly increased number of visitors – not all of them desirable from the trustee's point of view – spent time in Mount Royal Cemetery. Their presence raised issues of regulation and security. Enclosure of the cemetery became particularly urgent in 1905 when the old rail fence that circumscribed the property collapsed. Always keen on the latest technology, Roy recommended the "Pittsburgh Perfect Fence," a five-foot "electrically welded wire fencing" to which he added three strands of barbed wire "which makes the fence very efficient."[48] This enclosure remained intact until the 1920s, when the cemetery exchanged land with the city to permit construction of public transit up to Mount Royal Park. The exchange included a commitment on the part of the city to rebuild the southern part of the cemetery's fence, which had been demolished in the transfer, but it was years before the city fulfilled this promise. In the meantime, the cemetery complained, lack of a fence resulted in damage to "lots in our finest sections." Although extra men were detailed to guard against vandalism, it was "almost impossible to prevent the stealing of plants and damaging of flowering shrubs."[49]

The opening of the tram line along Shakespeare Road from Côte des Neiges Road to the park in 1924 and of a route up the east side of the mountain by 1930 forced the cemetery to give attention to the aesthetics and security of the rear gates, which gave access to the tram line and park. In 1935, the old park entrance gates near the charity lots were finally dismantled and moved to Hawthorn-Dale. Having acquired from the city, as part of the tram exchange, a strip of land running alongside Notre-Dame-des-Neiges Cemetery and additional ground near the tram line, the cemetery built a new entrance near the present location of the south gate. Visitors could now enter direct-

ly from the tram stop via the road alongside the Catholic cemetery, entering the grounds away from the charity lots and closer to the attractive Section A2.

Despite the disapproval of some trustees towards the growing number of visitors, Ormiston Roy remained an unabashed supporter of public access to the cemetery, particularly by automobile. In 1911, the trustees had decided to maintain their "rule governing automobiles ... viz that it is undesirable to allow Automobiles in the Cemetery and that Notices be posted to that effect." Roy had a different attitude and wanted to adapt the cemetery to the needs of drivers. In 1919, he began experimenting with concave roads, a form of construction that facilitated water runoff. Sponsorship by T. Howard Stewart of the Memorial Road to the crematorium permitted Roy to experiment with asphalt paving and, in 1924, he reported that the cemetery was one of the first locations in Canada to use "Amiesite Asphalt Pavement"; laid cold, this paving mixture was less slippery in wet weather than the traditional macadam.[50] By 1924, the cemetery had built a "spacious parking place for motors" near the superintendent's house. To keep the cemeteries accessible for year-round burials, Roy encouraged the latest equipment: by 1938, Hawthorn-Dale was equipped with a Caterpillar diesel tractor and a Baldwin snowplow.[51]

These improvements certainly added to the cemetery's attractiveness and accessibility to the automobile-owning public, although before the Second World War most Montrealers did not own cars. While allowing the elderly or infirm to tour the cemetery's beauty, moving cars also had the advantage of not being conducive to advanced courtship, picnics, or other sedentary pleasures. Visitors – as opposed to lot owners – were requested to drive steadily through from front gate to rear gate, and never to park or get out of their cars. Touring Mount Royal or Hawthorn-

Dale on Peony Sunday became a springtime tradition as popular as Peony Mile in Langport, Somerset, or the Lilac Sundays organized in Boston and Rochester. Thousands of peonies were planted along the long main driveway at Hawthorn-Dale and on Peony Sunday in 1935 police had to be employed to cope with the traffic jams. In 1939 the Mount Royal gates were left open in the evenings to accommodate visitors touring the peony beds: over 1,000 cars visited in a single evening and, again, police were hired to direct traffic.[52]

In 1935, thirty-six years after attending his first meeting of the Association of American Cemetery Superintendents and meeting Ossian Cole Simonds, Roy reiterated his mentor's view of the social contribution of the lawn-plan cemetery:

Our leading cemeteries should keep pace with the best thought of the times, with the best theories of religion, science and economics. They should be, as the name implies, sleeping-places – places of rest and freedom from intrusion. It seems natural that people should select for such a place the very best production of landscape art, a place where spreading lawns give a cheerful warmth and sunlight; where pleasing vistas show distant clouds or setting sun; where branching trees give grateful shade, furnish pleasing objects to look at, and places for the birds to come each year and sing again their welcome songs; where blossoming shrubs delight the eye, perfume the air, and make attractive resting places. Such places seem to exist more for the living than the dead, but the living are the ones that need them.[53]

Alongside his public status as a cemetery professional and landscape architect, Roy developed private interests, hobbies, and connections that gave him broad standing in English Montreal. A Mason, Rotarian, bird watcher, and

Funeral procession of Isabella Scott (née McMaster).

Feminist Isabella Scott was buried on 17 July 1942. The *Gazette* photographer chose his vantage point to give full play to the place of the automobile in the funeral procession. At the cemetery itself, roads were widened, reinforced, and paved with a view to receiving heavy automobile traffic.

Scenic trip for motorists, 1941.

The "Peony Sundays" promoted during the 1930s were followed by occasional special motor trips through Mount Royal Cemetery to view lilacs and crab apples in blossom. In this advertisement, the trustees' pride in the natural beauties on display was tempered by their disinclination to have people wandering about the grounds.

MOUNT ROYAL CEMETERY

— *Scenic Trip for Motorists* —
LILACS AND FLOWERING CRAB APPLES AT THEIR BEST

Motorists are invited to view the wonderful display of Lilacs and Flowering Crab Apples that are now blooming at their best, in Mount Royal Cemetery. From 5 p.m. until 8.00 p.m. today, and at the same hours Wednesday, Thursday and Friday the Trustees are permitting motorists to drive through the cemetery grounds.

Motorists are requested to drive slowly, keep off the grass, and refrain from parking (Parking cannot be permitted on any pretext).

Note especially the first half mile up to the Crematorium and back on the concave Memorial Road, passing the French Lilacs on the way, and on this part of the road ONLY motorists are warned they MUST drive to the left—as they do in England. When visiting the Cemetery proper for the next 2½ miles follow the one way traffic through to the exit at the Road of Remembrance (Shakespeare Road.)

ENTRANCE ONLY BY THE MAIN GATES
At the head of Mount Royal Boulevard.

EXIT ONLY BY
The Road of Remembrance.

Ormiston Roy (139a, Section PHS).

On his death in August 1958, Ormiston Roy was cremated and his ashes interred in Pine Hill Side. His headstone, erected by the trustees, reads: "Landscape naturalist, peony grower, collie dog fancier, curler, in the continuous service of the Mount Royal Cemetery Company from 1890 to 1958."

curler, Ormiston Roy was described in a 1912 biography as one of the continent's most successful breeders of collies. Secretary of the Montreal Horticultural Society and Fruit Growing Society, he also served as vice-president of the American Park and Outdoor Art Association. Roy's reputation, his well-placed friends, and his familiarity with complex technical and ethical issues such as cremation gave him increasing independence from the trustees. In 1934, he reported to them that he was giving press interviews to stress "a few points on which many citizens are misinformed." A year later, "having completed 45 years with the Company," he felt enough at ease to "reminisce a little" with the trustees, reminding them of improvements made over his tenure.[54]

Changes in the company's history of relations between trustees and management can be seen in Roy's evolving job description. His father's occupation had been "gardener" and "head gardener"; in his obituary, the trustees had paid tribute to Frank Roy's "practical experience as a landscape gardener."[55] Ormiston Roy's two brothers-in-law, who worked with him at the cemetery, were listed in their obituaries as "gardener" and "foreman." His own formal education was described vaguely as having been given by the Council of Arts and Manufacturers of the Province of Quebec. The council gave evening classes for boys over fifteen – principally "artisans and apprentices" – in subjects ranging from architectural drawing and wood and marble sculpture to plumbing and shoemaking; before coming to cemetery employment, his first work was apparently in the seed business.[56] Ormiston Roy perfectly

caught the turn-of-the-century wave of the professionalization of cemetery superintendent, rapidly distancing himself from his craft and gardening origins. He came to be described as a "horticulturalist," "landscape architect of genius," "botanist," or "philosopher."

An inveterate traveller to conferences, cemeteries, and parks around Europe, America, and Japan, and active in international cremation, horticulture, and cemetery societies, Roy returned from his trips invigorated by knowledge of the latest in technology, plants, and cemetery innovation. Entrepreneurial, he used his contacts, skills, and products developed in his cemetery career to spin off small businesses and a successful sideline as a consultant. He acted as landscape architect for the twenty-seven-acre estate of Eugène Lafleur in Hudson, Quebec, and, further afield, took consulting contracts with the Rockefeller estates in New York State, the Ford Motor Company in Deerborn, Michigan, the Grand Trunk Railway, the governor general for his estates in Ottawa and Quebec, and with Mackenzie King for his Kingsmere property in the Gatineau Hills.[57] Building on the reputation of the peonies he had developed at Mount Royal, he launched a peony-export business, entrusting his farms in Rouse's Point, New York, and in Laval, Quebec, to his son Carlyle.[58] At the cemetery itself, his job title progressed from superintendent to landscape architect and general manager; in 1918 he became landscape manager and crematorium manager. His headstone, erected in his honour by the trustees on a commanding site on Pine Hill Side memorializes him as landscape naturalist.

SEVEN

CREMATION, 1902–1974

Canada's first cremation was conducted on the grounds of the Mount Royal Cemetery in 1902. Ormiston Roy, recently named superintendent, was a strong proponent of the practice, and two of Canada's most powerful capitalists, J.H.R. Molson and William Christopher Macdonald, subsidized construction of the crematorium. Across Europe and North America, cremation was perceived by its advocates as clean, efficient, and technologically attractive, and it responded to public health concerns about air and water pollution emanating from burial grounds. Symbolically, the crematorium represented the superiority of modern science and the industrial furnace over nature's slow putrefaction process. Moreover, cremation could be assimilated to lawn-plan principles of cemetery development. By removing the physical presence of the body from the cemetery grounds, it was a means of diminishing the ubiquity of death. It presented a challenge to an older Romanticism and Victorian sentimentality represented by mausoleums, large headstones, and grave mounds. Cremated remains also permitted new land use and a reconfiguration of the cemetery. If buried – as opposed to being dispersed or stored – cremated remains required much smaller graves, which could be located in shallow-soil sections unsuitable for the burial of coffins.

The science of cremation had important business connotations: it helped cemeteries like Mount Royal regain the power over corpse and ceremony that had been undermined in the preceeding decades as undertakers professionalized into funeral directors. In one sense, rural cemeteries – with their distance from cities forcing new modes of transportation, communication, and organization – had encouraged services offered by the funeral director. The development of embalming, was even more important. Organized in the United States into the National Funeral Directors' Association in 1882, funeral directors had effectively used the science of embalming to capture centre stage in comforting families, organizing funerals, and arranging cemetery transport and grave committals. To facilitate embalming with its various apparatuses and waste, bodies were increasingly transported to funeral "homes" or "parlours." Here, as they organized coffins, flowers, viewing, and funerals, funeral directors were in a privileged position to advise families on cemetery transport and choice of gravesite and headstone. Cemetery superintendents such as Ormiston Roy objected to the high costs of burial, the crassness of funeral directors, and, particularly, their appropriation of authority over the cemetery site. His hope was that cemeteries with crematoria might regain their business initiative through the provision

Nurses leaving funeral home with casket, Winnipeg.

The substantial neighbourhood home recycled as funeral parlour, the wrought-iron fence, and the contrast of nurse pallbearers in white and male undertakers in black emphasize the increasing place of "funeral directors." Female pallbearers were unusual.

Chapel, Joseph C. Wray's Funeral Home, c. 1935.

The Wray Funeral Home had a long association with the Mount Royal Cemetery. The architecture of its chapel attests to the displacement of many funerals from a church setting to the funeral parlour. Cut flowers remained a mainstay of expressing condolences.

of chapels for funerals that culminated in cremation. This competition for territory between cemetery and funeral director made them uneasy partners and would culminate later in the twentieth century with the construction of crematoria by major funeral corporations and with the entry in the 1990s of the Mount Royal Cemetery Company into the funeral business.

Whatever its potential advantages for cemeteries, disposal of the corpse through incineration posed fundamental religious conundrums: an anathema to Roman Catholic, Jewish, and Greek Orthodox communities, it was a difficult issue for Protestants. Practised widely in the ancient Greek and Roman world but banished by Christian authorities, cremation revived in western societies in the late nineteenth century as part of the same public health impulse that had contributed several decades earlier to the building of rural cemeteries like Mount Royal. An 1876 report on burial grounds in industrial Glasgow emphasized that cremation was part of a larger strategy for eradicating urban stench and pollution: "On the side of public health, cremation has the best of it; it destroys the germs of zymotic disease, of offence, and of corruption at once."[1] New incineration technologies offered solutions to the problems of mass disposal of the urban dead or multiple victims of epidemics, catastrophes, or modern war. In 1873, Bruno Brunetti's cremation furnace was shown at the Vienna Exhibition and illustrations of William Siemens's furnace were widely published in the mid 1870s.[2]

In the United States, public health officials were increasingly concerned about the capacity of the country's rural cemeteries, built on the fringes of most major cities in the mid-nineteenth century, to meet the demands of burying the urban dead. The first American crematorium was built privately in 1876, and a public company, the United States Cremation Company, was incorporated in the same year. It

CANADIAN Illustrated News

VOL. IX.—No. 23.   MONTREAL, SATURDAY, JUNE 6, 1874.   SINGLE COPIES, TEN CENTS. $4 PER YEAR IN ADVANCE.

CREMATION IN GERMANY.—THE SIEMENS FURNACE FOR USE AT DRESDEN

The Siemens reverberating furnace.

Graveside rites are fundamental parts of Christian burial tradition. The combination of cremation with religious ceremony required some ingenuity, as this engraving from 1874 shows. The Siemens process suggested that a casket could be lowered into the furnace in rather the same manner as ordinary interments – and done so with great efficiency. The innovative technology of cremation was given wide publicity in the *Canadian Illustrated News*.

built the Fresh Pond Crematorium on Long Island, where the first cremation occurred in 1885. The National Cremation Association was founded in 1883. Within the decade, cremation societies or private cremation companies had been established in San Francisco, Buffalo, Boston, Lancaster (Pennsylvania), Worcester (Massachusetts), Cincinnati, Pittsburgh, New Orleans, St Louis, Baltimore, San Antonio, Los Angeles, and Detroit. By 1900 twenty-four crematoria in the United States handled 2,414 cremations. Yet, unlike embalming, which gained broad public acceptance, cremation advanced only slowly: in 1920, cremation followed less than 1 per cent of deaths in the United States.[3]

Similar trends were occurring in Europe. Despite the opposition of the Roman Catholic Church, cremation advanced most rapidly in Italy, where the first municipal crematorium in Europe was constructed in Milan in 1874.[4] To promote a "process which cannot offend the living, and [which] shall render the remains absolutely innocuous," the Cremation Society of England was founded in 1874. Its first president was Sir Henry Thompson, Queen Victoria's surgeon, and it received support from prominent intellectuals such as Anthony Trollope and Herbert Spencer.[5] The first British crematorium was built in 1879; the courts allowed it to begin operations in 1885, and by 1902 cities like Glasgow, Liverpool, and Manchester had crematoria in service.[6] Germany's first crematorium was built in 1878, and crematoria were soon in operation in Sweden (1887), Switzerland (1889), Denmark (1893), and Australia (1903).

It was physicians in both Europe and North America, particularly those with public health interests, who lobbied most strongly for cremation. At meetings of the British Medical Association in 1880, over 100 physicians signed a pro-cremation petition. In the United States, a committee of physicians reported that the "horrid practice" of earth burial "spread desolation and pestilence over the human race," poisoning "pure air, pure water, and pure soil"; this report was followed in 1886 by pro-cremation resolutions at meetings of the American Medical Association and American Public Health Association.[7] A periodical, the *Modern Cremationist*, was edited by a physician in Pennsylvania, while in Milwaukee supporters suggested that the local Academy of Medicine itself found a cremation society. Buffalo's crematorium was strongly supported by the *Buffalo Medical and Surgical Journal* and had a doctor as president. In Paris, arrangements were made to cremate the 3,000 bodies emanating annually from the city's two anatomy schools.[8] Such a practice was a sharp departure from transferring these remains to the city's boneyard, which was located in an underground quarry and to which the bones of generations of the city's poor had been moved from local graveyards. An 1885 German petition in favour of cremation was signed by 1,942 physicians.[9] In Adelaide, Australia, Dr Robert Wylde cited Louis Pasteur and went on to warn an 1890 audience that the cemetery could be the source of yellow fever, cholera, or typhoid: "The gases given off from dead bodies, which are sometimes sufficiently powerful to burst open lead coffins, must inevitably be a source of great danger to those who live in proximity to burial grounds."[10]

Business leaders added their voices. American steelmaker and philanthropist Andrew Carnegie declared cremation "one of the greatest hygienic improvements of a progressive age." Many architects had strong cemetery connections, designing entrance gates, memorials, and mausoleums. Perhaps not surprisingly, then, the *Canadian Architect and Builder*, repeated public health cautions drawn from Darwin and Pasteur. In just one acre, it stated in 1906, earthworms turned up fifteen tons of soil liberating germs that could fatally infect animals. "That in brief," Canadian architects were informed, "is the case for cremation."[11]

Proponents of cremation did, however, face broad opposition. Heading the secular charge were funeral directors, firmly entrenched in the public's mind as the primary professionals of death. Responding to the potential competition it posed to their embalming, coffin, and funeral operations, they denigrated cremation in journals like the *Casket,* pointing out its brutality to the human body. Strong religious objections came from the Roman Catholic Church, which passed repeated anti-cremation decrees, linking it to Freemasons, liberals, and later, communists. Canon law, reiterated in 1886, was adamant: "the bodies of the faithful must be buried; their cremation is forbidden."[12] The church was, of course, particularly powerful in Quebec; it attempted to prevent cremation even among non-Catholics by lobbying against proposed changes to the Mount Royal Cemetery's provincial charter. Most Jews also opposed cremation, although some Reform rabbis, at least in the United States, supported it and officiated at cremations.[13]

Given the rural cemetery's emphasis on respectability and the family, one of its important constituencies was the middle-class woman. This potential client eluded cremationists, who tended to view women as guardians of Victorian sentimentality and as advocates of in-ground burial. And, in fact, women did not seem impressed by the utilitarian arguments of radical cremationists that corpses might be burned to provide gas lighting, with the remaining ashes spread on fields as fertilizer. Fewer women than men chose to be cremated at the Mount Royal Crematorium. Nonetheless, a minority of women, usually university graduates, were active in American cremation societies. Six of the 113 members of the San Francisco cremation society were women, while in Los Angeles 12 of the 152 members were women. California activist Grace Greenwood visited the Milan crematorium, reported on its use-

The cremation of Dr William Price.

Before the development of modern furnace technology, cremation, as evidenced by this Welsh crematorium, remained marginal in Western society. The artisanal operations fascinated popular journalists but were decried by a broad range of opponents.

fulness for poor families, and described it as the "purest manner of rendering 'ashes to ashes.'" Advocates of cremation used social purity arguments, with their emphasis on the link between physical cleanliness and moral reform, to appeal to urban Protestant women: "it is easily conceivable," remarked one proponent, "that a woman of refined mind might choose cremation to escape what she dreads of worms, mould, eremausis, putrefaction, or any kind of profanation."[14] The benefits of cremation over slow rot in the ground were clear in the statements of Kate Field of Washington, who described incineration as "the healthiest," "cleanest," and "most poetical way" of disposing of the dead: "whoever prefers loathsome worms to ashes possesses a strange imagination."[15] The purging fire of cremation had clear links to purity, soap, and what the Methodist *Christian Guardian* called the "gospel of the toothbrush."[16]

Cemeteries – places constructed for in-ground burials – were perhaps not obvious locations for crematoria. Most of the early American crematoria were built by cremation societies who emphasized the scattering of ashes and who saw cemeteries as competitors. Many cemeteries in Britain and North America saw it otherwise. In Scotland, an 1876 report on cemeteries suggested that "well-devised inhumation and perfected cremation" could co-exist "side by side."[17] As early as the 1890s, the Association of American Cemetery Superintendents endorsed the construction of crematoria on cemetery grounds. In 1899, Ormiston Roy, back from the association's convention, informed the trustees that the issue had been "much talked of." In the same year, Mount Auburn Cemetery converted its chapel into a crematorium. In Milwaukee, Forest Home, a cemetery under the jurisdiction of the Episcopal Church, also built a crematorium.[18] By 1900, fifteen of twenty-four crematoria in the United States were located on cemetery grounds. In 1913, when the Cremation Association of North America was founded, its membership included a strong contingent of cemetery managers – including Ormiston Roy, who became its president in 1920. The Cremation Association was soon holding joint meetings with the Association of American Cemetery Superintendents and a possible merger was discussed.[19]

The cremation movement had spread into Canada by the 1880s. Hugo Erichsen, licensed as a physician in Ontario, an organizing member of the First International Cremation Congress, and chair of the Michigan Cremation Association, published *Cremation of the Dead Considered from an Aesthetic, Sanitary, Religious, Historical, Medico-Legal, and Economical Standpoint* in 1887. His book was for "all who like cleanliness, for all who love true sentiment, for all friends of economy, for all who venerate their dead, and for all who are not afraid of reform." He proposed obligatory incineration of the dead on battlefields and the establishment either of cremation corps in every army division or, better, a neutral society, the Black Cross, which would be

responsible for "gathering the dead and committing them to the flames."[20] He argued that in civil cemeteries, gravediggers were at particular risk from "dangerous graveyard gases." Citing an 1885 report from Montreal, he wrote of a gravedigger who dug a grave next to that of a recent smallpox victim: "At the time there was no smallpox in the village; but Robitaille, some days after digging the grave, sickened and finally died of smallpox, making it evident that he contracted the disease from the body of a man who had been buried for a month." Heavy drinking among gravediggers, Erichsen argued, was simply a form of resistance to "slow poisoning" from "the malignant influence of the vapours" from cemetery soil. Gin, he reported, had to be given to gravediggers moving bodies in a Surrey churchyard, while in Paris, three men perished from "inhaling the gas that escaped from coffins."[21] Erichsen's book was influential in Montreal, appearing in the library of cremationist John H.R. Molson.[22]

Members of McGill's Medical School added their voices, linking cremation to Darwinism, evolution, and the naturalness of death. William Osler, the university's star medical researcher, argued that cremation had to be put in a secular perspective: sciences like psychology and biology showed that death was not "a sacred encounter" but a "collective process" that was necessary "for evolution to occur."[23] McGill professor Dr George A. Baynes gave a public health course to theology students. His final lecture in 1875, published as a pamphlet, was devoted to cremation. Earth burial in urban areas, he told the class, was "high treason against life." The corpse was "an impregnated mass of contagion, only requiring the channel to engender the fatal malady." A careless nurse, opening the window of a room where a person had died of contagious disease, could "contaminate" the atmosphere. Funerals and "the parading of the dead through our streets was fraught with danger":

A child that died of scarlet fever was being taken in an open child's hearse to the Roman Catholic Cemetery along Sherbrooke Street. A little boy, attracted by the white pony, ran out of his house and followed the funeral and came back with an account of the pony and the carriage; a few hours after, the boy was taken sick and not many days after died of scarlet fever … I believe it is a wise precaution, nay, more, it should be a law, to have hearses always enclosed. It is proverbial, "caught his or her death at a funeral."[24]

A few years later, physician Dr H. Dalpi confronted Mount Royal trustees with a request to personally conduct the cremations of deceased patients on the cemetery grounds.[25]

Cremation was first mentioned in the Mount Royal Cemetery minutes in 1888, when Anglican trustee Wolferstan Thomas reported that individuals were willing to build a crematorium if the cemetery would "give the land and maintain the building."[26] No action was taken, and seven years later he raised the question again. While trustee Alexander W. Ogilvie vocally supported cremation, others worried about the $15,000 to $20,000 cost of building a crematorium and the ongoing expenses for maintenance. Critics also pointed out that the company's charter restricted it to earth burial and that construction of a crematorium would subject the trustees to Roman Catholic censure.[27]

The trustees' hesitation was symptomatic of a wider ambivalence to the incineration of corpses. Substantial Protestant theology emphasized that although the soul departed at the moment of death, the body would later be resurrected. The simple epitaph "Till we meet again" or the handshake chiselled onto many nineteenth-century headstones suggested that loved ones would be physically and spiritually reunited beyond the grave. Nonetheless, cremation was attractive to liberal Protestants, like the Unitarians

and to supporters of the social purity movement, particularly Methodists, and it was accepted by authorities in most Protestant denominations. In 1928 cremation was provided for in the Anglican Book of Common Prayer and that denomination's priests were authorized to accompany the body to the crematorium for a chapel funeral and to preside at the interment of ashes.[28]

In 1897, the debate over cremation at the Mount Royal Cemetery was revitalized by John H.R. Molson's $10,000 bequest to the trustees "for the erection and workings of a crematory furnace."[29] Given Molson's standing, his legacy, even if short of the total cost of a crematorium, could not be ignored. He had left instructions for his cremation, and after a service at his home, his body was taken by train to Boston. His cremation at the Forest Hills Crematorium received full newspaper coverage back in Montreal. One journalist wrote of the "scientific arrangements" and the "bright surroundings" in a "wealth of forest trees and wild flowers." Accompanied by "the chorus of song birds without," his body was reduced to ash in just over an hour:

The courteous superintendent of the crematory tells me that all the constituents of the casket and the clothing being lighter than the constituents of the body are dissipated and delivered up the flues, all of the ashes left in the retort being human ashes, practically the mineral matter of the bones. The combustion of the inorganic matter is complete and during a cremation there is not the least visible discharge from the big chimney.[30]

Still hesitant, the trustees put Molson's bequest in a trust account. The issue was pushed forward again on Ormiston Roy's return from the 1899 meetings of the Association of American Cemetery Superintendents. Describing cremation as a secular matter and an issue of efficiency, he reported that trustees of American cemeteries who had "looked

John H.R. Molson, 1890.

Son of Thomas Molson, head of the family brewery and Molson's Bank and senior governor of McGill University, J.H.R. Molson contributed widely to Protestant causes like McGill University, the Redpath Museum, and the Montreal General Hospital. While his father had been a prominent Anglican, J.H.R. Molson adopted the Unitarianism of his wife, Louisa Frothingham. By leaving instructions for his own cremation and a bequest of $10,000 for erection of a crematorium, Molson confirmed popular belief that Unitarians were the strongest Protestant denomination in favour of cremation.

on the matter as absurd a few years ago" were now erecting crematoria on their grounds and that American cemeteries were adopting it "simply to meet a growing demand."[31] Yet another year went by. Wolferstan Thomas, initial promoter of cremation among the trustees, was himself dead, and Molson's ashes had long been deposited in Mount Royal Cemetery, before the company agreed to build a crematorium.

The hands of the trustees were ultimately forced by tobacco manufacturer Sir William Christopher Macdonald. He had sat on McGill's board with Molson and, urged by Roy, took up his deceased friend's cause, telling cemetery officials he was ready to build a crematorium at his own expense. At a general meeting in August 1900, the cemetery finally accepted Macdonald's offer but only with the understanding that the crematorium would "at no time, and in no manner whatsoever, be a charge upon the funds of the Cemetery Company."[32] Building costs were reduced by Roy's suggestion that the crematorium be incorporated into the complex of new receiving vaults and conservatory-chapel then under construction on the high rocky ground at the eastern extremity of the cemetery. Building was underway by the autumn of 1900.[33] At this point, the trustees asked the provincial legislature to amend their charter to permit operation of a crematorium.

The trustees' trepidations concerning Roman Catholic reaction were immediately confirmed when the Archbishop of Montreal announced his intention to oppose the amendment. Monsigneur Louis-Adolphe Paquet, dean of Laval University's Faculty of Theology, attacked the project as "a pagan invention which fits badly with the spirit and traditions of a Christian country like ours."[34] Roman Catholic opposition to the bill was withdrawn only when, to Macdonald's frustration, the legislation was rewritten so as to restrict cremation to Protestants.[35] Other fears regarding cremation were assuaged by further restrictions in the 1901 legislation: the company could cremate only on condition that the deceased had expressed a wish, preferably in a will, to be cremated, that a medical certificate was produced, and that the deceased had not met with a violent death. On 18 April 1902, Senator Alexander Walker Ogilvie, a former president of the cemetery board, was the first person cremated at Mount Royal Cemetery.

To coincide with the opening of their crematorium, the trustees published a thirty-four-page pamphlet, 6,000 copies of which were distributed to newspapers and physicians across Canada. *Cremation: Its History, Practice and Advantages* presented the process as modern and scientific, part of the desire "to remove an undoubted menace to public health." Secular in its orientation, the pamphlet declared that science had taken the upper hand, demonstrating in cremation "the existence of a perfect plan. There is no religious scruple which should tie us to the sanitary errors of the past."[36] In contrast to the place given in the past to public grieving and memorializing in the cemetery, cremation was promoted as discreet, sterile, and essentially private, a practice that replaced "the gruesomeness of the open grave" with a "process performed with order, decorum and decency." Cremation had the advantages of modest cost, an unpretentious and disposable coffin, and a simple funeral.[37]

Macdonald, primary sponsor of the crematorium, would not accept the legislative compromise reserving cremation exclusively to Protestants, and the trustees accepted his suggestion to appeal to the legislature to have the crematorium's powers increased.[38] By 1903, Roman Catholic resistance made it obvious that the only recourse was to form a new federally chartered company empowered to cremate without religious restriction. In October 1903, a charter was granted. Legally separate from the Mount

Royal Cemetery Company, "The Crematorium, Limited" was authorized "to dispose of the bodies of deceased persons by incineration." The crematorium was administered by a manager who reported to five unpaid directors chosen from among the cemetery trustees. In March 1904, the crematorium's trustees bought the crematorium and the land on which it was built from the cemetery company. The crematorium company used the Molson bequest as an operating fund until 1916, when it received a bequest from Macdonald in the rather staggering sum of $100,000.[39]

Application for cremation was made by the executor or the deceased's nearest relative, who signed a declaration affirming to the deceased's wishes, preferably written, to be

William Christopher Macdonald (F440, Section F6).

Macdonald's interest in cremation remains obscure, although his support imitated that of American philanthropists like Andrew Carnegie. The product of a mixed marriage – a Protestant mother and a Catholic father – as a teenager Macdonald rejected all religion. While his support for cremation may have been to tweak tradition-bound Christians, it also reflected his generation's belief in the efficacy of modern science. Much of his philanthropy was associated with McGill University, where he strongly supported scientific agriculture, physics, engineering, and medicine. Macdonald died, age eighty-six, on 9 June 1917. His cremation, specified in his will, was carried out in the crematorium he had sponsored. His urn is buried alongside those of his mother and sister.

Floor plan of crematorium, conservatory, and vaults, c. 1901.

Planning of the conservatory and vault complex began before cremation at the cemetery became a critical issue. The original plan was to provide three additional winter burial vaults, one of which would be reserved for victims of contagious diseases. Of particular importance to the horticulturally inclined Ormiston Roy was the "conservatory-chapel." Stocked with plants, it was planned as a place, as Roy put it, where "those attending funerals might wait with comfort and pleasant surroundings, while bodies were being deposited in the vaults." This facility lent itself to adaptation to cremation, and a crematorium hall and furnace room were added.

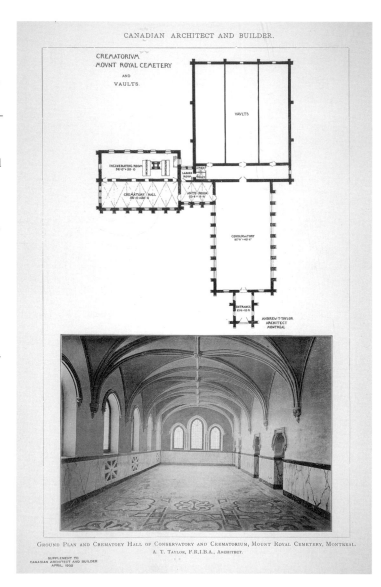

GROUND PLAN AND CREMATORY HALL OF CONSERVATORY AND CREMATORIUM, MOUNT ROYAL CEMETERY, MONTREAL.
A. T. TAYLOR, F.R.I.B.A., ARCHITECT.

SUPPLEMENT TO
CANADIAN ARCHITECT AND BUILDER
APRIL, 1902

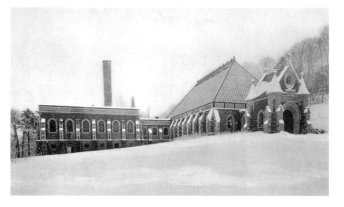

The conservatory and crematorium, c. 1901.

The main entrance and conservatory-chapel is at the right, the Crematorium Hall with its prominent chimney is at the left.

Interior of the conservatory.

Mourners passed through the conservatory to reach the crematorium proper. Early on, services were "held among the flowers," which apparently met "with the appreciation of all who have occasion to attend funerals in winter." The conservatory was stocked with ornamental plants from the cemetery greenhouses, although "a few purchases of large specimen ferns and palms from the McGill Botanic Gardens and elsewhere" added to the atmosphere. It became excessively expensive to heat the conservatory and it was demolished in the 1950s.

cremated. The applicant was also obliged to confirm that other family members had been informed of the cremation, that they did not object, and that the deceased had not died under violent circumstances. A second lengthy form was filled in by the attending physician.[40] The coroner's permission was necessary to cremate an individual who had died violently. In addition, the crematorium was required to hire a "Medical Referee" who, before a cremation could proceed, signed a "Confirmatory Medical Certificate." Specifically, he was to deny cremation in cases where it "appears that death was due to poison, to violence, to any illegal operation or to privation or neglect, or if there are any suspicious circumstances whatsoever."[41] On the other hand, and here public health concerns were evident, in cases of death from epidemic, cremation could be ordered by the Board of Health. In these circumstances, cremation could occur less than twenty-four hours after death.

The crematorium was designed by Andrew T. Taylor, Macdonald's architect on several projects, including the McGill science buildings that bear Macdonald's name. The decision to integrate the crematorium with the conservatory-chapel and vaults complex facilitated the incorporation of cremation into larger services offered by the cemetery. While early crematoria had been unaesthetic and frightful, Mount Royal's crematorium hall or chapel, like American counterparts built in the same period, was lavish, lined with marble, and conducive to a commemorative service. Rejecting the secularism of early cremationists and even the discourse of the cemetery's own cremation pamphlet, the facility was built with a view to responding to Protestant cultural needs concerning grieving and funerals. Mourners proceeded into the chapel through the glass conservatory with its furnishings of palms, exotic flowers, and year-round greenery. The chapel itself was planned to facilitate a Protestant service, and most crema-

The chapel.

Unlike the Protestant Burial Ground, Mount Royal Cemetery had never constructed a chapel on its grounds. Funerals were traditionally held in the city below in churches, funeral parlours, or individual homes, with a burial service following at graveside. Development of the crematorium necessitated a chapel in which services could be conducted prior to cremation.

tion services took the form of a traditional graveside committal service, with the casket placed on a central table.

The crematorium was built with the furnaces adjacent to the chapel. According to Donald Roy, this positioning "left a fearful reminder in people's minds of the cremation about to take place and possibly contributed little, by their ghoulish appearance, to promote the cremation movement." With the service over, mourners returned to the conservatory while employees removed the flowers and metal handles and, using a dolly, pushed the coffin through bronze doors into one of the two cremation chambers along the wall. Constructed of yellow fire-brick inside a steel casing, the incinerators were built by James Inglis, superintendent of the renowned Gardner Earl Memorial Crematorium in Troy, New York. Heated by kerosene, Mount Royal furnaces reached a temperature of some 2,000 degrees, incinerating a body in two hours.[42] During the first years of operation, cremationist John Howie had trouble controlling "heavy black smoke" that was produced "during the whole time of cremation."[43] This was alleviated somewhat in 1910 by changing the fuel but, as the board was told, "so long as we adhere to the system of putting coffins into a cold chamber, it is not likely that we shall be able to do away entirely with smoke."[44]

Cremated remains were removed from the incinerator the following morning and placed in urns for retrieval by families who might choose to scatter them, place them in a columbarium, or bury them in a grave. Unclaimed urns were a recurring problem, although ashes not collected within thirty days could in theory be buried by the crematorium.[45] Officials were always reluctant to bury remains without the participation of relatives, and indeed cremation itself was sometimes contested, as was the case with Thomas Roddick. By 1960, with some 2,500 unclaimed urns in the vaults, the trustees agreed to bury them in trenches opened in section B. The urns were tagged and their exact location recorded. The board also decided that, in the future, two years was a "reasonable delay" after which urns could be buried.[46]

Early cremationists had envisaged cremation and the scattering of ashes as an alternative to burial. The incorporation of crematoria into North American cemeteries – a practice quite different from that in Europe – gave impetus to the burying of cremated remains. Towards the end of the twentieth century, about half of cremated remains in the United States were placed in columbaria or graves.[47] Such trends provide the opportunity for crematoria to offer a wide array of service. Earlier in the century, Ormiston Roy recognized and developed the commercial potential of the crematorium in several ways. In 1918, the crematorium began to stock a range of ornamental urns.[48] He also planned tasteful sites for the burial of cremated remains, utilizing attractive sections too shallow for coffin burials. In 1927, Lilac Knoll, a central but rocky hillock, was developed as a section reserved for cremated remains. Purchasers were encouraged to buy large lots for their urns and, with its attractive landscaping, this section cannot be differentiated from adjacent ones devoted to in-ground burials.

For half a century, the Crematorium Company was managed by Ormiston Roy. At ease with an egalitarian and consumerist mentality, he promoted cremation as "convenient and inexpensive, imposing no financial burden on the survivors, thought of which frequently troubles the last moments of many."[49] His retirement brought a succession of Roys to the position: his brother John F. Roy, who retired in 1966; Ormiston's son W. Wallace Roy, who served in 1966–7; and then John's son Donald K. Roy. Donald's son Andrew began full-time work at the cemetery in 1981, was part of management 1990–7, and in 1997 became director of Funeral and Cremation Operations, reporting to the executive director.

Crematoria like Mount Royal experimented with different furnaces and wood, coal, kerosene, and petroleum fuels. Ormiston Roy sought to make Mount Royal's operation efficient and smoke-free.[50] In 1926, he convinced the

Roddick Gates, McGill University

Roddick Gates at the cemetery.

Sir Thomas Roddick (L1, Section L1)

Sir Thomas Roddick was a distinguished medical professor, dean of the McGill Medical Faculty 1901–8, and first surgeon-in-chief at the Royal Victoria Hospital. His wife, Amy Redpath, was scion of a distinguished Montreal family. His death on 20 February 1923 and in-ground burial two days later in Mount Royal Cemetery raised a sharp controversy over cremation. After the reading of his will six days after his burial, his executors asked the Quebec Superior Court to order his body exhumed and, in keeping with the wishes of his will, cremated. His wife successfully contested this request, testifying that her husband had "tacitly" rejected his testamentary wish. In 1925, she had the Roddick Gates, a McGill University landmark, built in his honour. At the cemetery, miniatures of the gates serve as his grave monument.

trustees to install the Balmfirth Combustion System in three of the crematorium's furnaces. This system cut fuel costs by 50 per cent by permitting the burning of cheaper grades of coal. Roy travelled widely to crematoria in France, Britain, and Germany. In Berlin, he was impressed to see a hundred coffins awaiting cremation and a round-the-clock crematorium that incinerated bodies in sixty minutes. Coffins were supplied at this crematorium: cheap and uniform in size and appearance, they had imitation handles and papier-mâché ornaments.[51] In 1949, in addition to announcing a new road that would relieve "congestion" when several funerals arrived at the same time, Roy speculated that Mount Royal would be the first North American crematorium to cremate by electrical power.[52] That same year saw the demolition of the conservatory, which was in poor condition and expensive to run. By 1955 renovations resulted in a more efficient crematorium with a more accessible entrance. Aesthetically, the loss of

the conservatory was offset by modernization of the furnaces and their removal from the side of the hall to the basement, giving the hall – now the official chapel – a decidedly less gruesome appearance.

In theory, cremation remained inexpensive – $10 in 1913, the fee was still a modest $50 for an adult and $35 for a child in the early 1960s.[53] At the same time, Mount Royal officials complained of funeral directors, their profits, and the expensive coffins they sent to the flames: "We hear a great many complaints about high funeral charges, Ormiston Roy told a Montreal *Gazette* reporter, especially where expensive coffins are used for cremation, but we are not in a position to be of much service to lot holders if they appeal to us only after all funeral arrangements have been made."[54] Despite its low cost, cremation was not popular in Montreal: only three were conducted in 1902, six in 1903, and seventy-one in 1912. The Spanish influenza epidemic of 1918 strained the cemetery's in-ground burial capacity and brought a sharp rise in cremations; between 10 October and 4 November 1918 there were twenty-four compared to three in the same period the preceding year. Over the next decades numbers rose only slowly: 200 in 1925, 407 in 1932, and 506 in 1942. The 573 cremations in 1948 represented 32 per cent of the bodies received at the cemetery that year. Numbers continued to grow slowly in the 1950s and early 1960s, reaching 607 in 1951 and 735 in 1962.[55] It was 1974 before the cemetery conducted more cremations (1,607) than burials (1,411).

Until 1963, the Roman Catholic Church continued to condemn cremation, although it was widely practised in heavily Roman Catholic countries like Belgium and France. Vatican II resulted in the modification of canon law to permit cremation. While the church continued to "recom-

Table 7 The popularity of cremation, 1902–72

Year	Cremations	Total registrations	Proportion choosing cremation
1902	3	1186	.25
1912	71	1901	3.73
1922	141	1875	7.52
1932	407	2043	19.92
1942	506	2045	24.74
1952	600	2302	26.06
1962	735	2328	31.57
1972	1136	2754	48.51

mend the pious custom of burying the bodies of the dead," cremation was permitted if the individual had expressed a written or oral wish to be cremated. Before cremation, a funeral mass was normally celebrated in church in the presence of the body with prayers following at the crematorium. Since 1985, the Catholic Church in Canada has permitted a funeral mass in the presence of cremated remains.[56]

Vatican II's effect was immediate. Before 1965, the cremation of Catholics occurred only occasionally: as late as 1964, they represented less than 1 per cent of individuals cremated in the Mount Royal Crematorium. Among the most notable was Montreal Mayor Honoré Beaugrand, who was cremated in 1906 and whose ashes were buried alongside those of his Protestant wife. With the growth in Catholic cremations, the number of cremations at the Mount Royal Crematorium more than doubled in a decade. By 1973, Catholics accounted for almost 24 per cent of cremations at Mount Royal,[57] but this marked the end of an era. In March 1974, the Bishop of Montreal gave permission for construction of a crematorium in Notre-Dame-des-Neiges Cemetery. Crematoria were also opened in the Montreal area by the Cimetière de l'Est and Montreal Memorial Park. Today cremation is utilized more in Quebec than elsewhere in Canada or the United States. In 1998, cremation followed 53 per cent of the deaths in Quebec; this compares to 42 per cent in Canada at large and a mere 24 per cent in the United States.[58]

EIGHT

MILITARY GRAVES

Across the cemetery's first decades, as we have seen, firemen, Masons, the Chinese, and national societies sought appropriate forms and space to commemorate their dead and to memorialize certain cultural and religious values. This was accomplished under the careful observation and sometimes veto of the trustees, who freely exercised their vision as to appropriate commemoration and use of the cemetery landscape. The trustees' capacity to treat commemoration as an essentially private phenomenon would change in the new century. Nationhood, empire, and human sacrifice became increasingly incendiary issues with the Boer War and World War I straining Canadian unity. Whereas the trustees in the 1880s had been able to deal in autonomous fashion with the issue of a cemetery memorial to the troublesome Orangeman Thomas Hackett, the new century saw commemoration – what Pierre Nora calls "les lieux de mémoire" – develop into a poignant and very public issue.[1] Pageants on the Plains of Abraham commemorating the heroism of Wolfe and Montcalm, construction of a 'bon-ententism' statute to father of Confederation George-Étienne Cartier on the slopes of Mount Royal near the cemetery, and emotions surrounding the establishment of the tomb of the unknown soldier brought powerful questions of public memory to the very doorstep of the cemetery.

For Mount Royal Cemetery, these issues took specific form in the burying of military veterans and in commemorating those who had died on foreign battlefields. The question of war commemoration and the cemetery was thrust to centre stage during the First World War, abetted by the famous poem "In Flanders Fields" – written by John McCrae, a Montreal doctor who served in France and Belgium – and by horrific Canadian losses in battles like Ypres and Vimy Ridge. Along with other cemeteries, Mount Royal – to that time a largely autonomous company – would feel the impact as both the federal government and empire-wide organizations like the Imperial War Graves Commission sought to impose their agendas of the memorialization of sacrifice.

Across early Canadian history, French, and British soldiers had been buried on the various battlefields where they fell or, as veterans back in their home communities, usually in churchyards alongside their civilian counterparts. By the 1830s, two military cemeteries had been opened in Montreal to serve the British garrison stationed in the city. The Papineau Military Cemetery was established in 1814 on a lot measuring 400 feet by 150 feet. At its closing in 1869, it contained some 1,000 British servicemen and their families from units such as the Royal Scots Fusiliers, the 23rd Welsh Fusiliers, and the Seaforth Highlanders. Among its graves was that of Lieutenant George Weir, killed by

Military Burying Ground
on Papineau Road, 1942.

Like many military burial sites
in Canada, the Papineau ground
was infamous for its dilapidated
and overgrown condition.

Patriotes at the outset of hostilities at Saint-Denis in the rebellion of 1837: his funeral concourse stretched half a mile along Papineau Road, which was "occupied by one living mass of men; and no one could get admittance to the ground, except those who immediately followed the hearse."[2] The military cemetery's most important monument was to General Benjamin D'Urban. A prominent officer in the Napoleonic Wars, and former governor of British Guiana, the West Indies, and South Africa, he died in the typhoid epidemic of 1849. After Confederation and the withdrawal from Montreal of the last British regiment in 1876, the cemetery was transferred to Canadian military authorities. Along with the adjacent Protestant Burial Ground, the military cemetery was considered as a site for

Montreal's smallpox hospital but was rejected on the grounds that "it would be bad for the patients to be hospitalized over a cemetery." St Helen's Island Military Cemetery was a smaller burial ground where service personnel and their families were buried from 1829 to 1870.[3] Early burials on Île Ste Hélène were conducted by the army chaplain, a function assumed after 1840 by the Church of England minister in the parish of St Mary's in Hochelaga. Many of the grave markers were wooden and the cemetery was particularly known for the ornamental chain fences that marked individual graves.

Until the development of historic parksites such as the Plains of Abraham in 1908, battlefields and military cemeteries such as the two in Montreal were neglected by both the public and the federal government, a practice in stark contrast to the construction of national memory in the United States through Civil War battlefield sites like Gettysburg or the repatriation of war heroes to national military cemeteries such as Arlington National Cemetery. In May 1902, the *Montreal Star* reported that veterans along with members of the Imperial Order Daughters of the Empire (IODE), would honour deceased British servicemen in Montreal by cutting the grass and whitewashing the fence around the neglected St Helen's Island Military Cemetery. Many of its grave markers had disappeared; indeed, by the 1930s little remained to mark the memory of the fifty soldiers, four women, and twenty-five children reportedly buried there.[4] The Papineau Military Cemetery was equally neglected; maintenance had fallen to volunteers, particularly the IODE. Newspapers compared the decrepit condition of these military cemeteries to the beauty of Montreal's rural cemeteries, the *Star* describing the former's weeds, fallen monuments, and unmarked mounds as standing in "a strange contrast to the well-kept cemeteries on the back of the mountain." After the Papineau Road Military Cemetery was vandalized in 1912, the federal government did contribute $7,000 to its repair.[5]

Connected to the issue of maintaining military cemeteries was the problem of providing decent burials for destitute servicemen who died in Montreal. In 1908 Arthur H.D. Hair, an English immigrant and veteran of campaigns in India and the Boer War, went to the press with his description of the miserable death of a "British pensioner" that he had witnessed. "Without friends or relatives," the veteran, honourably discharged after thirty-one years service, "sank in a doorway, ill and comatose." Taken by police as a presumed drunk to the Montreal General Hospital, where Hair worked as an orderly, he died without regaining consciousness. Refused burial by veteran's associations since he had not been a member, his body was sent for dissection on a McGill medical school slab. Shocked by this apparent humiliation of a British veteran, Hair proposed the establishment of a fund to bury "the Empire's fighting 'derelicts.'"[6] In 1909, the Last Post Imperial Naval and Military Contingency Fund was incorporated, with Hair as its organizing secretary.[7]

The fund was to act as "next of kin" under the Anatomy Act, protecting destitute veterans from anatomy tables and ensuring their decent burial. In 1910, it raised $211 from public contributions, $98 from the estate of a private donor, and $64 from military units. Last Post patrons included the Governor General of Canada, the Lieutenant Governor of Quebec, the Anglican Bishop of Montreal, Sir Montagu Allan, head of the Allan Steamship Lines and honorary Lieutenant Colonel of the 5th Regiment of Royal Highlanders, and Hugh Graham, Baron Atholstan, founder of the *Montreal Star* and organizer of the Children's Patriotic Fund for British soldiers. The honorary president was Reverend Frederick George Scott, chaplain of the 8th Royal Rifles; its accountant was George Durnford, a captain of the 68th Durham Light Infantry and secretary-treasurer of the Mount Royal Cemetery. Its $1 membership was open to both sexes, and although women were not named to the executive committee, the fund's seventy-seven members included four women. Subscriptions came from military units in Montreal, the IODE, the Literary and Dramatic Club of Trinity Church, and Anglican and Presbyterian churches. During the First World War, the Montreal Heavy Brigade held a euchre tournament and dance and sent $60, and officers in the Craig Street Drill Hall forwarded a $300 rental fee they had received.

Non-denominational, the Last Post Fund applied for options on gravesites in both the Protestant and Catholic cemeteries.[8] The Mount Royal Cemetery Company offered

The Last Post plot and cannon (N74 to N99, Section N2).

Last Post cannon looking to Military lot.

The placing of cannon at the Last Post site served to demarcate military sections from the rest of the cemetery, where classical, religious, and familial symbols dominated.

In the years after the First World War, the Last Post, operating from its Montreal headquarters, remained an influential force, especially when McGill principal General Arthur Currie accepted its presidency. Its regulations were included in a twelve-page document that encompassed details such as provision of Union Jack and naval or army ensigns for coffins, a $1 budget for printing obituaries, the naming of official undertakers (J.C. Wray or J. Brunet in Montreal), disposal of the deceased's effects, and arranging for the presence of a Last Post representative and duty officers from a local military association. Since Last Post rules forbade transportation from one district to another, the indigent veteran was to be buried in the area in which he died. Funeral costs were not to exceed $50; this included removal and preparation of the body ($7), provision of a shirt shroud ($3), a $25 coffin with nameplate and handles, $10 for hearse, and $5 for mourning coach. Burial costs were not to exceed $25 and the cost of the memorial, including lettering, $11.50. Leaving $12.50 for "unforseen" contingencies, the Last Post budgeted $100 for "an interment complete from 'A' to 'Z.'"

two possibilities: $20 gravesites in Mount Royal or $10 graves in Hawthorn-Dale. When the Last Post Fund opted for Mount Royal, it was sold two rows of five graves in Section N with an option on eight other rows.[9] Placement in Section N near the Catholic fence, the new Free Ground, and the Chinese concession emphasizes that the trustees saw destitute soldiers as a marginal group best distanced from the cemetery's family core. Prior to the First World War, the trustees' ambivalence about giving place to the commemoration of the martial and the violent was reflected in their reluctance to sanction installation on the Last Post Fund plot of two nine-pound cannons from the fort at St Helen's Island. Although cannons from the American Civil War or Spanish-American War regularly marked veteran's sections in private cemeteries in the United States, such accoutrements clearly clashed with lawn-plan principles and Roy's opposition to flagrant commemoration. Clearly ill-at-ease, the trustees accepted the application in 1912, while expressing fears that the cannons, cast in Britain in 1875, "might be tampered with by youth": the weapons can still be observed on the site.[10] Not surprisingly, given its reaction to the commemorative guns, the cemetery imposed strict regulations on Last Post graves. Markers were limited to headstones measuring 10 inches in height by 20 inches in width. Graves were not sold to the Last Post Fund with perpetual care. The fund was responsible for cutting the grass, repairing monuments, and levelling sunken graves.[11]

From 1910 to 1913, the Last Post Fund gave financial assistance to thirty seven burials – twenty-nine Protestant, eight Catholic – in several cemeteries. While most were buried in Last Post Fund plots such as in Section N, three were buried in family lots with financial assistance from the Last Post Fund. In 1914, the fund broadened its mandate from burying destitute ex-servicemen to include "all such charitable contingencies" associated with deceased military personnel, in particular petitioning government on behalf of widows and orphans. By the end of the war, the cemetery had increased the number of graves reserved for the Last Post Fund from fifty to ninety-seven. The fund was now authorized to buy graves in rows of ten; the new graves, priced at $20, could hold two coffins, one on top of the other. Gravedigging charges for a Last Post grave were $4 in summer and $10 in winter.[12] Mount Royal Cemetery officials, convinced that the fund was buying graves "at indigent rates and selling to the government at a profit," urged the federal government to buy military graves directly from the cemetery.[13]

The First World War shook English Montreal's sense of itself, its institutions, and its conception of death and memorialization. The death in Europe of 66,655 Canadians – an utterly unprecedented Canadian loss in war – changed the focus of customs of commemoration and gave an urgency to the recognition of Canadian nationhood and of the sacrifice of its men. Whereas the Mount Royal Cemetery, particularly in its better sections, had focused on individual achievement, the family, and Protestantism, the slaughter of the First World War gave emphasis to the democratization of death, to sacrifice, and to the war's "transgression of the limits of the human condition."[14] William Douw Lighthall, poet and amateur historian, former mayor of Westmount, and owner of a Mount Royal lot, told the Royal Society of Canada in 1918 that the war was Canada's "Homeric Age," a story "too grand to be forgotten."[15] The war put the trustees' long-time credo to the test. Their fussing over Last Post graves seemed misplaced, and cemetery landmarks like the Molson mausoleum appeared anachronistic and even decadent alongside the stark simplicity of soldiers' gravesites and, later, the egalitarianism of those memorialized in war cemeteries like

that at Vimy Ridge. In the two decades after 1914, Mount Royal authorities struggled with the issue of the relation between national memory of war and the commemoration of civil deaths. They probably never satisfied what Lighthall called "the trumpet of the breast": their unsuccessful and unglamorous attempts to construct "Memorial Roads" and cenotaphs placed flush to the ground contrasted sharply with the outpouring of memorials constructed in parks, railway stations, hospital entrances, and public squares across Canada.

Whatever the ambivalence over military commemoration on its grounds, the cemetery was not insensitive to the realities of the war. Secretary-treasurer J.A. Ryan enlisted, two trustees served at the front, and gate porter Percy Potter was decorated for five years of overseas service. In 1916, in response to a request from the Canadian Patriotic Fund, the company offered twelve graves in Hawthorn-Dale at "charitable institution rates" for the burial of destitute wives and children of men at the front.[16] For his part, Ormiston Roy arranged with the trustees in early 1917 to offer his unpaid services to the federal government with a view to developing a plan for providing graves for servicemen who died in Canada. Paying his salary and apparently warming to the idea of burying veterans, the trustees endorsed his "National Burial and Memorial Scheme" by which Ottawa would provide "a suitable and last resting place for every soldier of the great war who may die in Canada, whether rich or poor."[17]

Roy's initiative was eclipsed by establishment of the Imperial War Graves Commission (IWGC) in May 1917 following a resolution to the Imperial War Conference by Canadian prime minister Robert Borden. With over one million war dead across Britain, the colonies, and dominions, the commission assumed responsibility for developing suitable cemeteries on various battlefield sites, for determining the form of memorial, and for the treatment of rank in war cemeteries.[18] An early decision was made that the bodies of Canadian soldiers who died in England could be repatriated to Canada but those who died at the front would be interred in European military cemeteries. This would emphasize the egalitarianism of death among soldier-comrades, would keep Canadian policy in line with British practice, and would solve the logistical problems of having to transfer thousands of dead from the continent.[19] A committee of artists suggested a standard headstone, which was copyrighted by the IWGC. An upright slab thirty-two inches high and fifteen inches wide, each headstone featured an emblem at the top, usually the maple leaf for Canadians. Beneath the emblem was the individual's name followed by the service or regiment, the date of death, and the age at death. A religious emblem such as a cross or the Star of David was optional as was a personal inscription of up to sixty letters at the bottom of the stone, which could be suggested by next of kin.[20]

As the IWGC's planning went ahead, in 1918–20, Roy's repeated requests for government support of his scheme went unanswered. In 1921, Roy visited European battle-fields and cemeteries with a view to evaluating how Mount Royal Cemetery might best honour veterans. In his view, British military cemeteries were the most tasteful, albeit "stiff, formal and stereotyped, with more stone and less trees, shrubs, grass and flower than a naturalist in landscape could desire."[21] He was clearly frustrated with the centrality the commission gave to upright stone slabs. Instead of headstone rows and central cenotaphs, he called for sites modelled on the lawn plan. These would be easier to maintain: "I hoped [the lawn plan] might have been adopt-ed there with a saving of millions and millions of pounds sterling – one with flowers and trees and shrubs and gar-

dens and bird sanctuaries – instead of row upon row of cold stone and artificial lines – that make up-keep so expensive, and that sooner or later must fall into neglect for want of funds to keep them up."[22]

Other relationships were modified by war and these new issues of public memory. Since their establishment in the 1850s, the Protestant and Roman Catholic cemeteries had maintained a distant relationship across the "Catholic fence," as it was termed on the Mount Royal Cemetery side. Close mountain neighbours and fellow travellers in the business of burying, they observed but rarely spoke to each other. The Guibord affair, the burial of Charles Chiniquy in Protestant soil, and differences over cremation were reminders that religion remained a palpable fault line on the mountain. Periodically, the Protestant trustees had been asked – and had systematically refused – to open a gate between the two cemeteries, although by the 1880s each had a rear entrance giving onto the lane leading to Mount Royal Park. This arrangement was far from ideal so far as the trustees were concerned: in 1909, they complained of the "use made as a highway of the [Protestant] Cemetery by means of Roman Catholics who visit the adjoining Cemetery at certain seasons and festivals [and] who treat ours with scant decency and much to the injury of Flowers and Plants."[23] Yet after the First World War, the cemeteries were obliged to open the fence following the purchase by the IWGC of adjoining properties in the Protestant and Catholic cemeteries and construction of a cenotaph with both a French and an English face. The fraternity of military service would be emphasized by conjointly organized military ceremonies and the uniform headstones placed on military graves on both sides of the fence. In 1921, the IWGC finally purchased a "Soldiers' Plot" in Section G for $16,500 (300 graves at $55 each). Bordering the Roman Catholic cemetery, where an identical plot was also bought, the commission insisted on an open passage between the two plots. In a city scarred by the conscription crisis, the Protestant and Roman Catholic Soldiers' Plots emphasized outside imposition of the principles of comradeship and uniformity of sacrifice. In addition, war graves commission policy permitted no favouritism to be displayed for rank or gallantry, and all service personnel, even if court-martialled or convicted of a crime, had the right to burial in the military section.[24] The Mount Royal Cemetery's sale included acceptance of regulations applicable to all IWGC gravesites except, in deference to the Montreal climate, stones were to be granite and were to be placed on foundations conforming to the cemetery's rules. Only one soldier was to be buried per grave.[25] The sale included a provision for perpetual care except for "unforseen circumstances" such as the trampling of grass during funerals.[26]

In 1922, the Cross of Sacrifice, the IWGC's memorial for sites containing at least forty war dead, was built on the fence line between the Protestant plot, where 450 war dead are buried, and the Catholic, which holds 469 soldiers.[27] Designed by Sir Reginald Blomfield, the large stone cross bears a downward pointing bronze sword: the memorial has inscriptions in French facing the Catholic dead and in English on the Protestant side. There is a small but important difference between the two inscriptions. On the Mount Royal side, the inscription on the monument reads: "To the memory of those who died for King and country in the great war 1914–1918"; on the Roman Catholic side, the French inscription omits any reference to the king: "À la mémoire des soldats morts pour la patrie dans la grande guerre 1914–1918." The difference succinctly sums up the divergent views of empire and nation that, officials assumed, characterized English- and French-speaking soldiers. To

Imperial War Graves Commission gravesite.

The egalitarianism, spareness, and uniformity of these twentieth-century military graves contrast sharply with the individuality and character of nineteenth-century lots in the better sections.

Cross of Sacrifice.

As well as marking the burial site of veterans of diverse religious faiths, the Cross of Sacrifice symbolized the opening of the fence between the Protestant and Catholic cemeteries.

the Protestant solider, king and mother country were important concepts; to the French-speaking Catholic, "la patrie" – the homeland – was central.

The placing of war cannon on the Last Post Fund plot, the geometric lines of headstones in the Soldiers' Plot, and the opening of the Catholic fence represented challenges to the coherence of a cemetery based essentially on Protestant conceptions of the family, privacy, and individualism. Decoration Days held at the Last Post plot on Queen Victoria's birthday became popular, bringing crowds and noise into the furthest reaches of the grounds: military bands, a piper, and bugling of the Last Post accompanied volunteers in the tasks of grave cleaning and decoration of the site by Union Jack flags.[28] By the early 1920s, politicians were participating in Decoration Day along with Boy Scouts, the Imperial Order Daughters of the Empire, and veterans' associations.

Unsatisfied with the architecture, isolation, and cold granite imposed by the Imperial War Graves Commission at the Soldiers' Plot at the back of the cemetery, Ormiston Roy turned to private benefactors and a commemorative project that might extend his lawn-plan ideas into the core of the cemetery. In 1923, T. Howard Stewart, one of Sir William Macdonald's heirs, sponsored construction of a "Memorial Road" from the main entrance to the crematorium. In his gift, Stewart emphasized that commemoration along the road had to remain consistent with lawn-plan principles: "the open lawn spaces and ornamental grounds adjoining it shall always be maintained as such and shall never be encroached upon for burials." Roy hoped to extend this concept by constructing soldiers' memorial roads throughout the cemetery. Sponsored by philanthropists, these roads would be bordered by grassy zones in which families might install flush-to-the-ground bronze markers. In sharp contrast to IWGC gravesites, the Mount

Inaugural ceremony of the Last Post plot, 1910

Fly-by over George-Étienne Cartier monument on Mount Royal, Decoration Day, 24 May 1921.

With their noise, picnics, and festive crowds on the slopes of Mount Royal just a short distance from the cemetery fence, Victoria Day celebrations represented conflicting public uses of mountain space.

Royal cemetery roads would be, in the words of Ormiston Roy,

lined with bronze maple leaves – with cenotaph inscriptions to our Heroic Dead – an adaption of the scheme that I devised for the Battlefields of Europe … These bronze leaves placed level with the turf, so as not to impede the lawnmower, would, with artistic landscape settings and backgrounds of flowers and trees, make our Cemetery a world-noted shrine and would be an example for future generations – in showing them that bulky ostentatious monuments and headstones are not needed to make quiet, peaceful resting-places for our dead.[29]

The reference to bronze markers clearly showed the influence of the highly successful Forest Lawn Memorial Park, established in Glendale, California, in 1913. The only marker allowed in that cemetery was bronze, a material that offered durability, lightness, and, as it aged and oxidized, greenness. Offered by a variety of producers, bronze also freed cemetery officials like Roy from reliance on local stone dealers and offered new entrepreneurial opportunities.[30]

Roy also hoped to imitate Forest Lawn's importance as a tourist attraction. To give artistic weight to the "world-noted shrine" he envisaged at Mount Royal Cemetery, Roy proposed hiring George W. Hill to design the bronze maple leaves. Hill had sculpted Montreal's South African War Memorial (1904), statues of fathers of Confederation George Brown and Thomas D'Arcy McGee, and, most notably, Westmount's War Memorial. Untouched by the passing lawnmower and set on solid granite bases, Hill's maple leaves would serve as "Cenotaphs to Montreal's Heroes in the Great War," a "practical demonstration" of how Canadians "on a large scale" and in a "dignified and fitting manner" could "perpetuate the names of those gallant men and women who took part in the great war." Roy saw the memorial roads as a means of encouraging civic pride in the cemetery: "What more appropriate way could the citizens of Montreal take to honour their dead in the Great War, than to make Memorial Roads in our Cemeteries – Institutions as deserving of their support as any charity or hospital in the land."[31] Finally, Roy told the trustees, the roads would reduce maintenance costs by permitting elimination of several intersecting roads, some of which could be converted to gravesites.

Roy's plan to make the lawn cemetery a focus of war commemoration and popular visits never materialized, superceded by the bolder war memorials built in squares, parks, and other public places. His plan may also have clashed with the trustees' sense of the cemetery's Protestant respectability. In any case, it failed to attract the necessary philanthropic support, and, when Roy became sick in the summer of 1925, the project slid gently into abeyance. An important sign of the Mount Royal Cemetery's marginalization as a site of military remembrance was the Last Post Fund's decision in 1930 to end burials at that cemetery in favour of a Field of Honour opened in Lakeview Memorial Gardens Cemetery in the west-end suburb of Pointe Claire. A lawn cemetery with grave markers flush to the ground, the Field of Honour was reserved for veterans and their wives.[32]

City of Westmount war memorial.

Overlooking city hall, Westmount's impressive war memorial became an important site of commemoration.

Funeral procession of Sir Arthur Currie advancing up Park Avenue (1933).

Some of Montreal's most impressive funerals have been reserved for military leaders. General Currie's funeral competed in importance with the 1849 funeral of General Benjamin D'Urban, when shops closed and 10,000 Montealers lined the streets.

By the 1930s, military cemeteries like Vimy Ridge, with its imposing memorial, were being constructed as major sites of public memory, their emotional and nationalist overtones challenging the norms of civil cemeteries in Canada. Once again, Mount Royal trustees, always awkward with military commemoration, gunfire, bands, and similar markers of masculinity, were drawn into debates as to how to recognize military heroes buried in their grounds. The funeral of General Arthur Currie, and his burial at Mount Royal Cemetery in December 1933, was a major public event. Children were dismissed from school and the committal service was broadcast by radio from grave-side. Aside from his generalship in the war, Currie had served as national president of the Last Post Fund in 1924–32, while his position as principal of McGill University assured him top standing in civil society. In an Armistice Day address written just weeks before his death, Currie lamented that Canada had not kept "faith with the unreturning dead" and that the sacrifice of the soldier had not turned to glory.[33]

With the cemetery slow to commemorate the presence of Canada's most important soldier within its grounds, the Last Post Fund moved to open Currie Circle in its Field of Honour at Pointe Claire. It was at least two years after the general's burial that Mount Royal officials undertook negotiations with his family with a view to his removal from their family lot (Section I64) well back in the cemetery near Pine Hill Side to a more central site on which a war memorial could be erected. With the cemetery agreeing to contribute one-third of the cost of the new lot, and Ormiston Roy providing a plan for both the monument and lot layout, on 28 November 1936 Currie's body was removed to E.168, a prominent crossroads site near the entrance. On the third anniversary of his funeral, the Cur-

rie monument was unveiled. Its design, the Cross of Sacrifice, was a duplicate of that erected in Imperial War Graves Commission military cemeteries – including the Soldiers' Plot at Mount Royal – and special permission was granted for its use on a private lot in which other family members would be buried.[34] The memorial site included soil brought back from Vimy, Ypres, the Somme, and Mons – the sites of some of the bloodiest battles in which Canadian troops fought.[35] In his layout of the Currie lot, Roy came back to his plan, dormant since the mid 1920s, for ground-level cenotaphs that military families might place around the general's monument: no other country, he reported, "has provided a soldiers' plot where bronze tablets, set level with the sod might be placed, not only to those who fell on the battlefield, or died overseas, but to soldiers who died in later years after returning."[36] Writing for the unveiling, Roy described the Currie site as a potential "shrine or Valhalla for soldiers of the Great War." Looking to American models, he suggested an annual memorial service in which "thousands of people attend and loudspeakers are sometimes installed in the trees, and church choirs and military bands assist."[37] Roy's project apparently clashed with the trustees' conservatism and their reluctance to transform the cemetery into a Valhalla with loudspeakers: neither cenotaphs nor ceremonies materialized at the Currie lot in the interwar years.

The Second World War gave renewed impetus to the issue of military graves and the commemoration of the war dead. In Mount Royal Cemetery, the Soldiers' Plot bought by the Imperial War Graves Commission in 1921 was nearly full, despite purchase in 1938 of an adjoining piece of land (G942–4). Yet, once again, the trustees hesitated. In 1950, they offered the Department of Veterans' Affairs, which had taken over local administration from the IWGC,

Sir Arthur Currie monument (E169, Section E5).

As one penetrates into the cemetery from the main gates,
the Currie monument cannot be missed.

Department of Veterans' Affairs lot.

The absence of above-ground markers in this military section emphasizes the acceptance of lawn-plan cemetery principles across Canada.

a large but undistinguished lot along the Catholic fence on the site of the old park entrance. Alternatively, they proposed a suburban site in Hawthorn-Dale Cemetery. The federal government opted to purchase 28,800 square feet at the park entrance site for $72,000, including $11,200 for perpetual care.[38] It bought a similar section on the Roman Catholic side. In both cemeteries, the pattern of burials is chronological with no regard for rank, the first to die lying in the front-left corner. The trustees' uneasiness with this section remained: they tried to integrate the area, its architecture, landscaping, and theme of war sacrifice with the modest gravesites in nearby sections, many of which had been purchased by individuals of minority ethnic groups. Retaining the coherence of the cemetery and responding

to the needs of its ethnic constituencies was important as the company faced increasing competition from suburban memorial parks. Within a few years of the opening of the new military section, the trustees were expressing displeasure with its appearance, which, from the road, gave a banal impression of a stretch of grass leading to the fence and the adjoining military section in the Roman Catholic cemetery. It may have been coincidental, but in 1958, the year of Ormiston Roy's death, the trustees ordered removal of the nearby greenhouse and a year later asked Veterans' Affairs to erect a suitable monument, which, they suggested, might be set off by an avenue of Gingko trees. It was 1965 before a monument between the military lots in the Mount Royal and Roman Catholic cemeteries was completed.

NINE

CONTINUITY AND ENTITLEMENT

By the 1920s, the management, technological, and lawn-plan transformations begun at the cemetery in the 1890s were essentially complete. After a quarter century as superintendent, Ormiston Roy gravitated to landscape architecture at the cemetery as well as his consulting and nursery businesses on the side. Although he remained in the employ of the cemetery, he ceded day-to-day, direct involvement in burial and administration to his brother John. Over the next decades, management of the cemetery remained firmly in the hands of successive generations of Roys, who, in the tradition of Ormiston Roy, ran it with a sure hand for the needs of the Protestant community.

At the same time, the post-war period, and especially the 1960s and 1970s, saw Quebec undergo fundamental mutation. The growth of Quebec nationalism, of the welfare state, whose benefits ensured decent burial, of increasingly secular leisure pursuits, and of environmental concerns for green space on the mountain, all served to diminish the vitality of the lawn cemetery, its peonies, war memorials, and Sunday visits to family graves. The cemetery ignored and sometimes resisted the changes shaking the society around it, digging in its heels as propertied, Protestant, and private. By the 1980s, however, it was less clear that competent management and reliance on the entitlement of property rights would be sufficient to protect the cemetery from decline as a vestige of a slowly collapsing Protestant community.

In 1924, John F. Roy took over management of a company in which professionalization was well advanced. Full-time administrators and secretaries served the public in a newly acquired downtown office building on Drummond Street. On the cemetery grounds, the capacity to conduct winter burials permitted more efficient organization of the labour force after 1919. Fascinated with mechanical devices and a lifelong tinkerer and traveller, Ormiston Roy had seen to the application of new technologies. The mechanized lawnmower, the telephone, and backhoe, improved fencing and asphalting, the growth of tramway service to both cemeteries, and expanded use of trucks, tractors, snowplows, and especially automobiles had permitted the creation of new burial sites and a changing landscape with new vistas, shrubs, and greenery. This technology brought better communications between the various cemetery sites, improved control of public acccess, and the construction of roads, ditches, and drains that permitted heavy vehicle traffic and year-round access. Implementation of the lawn plan had resulted in a modern-looking cemetery in which railings and enclosures had given way to smaller markers. The increasing use of ground-level bronze markers further reduced the impression of the cemetery as a massive repository of granite. With the opening of Hawthorn-Dale, the trustees had effectively created a two-tiered Protestant cemetery system in which middle-class family lots still dominated Mount Royal; all of the poor and an increasing number of the modest were directed to suburban Hawthorn-Dale. Only in the 1950s was substantial landscaping and filling done at the Mount Royal site to accommodate growing Orthodox, Middle Eastern, and Asian populations.

The opening of the crematorium in 1902 had positioned the cemetery as Canada's first – and, for decades, only – provider of this service. Alongside the cemetery's traditional in-ground burial service, cremation developed as a significant business activity, with bodies brought for incineration from across central Canada. With their smaller space requirements, urn burials had permitted the opening of new sections and the creation of a more integrated lawn landscape across important parts of the cemetery. Cremation had also given the cemetery control of an important technology, renewed direct contact with the public and with Protestant ministers through construction of the conservatory and crematory chapel, and some means of competing with the city's funeral directors, who had assumed dominance in the funeral and burial business through their use of funeral parlours and embalming technology. Finally, the First World War had forced reflection on the cemetery's role in the formation of public memory. And, whatever the trustees' ambivalence, construction of military sections on the initiatives of the Last Post Fund and the Imperial War Graves Commission had brought a different character and visitor traffic to extended areas of the cemetery.

The Judah Mausoleum (C28, Section C2).

Because of neglect and vandalism, several mausoleums have been sealed.

On his retirement in 1966, John F. Roy spoke of his forty-two years with the Mount Royal Cemetery Company. Recalling his family's identification with the cemetery since 1890, he suggested that his life's work, in contrast to the striking innovations introduced by his brother, had been one of continuity, of technological adjustment, and of physical renovation of the property. He did not feel called upon to address the issue of the relationship of the cemetery to the social and political change occurring in Quebec society: "Three outstanding features in which I have taken great satisfaction, were the regrading and surfacing the gravel roads with bituminous concrete, the general overhaul of the whole Cemetery since 1956, and the modernizing of facilities at The Crematorium."[1] In 1949, he had overseen the opening of an important road across Rose Hill, connecting Pine Hill Side with Section C2 and enabling development of "the most valuable site for landscaped lots in the Cemetery."[2] A year later, paving of the main roads was undertaken in preparation for the cemetery's hundredth anniversary celebrations in 1952. As part of an overhaul of the cemetery's landscape, experiments were undertaken in 1955 with two "overgrown" but prestigious sections (L1 and F4) with a view to "making these areas into well-cared for lots."[3] The success of the experiment led to a long-term program "to renovate the grounds … [with the] removal of unwanted trees and shrubs, straightening up of monuments and markers, rotor-tilling, spreading of thousands of yards of topsoil, regrading, fertilizing and seeding, also improvement of roads."[4] The cleanup extended to the removal of "decrepit enclosures" for which owners could not be located and to the repair, sealing, or even removal of dilapidated mausoleums.[5] In 1949, the conservatory was removed, and over the next few years the crematorium was substantially modernized. The 1940s and 1950s saw the introduction in North American cemeteries of improved lawnmowers, gas-generated trimmers, and of the soon ubiquitous backhoe.[6]

In 1966, the year his father John F. retired as manager, Donald Roy left his job at Canada Starch, to become assistant manager and registrar of the company and crematorium. Venerating the work of his father and "his favourite uncle," Ormiston Roy, he slipped comfortably into cemetery administration. He had grown up in a house, built by his father, that backed onto the cemetery. Active in sports, the school board, and the Presbyterian Church, the Roys were prominent in Outremont, a suburb that retained a strong Protestant influence and whose architecture and green spaces complemented the cemetery. John and Wallace Roy had a strong sense of place and local environment. They were part of the attempt of the Verdun and District Sportsman's Association to increase the pheasant population on Mount Royal. They grew pheasants in captivity and then released them; by 1960, cemetery employees were feeding some 150 pheasants through the winter.[7]

Although he had grown up during the Depression, Donald Roy remembered his youth on the mountain as Arcadian. Family and daily life were inseparable from the cemetery: his father took a path through the back fence to work, came home for lunch, and had his car washed daily by cemetery employees. Ormiston Roy and his family lived just down the mountain in a home built for them on the cemetery's grounds. Donald tobogganed on Mount Royal and worked part-time around the grounds learning horticulture, landscaping, labour management, and the cemetery trades from the hands of family members and employees he had known all his life. Like his father, he studied agriculture at McGill's Macdonald College, and, from him, inherited an interest in the technology of cremation; he continued a family tradition by becoming president of the Cremation Association of North America in 1983–4.

Despite the deepening emphasis in twentieth-century society on specialization and professionalization, Mount Royal managers persisted as generalists – dealing with both labour and the public; lending a hand in surveying, land-scaping or quarrying; expert in both the technique of burial and the art of coping with grieving families; familiar with growing government regulations concerning public health, the environment, and emission standards for crematoriums; and cognizant of cremation technology. Until the Drummond Street building was sold in 1958, manager John F. Roy spent mornings in the downtown white-collar world of accounting, registrations, and budgets, travelling to the cemetery grounds in the afternoons to deal with labour problems, flooding, black smoke at the crematorium, or a backhoe breakdown. Expertise in a variety of métiers from quarrying and iron-working, to construction and forestry was available from long-time employees. Surveying was the purview of the general superintendent of operations, Bill Chapman, and, without consulting engineers, landscape architects, or planning commissions, he laid out and managed development sites around the grounds. Secretary in the downtown office and responsible for many of the lot sales was McGill law graduate Albert Swindlehurst; part of his compensation included accommodation in a cottage on the company's Hawthorn-Dale site. Senior employees travelled the world to conventions or cemetery sites, where they kept abreast of crematorium and cemetery technology.

Cemetery employees were trained to deal respectfully and effectively with the public. For those without a pre-arranged lot, sales usually occurred when the bereaved came to the downtown office; there, sympathetic cemetery staff, much in the tradition of the church sexton, would show them diagrams and grave options. If they visited the cemetery instead, the manager, using his large company car, might chauffeur buyers around to inspect different lots.

Growing up on the mountain – Betty Roy.

Born in 1911, Jessie Margaret ("Betty") Henderson moved with her mother and brother into her grandparents' home after her father's death in the First World War. Her grandfather, John Henderson, was superintendent of Mount Royal Park, and she grew up in Smith House, a stone mansion built on the mountain in 1858. Renovated in 1999, it now serves as a welcome centre in the park. Also growing up nearby in a cemetery-owned house was Wallace Roy, son of Mount Royal Cemetery superintendent Ormiston Roy. Youngsters on the mountain rafted on the swamp, rode horses, and tobogganed. Enthusiasts in sports clubs like the Montreal Snowshoe Club and the Montreal Hunt Club used the mountain winter and summer. Although walkers and those who rode the incline railway to the summit used the park in increasing numbers, Betty Roy recalled that "you figured the mountain was controlled by the wealthy people who could ride and use it." The 1932 marriage between Betty Henderson and Wallace Roy, which joined the most prominent families of cemetery and park, speaks to the cloistered nature of life on the mountain. Wallace Roy spent his career on the mountain, working at the cemetery as general superintendent, assistant manager and registrar, and then as manager until his retirement.

Before a cremation, family members were obliged to produce documents and sign forms at the cemetery. During this visit, discussions might occur concerning purchase of a gravesite for urn burial.

In contrast to technological advances enthusiastically instituted at the crematorium and on the outside grounds, the cemetery's office and record-keeping systems remained artisanal and handwritten. Its card-index registration system, modelled on that used by libraries to locate their books, had been introduced by Ormiston Roy in 1899. For burials, individual diagrams were made by the site foreman, signed by him on the back, and then transcribed into cemetery records. Two sets of lot books were kept, with a daily messenger taking up records from the downtown office. Since payment was due before either cremation or burial, funeral parties, accompanied by funeral directors, usually stopped inside the cemetery gates as the registrar entered information and took payment.[8] Although maps were issued showing mourners cemetery locations and how to travel from the downtown office to the cemetery, complaints were received that downtown staff were not "well-acquainted with the Cemetery grounds," leading several mourners to miss funerals. This administrative division between cemetery and downtown became unnecessary as post-war prosperity made the private automobile increasingly ubiquitous. With clients driving directly to the cemetery, the downtown location, opened just a generation earlier, became a liability. In 1958, the Drummond Street building was sold; the head office and public reception area moved to refurbished quarters inside the main gate.

Through activities like the sale of products from its greenhouses, the cemetery had long engaged in revenue-producing pursuits. Ormiston Roy's multiple entrepreneurial activities in flowers, bronze plaques, and a patent were accompanied by the sale of Christmas holly wreaths for gravesites, a practice begun in the 1930s. At the same time, the cemetery was suspicious of many of the money-making schemes presented to it, maintaining a clipping file of doubtful projects and keeping most at arm's length by reiterating its status as a non-profit company. Builders of "community mausoleums" were one group of entrepreneurs, usually American, who tried to buy sites in Mount Royal Cemetery. These massive mausoleum complexes might offer up to 8,000 crypts in which individual coffins could be placed and they advertised heated space and chapel service as alternatives to winter burial or cremation. The best-known was Forest Lawn's Great Mausoleum.[9] Part of a California culture that included the aggressive marketing of burial facilities, Forest Lawn's mausoleum was modelled on the Campo Santo in Pisa; admission was charged to view the mausoleum's stained-glass Last Supper.[10] Ormiston Roy, no fan of large monuments, turnstiles, or cemetery crowds, joined in the Association of American Cemetery Superintendents' condemnation of these community mausoleums. In 1913, he protested propositions made by the Quebec Mausoleum Company, which, according to him, nearly hoodwinked Mount Royal trustees into selling a site for a 900-body vault. Company salesmen, Roy recounted, had offered him $40,000 in stock "to allow my name to go on the prospectus, and not to raise any objections, or advise the Trustees against building."[11] In the mid-1930s, other mausoleum schemes were proposed to the cemetery. One company formed by what Roy called "outside racketeers" later collapsed in Toronto with $400,000 outstanding in subscriptions. Another mausoleum proposed for the Mount Royal grounds by entrepreneur Maxwell A. Holliday was dismissed by Ormiston Roy as a "filing cabinet for the dead." Holliday was arrested in 1940, accused of having swindled $49,000 from Notre-Dame-Des-Neiges Cemetery for another ill-fated mausoleum project.[12]

Managing labour was among the superintendent's most critical tasks. As already noted, Mount Royal Cemetery effectively used nepotism and paternalism to encourage loyalty. Yet, below the key employees, much of the labour force was traditionally seasonal and unskilled, involved in quarrying, constructing roads, working in the forest, landscaping, or digging graves. Wrongly, authorities often saw these cemetery workers as unstable or migratory. As with any large employer, cost and productivity were fundamental issues; like most North American cemeteries, Mount Royal took a dim view of labour solidarity or unions. The cemetery was able to utilize mechanization, outside contractors, and periods of labour surplus to offset labour militancy. Donald Roy recounted childhood memories of unemployed men in the 1930s begging for cemetery work or just food. Men seeking work breaking stone or digging graves gathered in the morning below the balcony of the contractor who lived over the cemetery workshop. Lucky ones came away with chits good for a day's work.[13] Ormiston Roy reported that cemetery cleanup work in 1931 had provided "much needed and greatly appreciated work for several weeks to upwards of a hundred of the City's unemployed."[14] This cheap labour force permitted broad physical improvements: the 1930s marked the first time grass was cut across the entire cemetery regardlless of whether perpetual care had been paid for.[15] Through the Depression and into the Second World War, the company consistently applied for exemptions from the Workmen's Compensation Act, the Fair Wage Act, and the Unemployment Insurance Act, arguing that it was a non-profit corporation, that it provided free burial to the poor, and that most of its workers were in horticultural work exempted under the acts. In 1941, for example, John F. Roy sent the following petition to the Unemployment Insurance Commission:

With the exemption of our blacksmith and carpenter and the office staff, the rest of our employees are engaged in such horticultural pursuits as grass cutting, planting flowers, weeding and hosing, watering, raking leaves, making hotbeds, growing of grain and other fodder for our own use, trimming of shrubs and trees etc. ... I did not mean my request for exemption to apply to all cemeteries, but only to Mount Royal, because it is probably the only cemetery in the country having an obligation to bury free of charge the Protestant poor.

I would submit the Mount Royal Cemetery is as much a charitable institution as any hospital, inasmuch – as in hospitals – the poor are provided for out of revenue: the rich bearing the major burden, but, unlike hospitals, we do not receive any money grants from the Municipal or Provincial authorities, although they recognize the charitable nature of our company by various tax and other exemptions.

I would therefore ask you to limit the application of the Act to specific tradesmen in our employ and the office staff ...[16]

Increasing shortages of manpower during the Second World War meant that in 1943, the Cemetery was able to hire only 60 men, compared to the 190 it had employed the previous year. Merchant seamen waiting for their ships to sail were hired temporarily and a five-cent-an-hour bonus was paid to regular workmen. Labour militancy, present in Quebec long before the Quiet Revolution of the 1960s in industries like textiles and mining, penetrated the cemetery in the post-war period. As early as 1949, when trustees were told of union organization at the neighbouring Roman Catholic cemetery, working conditions and pay rapidly improved. By 1951, hourly wages at the Mount Royal Cemetery had doubled from their 1943 level to $1 an hour for "key-men." In 1955 a pension plan was introduced for permanent employees with three years' service. In addition to its twelve salaried employees, an internal report showed that the company's full-time, hourly paid labourers "were not, as had been assumed, necessarily transient workers." Rather than "a migratory class of workmen," twenty-eight labourers had served at least three years and eight had more than twenty-five years service.[17] In 1964, the company increased salaries 15 per cent across the board and improved holiday benefits; henceforth all workers were registered under the Unemployment Insurance Act.

These concessions did not stave off union organization. The workers had several grievances. Industrial accidents had occurred at the cemetery: in 1947, worker Henri Pilon died from injuries sustained in a work accident; in 1959 three workers were injured when a greenhouse wall they were demolishing fell on them. Workers were increasingly outspoken in criticizing their wages and the fact that, on cemetery time, they had been diverted to work on the manager's property. In 1953, the trustees received a letter signed the "Employees of Mount Royal Cemetery" charging that "considerable work was being carried out for the personal benefit of the Manager at the expense of the Cemetery Co. and if this were not so wages could be increased without additional cost to the company." After investigation, the trustees passed a vote of confidence in John Roy, noting that they were "fully satisfied that the allegations made are totally unfounded."[18]

Strained labour relations were typical of many other cemeteries where superintendents complained of being "betrayed" by long-time employees and of militant and "subversive outsiders."[19] Cemeteries found themselves in a delicate position. On the one hand, technological developments resulted in decreasing dependence on seasonal labourers; as a consequence the trustees were not highly motivated to deal with dissatisfaction from that quarter. For example, while digging a grave took a minimum of three hours in good soil, and a full day in tougher sites, the intro-

Digging a grave, 2002

duction of the backhoe permitted the opening of a grave in twenty minutes, year-round.[20] Yet the cemeteries could ill afford the negative public relations associated with labour difficulties. Well-publicized strikes, replete with accounts of the backup of bodies awaiting burial, weakened the public image of several prestigious cemeteries.

In 1966, Mount Royal workers joined the Building Services Employees Union. Despite arbitration and the company's hiring of a labour lawyer, the men struck on 25 November of that year: for fourteen days, no burials or cremations took place. Ultimately the strikers received "a very substantial increase" in wages and benefits, the costs of which were passed on in increased burial fees.[21] In the mid-1970s, the cemetery again faced work stoppages; the issue was working conditions, which compared unfavourably with those at other Montreal cemeteries.

Anxious to avoid another strike, the company felt "virtually compelled" to match the five-day week and pay rates offered at Notre-Dame-des-Neiges Cemetery.[22] In 1978, workers struck again, this time when the cemetery cut back its unionized seasonal workforce by hiring outside landscape contractors who promised "superior" grass-cutting skills and more "efficient use of modern machinery." When the regular workers respected the seasonal workers' picket lines, ugly scenes erupted as funeral processions arrived at the gates. The three-day strike ended with a compromise by which the union accepted outside contractors in return for the cemetery's hiring of ten summer workers.[23]

Nativism and a sense that the collegiality of the cemetery workplace had been jeopardized by unionization and the disappearance of a largely British workforce is quite discernible at the Mount Royal Cemetery. In the 1960s its seasonal labour force became largely Italian and then Portuguese in the 1980s. The minutes of a board meeting in 1969 reported that the men did not show "the same degree of personal interest and pride of former years." In 1975 trustees were told that "the talents of the summer workers have not been very satisfactory, principally because many of them were recent immigrants from foreign countries where mechanical knowledge and skills are, by Canadian standards, at low level."[24]

These changes in the ethnicity of the cemetery's outside workforce were a reflection of demographic change in Montreal. While people of French origin continued to constitute about two-thirds of the city's population, those of British origin declined steadily. In 1901 they had represented 33.6 per cent of the city's population; that proportion dropped to 24 per cent in 1921, and 12.4 per cent in 1961.[25] As late as 1939, the cemetery was still confidently describing its service as one that was "solely in the interests and for the benefit of the Protestant population of Montreal."[26] By

that time, this emphasis on Protestantism was already short-sighted; later in the century it became untenable as the percentage of the Quebec population that was Protestant fell from 8.1 per cent in 1961 to 4.9 per cent in 1981.[27] This decline, at least in Montreal, coincided with heavy immigration, first from continental Europe and then from Asia and Latin America. In the decade from 1951 to 1961 the number of Italians in the city almost trebled to 79,841.

Montreal's increasing pluralism brought the trustees face to face with changing realities: their traditional Protestant constituency was being replaced by new Canadians, particularly Greeks, Ukrainians, and people from the Middle East. Much of this growth in the non-Protestant population took place in the very environs of the cemetery. By 1940, for example, Outremont had a substantial and steadily growing Jewish population; Mile End, Park Avenue, and Côte-des-Neiges – neighbourhoods where Protestants had been strong – developed strong ethnic populations in the postwar decades. Anglican burials, which had represented 44 per cent of interments in 1911 and 37.3 per cent in 1951, fell to 12.4 per cent in 1998. Similar declines can be charted in the Presbyterian and United Church. The latter counted for 24.9 per cent of burials in 1931 but only 5.8 per cent in 1998. The growth of Greek, Ukrainian, and Russian Orthodox burials was of particular importance; by 1991, these constituted almost one-quarter of the cemetery's burials. The Orthodox had become the cemetery's most important denomination, reflecting growth in Montreal. The city's Greek population, for example, grew from about 1,000 in 1906, to 2,100 in 1940, and 23,623 in 1961.[28] The Greek Ladies' Benevolent Society, which was chartered in November 1922, had bought a gravesite in 1933.[29] The Hellenic Ladies' Benevolent Society bought a 720-square-foot lot in 1945; by 2002, it had been the site of forty-two charitable burials. At the same time, as increasing

THE MONTREAL CHURCHMAN

MOUNT ROYAL CEMETERY

ave often wonder-
now many Angli-
, as well as our
r Protestant
nds, appreciate what
onderful beauty spot
haven of rest they
n right in the very
art of this City of
ontreal, yes, do not
surprised at the
atement, because it is
rue, perhaps you have
never realized that The
Mount Royal Cemetery
Company which owns
and operates the Mount
Royal Cemetery, The
Mount Royal Cremator-
ium and The Hawthorn-
Dale Cemetery is ad-
ministered by a Board
of Trustees who are
elected by the various
Protestant Denomina-
tions, and act without
remuneration, solely in
the interests and for the
benefit of all the Protestant population of Montr

One of the outstanding features that will attra
tention on entering The Mount Royal Cemetery
the entire absence of pruning ,that exposes the
branches of trees and shrubs, the foliage line
comes right down to the ground just as they do :
Royal Gardens at Kew, England.

The Shrubs are treated in a naturalistic manne
sequence have a smooth flowing appearance a
beds are a joy to behold.

Mr. W. Ormeston Roy, who this year entere
year with the Mount Royal Cemetery, of wh
scape architect, is justly proud of his accompl

During the spring and early summer the Tru
in the newspapers that on certain evenings the gates of
Mount Royal Cemetery, which usually close at 5 o'clock, would
remain open for visitors in automobiles to drive through the
grounds and hundreds availed themselves of this unusual opportunity of seeing the flowers, shrubs and park-like beauty
of the grounds, if this privilege is again extended in this
manner do not fail to take advantage of it, you will never regret it.

WEDNESDAY AT 9 A.M.

The day of week has a lot to do with getting married in
the Netherlands. There are different prices for different days:
Mondays cost 75 florin; Tuesday, 100; Wednesday at 9 a.m.,
free, later in the day in groups, 7.50 florin; and, individually,
15; Thursdays is another 100 florin day; but on Friday it is
possible to be married in groups for 12.50 florins each. Sat-
urdays cost 75 florin.

A beautiful symphony of colour is unfolded before our eyes as we pass along the
in The Mount Royal Cemetery. Beautiful vistas are beheld at every turn, a veritable
—(Photo by courtesy of The M

describable natural beaut

---

follows,
care:—
Adult graves
as low as $35.00
Children's graves
as low as $14.00

Adult g_____
as low as ....
Children's graves
as low as $5.00

MOUNT ROYAL CREMATORIUM

The Crematorium was established in Mount Royal
Cemetery 38 years ago and renders a similar service to
those preferring cremation.

The Mount Royal Cemetery Company is administered by a
Board of Trustees, who act without remuneration, solely in
the interests and for the benefit of the Protestant population of Montreal.

MOUNT ROYAL CEMETERY CO.
1207 Drummond Street   MArquette 8059

Far left Advertisement, 1939

Above Advertisement, 1988

Left Advertisement, 1990

These advertisements show the cemetery's changing services.
In 1939, it still strongly associated itself as "solely in the interests"
of the Protestant community. Its services, with prices including
children's graves, emphasized burial at its two locations. By the
1980s, when the cemetery was giving much more prominence to
cremation, ads noted the completion of its new chapel and columbarium niches for cremated remains. In the decade that followed,
cemetery ads became more bilingual and more democratic, with
the emphasis on "choice." Broadening the cemetery's services to
include monuments, plaques, and crypts was accompanied with
a new emphasis on heritage and the cemetery's "proud record"
as Canada's first crematorium. Inquiries in 1939 were directed to
the downtown office, but visitors in 1990 were encouraged to visit
the grounds itself for "At Need or Before Need Arrangements."

Greek Orthodox monument.

This monument, located in Mountain View section, reflects the cemetery's broadening constituencies.

numbers of Roman Catholics opted for cremation, their representation in Mount Royal Cemetery rose. By 1971, 11.4 per cent of the hearses that moved into the cemetery and past Orangeman Thomas Hackett's memorial contained Catholic remains.

Although it continued to serve Protestants poor and modest means, Hawthorn-Dale Cemetery suffered from its increasing isolation from Montreal's English-speaking population. Over the course of the century, the Anglophone minority in the area of Pointe-aux-Trembles dwindled sharply. Symptomatic of this isolation was the trustees' 1927 decision to discontinue its funeral tram service from the Papineau Avenue terminal, an operation that had never been profitable. Subsequently, funerals accessed Hawthorn-Dale by automobile. Within a few years the Papineau Avenue burial grounds and the cemetery's former office there were demolished to make way for the northern approach to the Jacques Cartier Bridge. Almost nine hundred bodies were removed from the bridge site and placed in graves at Hawthorn-Dale that had been purchased by the city.[30] The physical approaches to Hawthorn-Dale were enhanced by a cast-off from Mount Royal: the old park entrance gate, no longer needed after the exchange of land for the new tramway, was installed on Notre-Dame Street at the southern end of Hawthorn-Dale. The extension of Sherbrooke Street eastward cut the cemetery in two. Although the company received compensation for this inconvenience, the division effectively meant the abandonment of the southern half – which luckily contained no graves – as burial space.[31] This southern-most portion was expropriated by the municipality for a park. The trustees received many offers to acquire other parts of Hawthorn-Dale, all of which were rejected in the interests of maintaining a reserve of land for burials. Yet, despite low grave prices, the cemetery remained underused. Consequently there was little incentive to improve its facilities. In 1965 Hawthorn-Dale began to offer winter burials, but this was discontinued a decade later because of the expense of operating the cemetery through the winter and the cemetery reverted to keeping bodies at the Mount Royal crematorium vaults from December to April. During the winter of 1977 the vacated office building at Hawthorn-Dale was destroyed by fire; it would not be replaced for nearly two decades.[32]

The trustees also had to face municipal projects to dissect the mountain with traffic arteries. In 1949, city traffic officials proposed tunnelling a thoroughfare under the Mountain from Pine Avenue and Drummond Street to Mount Royal Boulevard. Given its expense, the project was shelved, only to be replaced in January 1955 by Mayor Jean Drapeau's startling announcement of the construction of two north-south boulevards that would be built across the mountain and which would directly affect the cemetery: "I respect − even if I do not share it − the opinion of those who believe that Mount Royal [ie., the mountain], for aesthetic or other reasons should be preserved as a secluded spot," Drapeau told the Canadian Club of Montreal. "But the fact that the most important commercial artery of the city abuts on one of its flanks, deprived of north-south arteries, seems to justify a different point of view."[33] By August of the same year, after consultation with a firm of New York landscape architects, the city had shelved its plans for a north-south thoroughfare in favour of converting the tramway line on the mountain into a scenic parkway.

Although a non-profit company, the trustees were not immune to projects that promised a return and that encroached on only peripheral parts of the grounds. In 1952 and without public fuss, Bell Telephone built a tower on land purchased at the upper end of the cemetery. In 1959, the trustees decided to involve the cemetery in a real estate project along Mount Royal Avenue. They had already attempted to subdivide the area in 1914 but had withdrawn the plan upon realizing that their tax-exempt status had recently expired and that they might be left paying property taxes on unsold residential lots. In 1931, the City of Outremont had tried unsuccessfully to revive cemetery interest in a subdivision; later, in 1953, the cemetery briefly considered buying land on the opposite side of Mount

Table 8 Religion of those buried in Mount Royal Cemetery (January–April)

Year	Anglican	Presbyterian	Baptist	Methodist	Lutheran	Congregational	United	Orthodox	Catholic	Protestant	Not mentioned	Other*
1911	44	29.4	2.3	12.1	0.8	2.3	0	1.8	0.8	0.5	4	2
1931	40.7	21.2	3.9	0.5	0	0.9	24.9	3.5	0.2	0.7	0.2	3.3
1951	37.3	19.4	2.4	0.4	0.8	0	28.3	5.6	0.6	0	0.8	4.4
1971	30.3	15.9	1.3	0.1	3.5	0	22.8	7.1	9.5	1.3	2.8	5.4
1991	19.8	6.6	0.4	0	2.2	0	15.8	24.3	11.4	12.9	2.2	4.4
1998	12.4	5	0.4	0	1.2	0	5.8	19.8	9.9	11.6	26	7.9

Source: *Register of Internments*, Mount Royal Cemetery; table compiled by Sophie Mathieu
* Includes Jehovah Witnesses, the Apostolic Church, the Salvation Army, the New Church, the Temple Emanu-el,
   the Unitarian Church, the Pentecostal Church, etc.

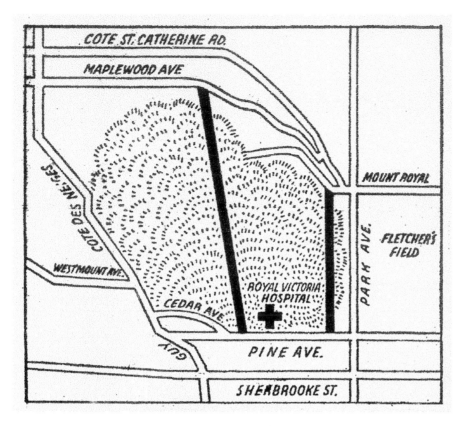

Mayor Jean Drapeau's project for two boulevards across Mount Royal, 1955

Royal Avenue as a means of controlling construction around the main entrance.[34] The trustees responded more favourably in 1959 to the idea of a $4,000,000 real estate sale, particularly because of their interest in investing in a new cemetery site on the western part of the island of Montreal, where the Protestant population was increasingly concentrated. The Mount Royal Avenue development called for an investment of $100,000,000 in the construction of 4,675 housing units in 26 buildings, the highest of which would be sixteen stories.

Although rocky and unsuitable for burial, this part of their grounds was an easily accessible and highly visible part of the mountain and the cemetery company soon found itself embroiled in a major public controversy with both environmentalists and nearby Outremont property owners. Besides opposition from the newly formed Comité de Vigilance d'Outremont, the land sale was opposed by groups as diverse as Save Montreal, the Montreal Association of Parks and Playgrounds, and the Montreal Council of Women. Faced with hostile French and English editorials, with the provincial government blocking any zoning change, and with a dispute between the City of Montreal and Outremont about jurisdiction over the land and whether it should be expropriated for Mount Royal Park or developed as real estate, the developer withdrew his proposal. Supporting the City of Montreal's claim to the right – over strong cemetery protest – to impose zoning restrictions over the entire mountain area, the Provincial Legislature decided in February 1962 that the contested land lay in Montreal's jurisdiction. In 1975, with expropriation for park use hanging over it, the cemetery finally accepted $1,567,025 for the sale of its land to the city.[35]

Despite the public confrontation with heritage and environmental groups, the cemetery company was slow in perceiving its vulnerability. While the public had a tendency to confuse institutional and public space, assuming it had right-of-way access across Mount Royal, the cemetery persisted in claiming its property rights as a private company. In 1955, the trustees responded to newspaper complaints concerning the absence on the grounds of drinking fountains, toilets, and benches. The cemetery "is not a park," they reminded Montrealers, and "a lot of benches might mar the general appearance or might encourage picnicking which may not be desirable." In 1959, the cemetery did reopen its gates on summer Sundays, hiring Barnes security guards to patrol the grounds.[36]

Funeral procession, c. 1930.

The increasing centrality of the automobile in the cemetery did not obliterate the traditional. This all-male funeral procession, with some mourners attired in top hat, is following on foot, the motorized hearse en route to one of the mountain cemeteries.

Inauguration of the Camillien Houde Parkway, 1958.

This photo, taken at the opening of the motorway that replaced the tramway on the mountain, gives a strong sense of the growing place of the automobile on the mountain – and within the cemetery.

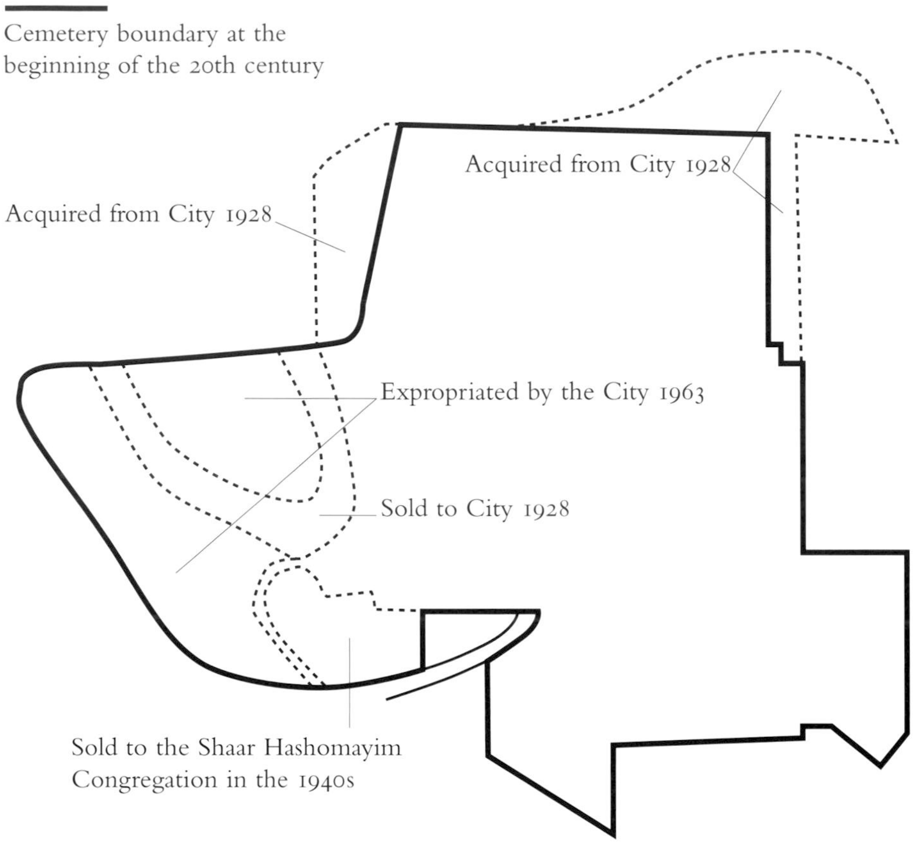

Cemetery boundary at the
beginning of the 20th century

Acquired from City 1928

Acquired from City 1928

Changes to Mount Royal Cemetery's
boundaries, 1928–63.

The cemetery exchanged large portions of
land with the City of Montreal in 1928 at
the time of the building of the tramway
which looped up the eastern side of the
mountain from Park Avenue. Several pieces
of land north of the crematorium were sold
to the Shaar Hashomayim Congregation
during the 1940s. The remaining eastern
portions of the cemetery were expropriated
by the city during the 1960s and incorporated into Mount Royal Park, after a failed
attempt by the cemetery to sell the land to
a real estate developer.

Expropriated by the City 1963

Sold to City 1928

Sold to the Shaar Hashomayim
Congregation in the 1940s

With many of its upper prestigious sections approaching
capacity, the cemetery turned in the late 1970s to develop
gravesites on the summit of Mount Murray. This action
would unleash a new controversy over the cemetery's public responsibilities in determining land use on the mountain, in shaping its nature and geography, and in regulating
public access. As well as raising the ire of environmentalists
and advocates of a more democratic use of the mountain,
the clear-cutting and landscaping project took place in the
midst of rising Quebec nationalism. Some nationalists por-
trayed English Montreal – and by inference the Protestant

cemetery, with its mountain location, its unilingualism, and
its mausoleums for the English rich – as the top of a colo-
nialist pyramid, what Léandre Bergeron called a source of
"collective frustration."[37] English Montreal had felt directly threatened by the FLQ crisis and just a year earlier, in
1969, McGill University had faced 15,000 'Operation
McGill Français' demonstrators assembled before the Roddick Gates to challenge the place of English institutions in
Quebec. Hospitals, the YMCA, churches, museums, and the
Protestant cemetery had to confront similar accusations
that they were obstacles to the emergence of a nation in

which Québécois culture must predominate. In reality, the cemetery was subjected to few nationalist demonstrations. Exceptions occurred in June 1975 and again in 1976, when Mount Royal Park, adjoining the cemetery, was the site of huge nationalist rallies organized over several days by the Société Saint-Jean-Baptiste. An observer myself, I remember the "Mon Pays" sentiment as thousands of Montrealers celebrated on the mountain: crowds, drinking, entertainment, music, and litter, left the impression of a joyous medieval carnival. The cemetery viewed the occasion differently. Honouring French Canada's patron saint, the celebration's noise, beer, and sense of personal liberation were indirect cultural strikes at the very origins of the cemetery, trespassing on its sense of privacy, Protestantism, and respectability: the thousands who walked the grounds at night to reach the park and the few who vandalized headstones violated a carefully constructed territory and place of Protestant memory.

This was the political setting in which the Mount Murray project was launched. In 1959, one section of Mount Murray had been developed with single graves and flat markers.[38] Two decades later, a more ambitious scheme to develop the upper part of the area was undertaken. It was, after all, the roughest part of cemetery property: its slope was severe, the land was forested and rocky, access was via an old lumber road, and its out-of-the-way location had made it the site of the cemetery dump. At the same time, its views as the cemetery's highest summit gave it great development potential for exclusive burial sites. The decision to clear-cut the summit was made by the manager; the trustees were apparently not consulted. As manager Donald Roy recalled simply: "I was Captain of the Ship." Merle Christopher, then his assistant, described the clearing as having been done in "the old way."[39] Working under Roy's supervision, contractor Jack Orr was hired to clear the land, to

Workmen repair tombstone after Saint-Jean-Baptiste celebrations on Mount Royal, 1976.

According to the cemetery's *Annual Report, 1977:* "Unruly groups returning from the festivities created havoc in some of the sections. Monuments by the dozen were seriously damaged; others, some 350 in all, were simply toppled over. The Cemetery took on an appearance never seen before in its entire history. Cemetery crews were assigned to re-erect the fallen monuments and many were raised without damage. However, others were too large and cumbersome and the services of a properly equipped monument dealer had to be retained. Aided by Cemetery labour, so as to keep the costs as reasonable as possible, the monument dealer was able to erect the remaining monuments and, in a few cases, effect minor repairs on site. Some had to removed for shop repairs but all have since been returned. Unfortunately, however, some monuments were damaged beyond repair. These were old monuments of thinly slabbed marble which, after being broken, could not be placed in an upright position but only laid out flat on the ground. The tidying up process was completed in about a three-week period. In protest against this malicious abuse of private property, a letter was written to His Worship the Mayor of Montreal."

Aerial view of Mount Royal (1956).

This view from the north shows the Université de Montréal bordering on the two cemeteries. The Mount Royal Cemetery's forests on Mount Murray are clearly evident. Also of importance is the extensive urban expansion north of the mountain.

"Centennial Trees Felled on Mont-Royal."

With this headline, 8 August 1979, *La Presse* explained that the cemetery's magnificent Mount Royal site was being bulldozed to provide more burial space for Protestants. On 1 February 1980, *La Presse* returned to the attack publishing a winter photo of the site, which it described as "a desert." Snowshoer and geography professor Léon Gagnon decried the "catastrophe," calling on government to impose environmental-impact assessments before such "modifications of the natural order of the landscape."

improve the old lumber road, and to build burial terraces with fill hauled from construction sites around the city.

While the cemetery described the project as a "landscaping feat," environmentalists described it as brutality towards the mountain. Widening the old road up the slope and asphalt paving at the top further aroused critics. Pointing out that the cemetery was both private and Protestant, *La Presse* journalist Huguette Roberge complained that property rights were more *sacré* than protection of the mountain. Except for administrative matters like building permits, she charged, the cemetery was barely subject to municipal authority. Ethnic suspicions were evident in her questioning of the need for more Protestant burial space in a period when cremation was gaining popularity: the implication was that, even as they were fading in numbers and significance, Protestants, were a narrow elitist group

holding on to the best situations.[40] In February 1980 another *La Presse* journalist charged that the cemetery was collecting revenues from its use of the mountain as a landfill site. Relying mostly on arguments of entitlement, the cemetery response was ineffective: Donald Roy told *La Presse* that "his company had the entire right to cut all the trees it wished on its property" and that, like any other corporation, it had the right "to make profits."[41] It would be another decade before the cemetery moved from confrontation to alliances with environmentalists in preserving the mountain, its flora, and its birds. Only in the 1990s would it approach change, as it became bilingual and more integrated into Quebec society, as it emphasized its historic role as a pluralist (albeit Protestant) institution, and as it developed a public relations strategy built around its importance as a heritage and natural site.

TEN

NEW RESPECTABILITY:
BUSINESS AND HISTORY AT THE
CEMETERY TODAY

Today, a visitor to the Mount Royal or Hawthorn-Dale Cemetery facilities is likely to be struck by the contrast between Victorian landscapes and Gothic architecture on the one hand and state-of-the-art crematorium technology on the other. Compare, for example, the warmer, more quaint and cramped setting of the business offices in the old superintendent's house just inside the historic main gate with the elegance, efficiency, and modernity of the funeral complex/crematorium. The explanation for this juxtaposition of the traditional and the futuristic, of nature and computer screens, of bluebird houses and a staff electric golf cart, is to be found in a fundamental shift in business strategies at the cemetery since 1990. Recall that across most of the twentieth century and strongly influenced by Ormiston, John, and Donald Roy, the cemetery had steadfastly emphasized qualities of reliable and, efficient service to its largely Protestant constituency. While historically it had officially welcomed all communities, the cemetery's cultural bedrock remained an essential Protestantism and Britishness, what we have tried to encompass in the term "respectability."

Failing to defend itself in the clear-cutting fiasco on Mount Royal in 1979 with misplaced arguments based on

Interior of the archives vault, main office.

Containing the cemetery's excellent archives, the vault epitomizes the traditional at the cemetery and the importance given across the cemetery's history to exact record-keeping.

an entitlement rooted in private property and Protestant privilege, the cemetery slowly came to perceive the public relations significance of promoting more positive features of its past – its links to philanthropy and Christian compassion for the needy, its status as a non-profit institution with roots in the local community that stretched back to 1799, and, above all, its reputation for inclusiveness. This transition to a focus on heritage and the cemetery's legitimate place in the community was part of its transition into a third phase of its history, if we view its rural cemetery and lawn–plan phases as the first two. These changes were driven by competition from the "death care industry," especially multinational corporations. For his part, Merle Christopher, the new executive director, focused on administrative organization, sales, marketing, and public relations rather than technical issues. Rather than pursuing autonomy from his board, he worked to reinvigorate relations with the trustees, who in turn, reverted to the activism of their nineteenth-century predecessors. Policies of transparency with the public, bilingualism, and an enthusiastic reaching out to non-Protestant clientele became central. Changing public perceptions of heritage and awareness of the environmental and leisure potential of Mount Royal and Hawthorn-Dale led the cemetery to provide walking tours and guides to the famous personages buried in its grounds. The birdhouses, the incorporation of niches for cremated remains as part of a sculpture garden at the summit of Mount Murray, the employment of a landscape architect and public relations officer, and the cemetery's entry into the funeral business were part of this new business perception. Hawthorn-Dale was transformed from a white elephant by its integration into the park system of the eastern end of the island of Montreal and its development as a regional and multicultural provider of funeral, burial, and cremation services.

To situate this transition, one has to step back several decades. In 1952, Mount Royal Cemetery celebrated the hundredth anniversary of its first burial. For that occasion, the cemetery admitted cars on specific evenings from 17:00 to dusk so that people could tour the grounds and admire the blossoming trees. The trustees also decided to provide perpetual care for the gravesite of the first burial "in view of the historic interest of this Lot and the saintly character of the Rev. William Squire."[1] The principal event in celebration of the anniversary was a commemorative service on 22 October. The souvenir leaflet included the order of service, the president's remarks, some historical information, and a poem written by Wilson MacDonald and dedicated to Ormiston Roy, "One Hundred Years of Peace":

They yearned for rest, and now how deep their sleep!
The cool, white arm of clay about them thrown:
Their laughter all gone homeward to the sun
And all their woes unto the friendly winds
That tent upon this mountain. They have lost
The gardens of our roses, and their hands
Shall waft upon our air no more adieus,
The valiant dust that imprisoned for a day
The glory of the great lies here as prone
As temples where no god was visitant:
For the humility wherein men take
The lowely sod for consort doth resolve
All summits to one level. Here no robe
Of purple silk, or majesty of mien,
Or ancestry, or name, or high estate
Has power to add one favour to their rest.
The seer and clod are sleeping. Both have gone
Upon the same adventure: pride or caste
Shall keep apart no more their warring clay;
But, to the measure of a summer breeze,
Their dust shall sing together in a song,
Shall meekly blend within the proudest flower
In some new, royal garden of the sun.

Cemetery history represented only a minor part of this ceremony. The coverage in the *Montreal Gazette* included an article by Edgar Andrew Collard, which provided anecdotal material concerning extravagant funerals and other singular incidents but made little of the cemetery's historical

Elsie Reford at Grand-Métis (258, Section PHS).

A Meighen by birth, Elsie Reford (1872–1967) married into one of Montreal's most prominent shipping families. Important Anglicans and philanthropists, Refords served the Protestant community at the university, hospital, and cemetery. Elsie was particularly known for the spectacular garden she created at the family's summer estate at Grand-Métis.

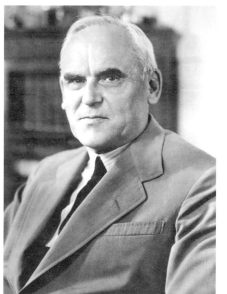

C.D. Howe (507, Section Rose Hill).

Alongside well-known Conservative politicians such as Alexander Tilloch Galt and J.J.C. Abbott, many prominent Liberals are also buried at Mount Royal. As minister of munitions and supply in the Mackenzie King government during the Second World War, Clarence Decatur Howe (1886–1960), an American-born engineer, played an important role in organizing Canadian wartime participation. In the postwar deconstruction of government controls, Howe acted as the link between government and business, serving as minister of trade and commerce, 1948–57.

Anna Harriet Leonowens (née Crawford) (F738, Section F9).

Immortalized in the book *Anna and the King of Siam*, in several movies based thereon, and in the Broadway musical *The King and I*, Leonowens retired to live with her daughter in Montreal. She died in 1915. Today her monument often serves as a movie set.

Canada's Hangman: Alexander Armstrong English (aka Arthur Ellis).

Taking up the occupation of hangman at age forty-seven after a career in the British army, English (1865–1938) conducted over 600 hangings across Canada in the period 1912–34. Nephew of a well-known British hangman and trained in mechanical engineering, English emigrated to Canada in 1912. Paid $200 and expenses for a hanging, he travelled with a black bag that included his ropes, straps, and black cap. For smaller centres unequipped with a permanent gallows, he provided a portable scaffold. "Ellis" was well-known to the police in Montreal's east end as a violent individual sometimes seen on the streets with a .38 revolver in his belt. Arrested at one point for wife beating, he was apparently freed without trial because three condemned men awaited him in Vancouver. Separated from her husband for a lengthy period and surviving him for twenty-two years, Edith Grimsdale chose to be buried alongside him in Hawthorn-Dale Cemetery.

importance or its place in the life of the city. The *Gazette* went on to emphasize the good work of the original trustees but, apart from a paragraph on Squire, made no reference to famous people buried at the cemetery or to unique features such as the crematorium.[2]

In 1959, the cemetery was opened to cars on Sunday. By the end of the summer 3,184 cars had been counted passing through the main gates.[3] The pride with which the trustees noted this statistic reveals their growing awareness of the public's appreciation of greater access to the cemetery. At the same time, this kind of visit was entirely in keeping with Ormiston Roy's sense of the cemetery as a floral showcase that visitors would tour in their cars. This philosophy might welcome use of the cemetery as the subject of a Kodak Brownie snapshot but it failed to promote the site as a complex pocket of nature or a place for quiet outdoor reflection. Heritage, too, remained a nebulous concept, as was clear in the trustees' discussions on possible cemetery participation in Canada's centenary and in the international exposition planned for Montreal in 1967. As part of what it called "general beautification," the board considered replacing the historic gates at the main entrance.[4]

Despite such questionable attitudes, by the late 1960s the cemetery had begun to perceive the importance of openness and candour in its dealing with the public. The cemetery's public image had suffered in the attempt to sell land along Mount Royal Avenue to developers in 1959, with the trustees admitting that "the Company has come very much more in the public eye because of the land situation. There is a rather definite feeling that under the present somewhat tight system of administration ... there might be reason for some criticism which could, at least, be allayed or better defended if a wider dissemination of knowledge as to the Company's affairs were made."[5] It was during this

misadventure that the idea of commissioning a history of the cemetery was broached for the first time. The idea was revived in 1973 by Donald Roy, who suggested Edgar Andrew Collard, former editor of the *Gazette*, as author: "Such a document," he told the trustees, would be "a useful publication for public relations as well as an historical document."[6] Again, the suggestion was a response to unfavourable publicity, a *Gazette* article having accused the cemetery of cavalier treatment of "pauper's graves." The trustees angrily retorted: "In neither cemetery is there a welfare section and in neither are services performed in a manner as described in your article. While our cemeteries serve families under welfare, all welfare cases are treated in the same way, and with precisely the same high standards, as every other interment; at neither cemetery are trenches dug nor caskets left exposed to view." Their response to these accusations was to draw attention to the company's 120 years of public service and to voice their outrage at the *Gazette's* "degrading the prestigious history of Mount Royal Cemetery."[7] Collard was set to work preparing a history of the cemetery, but since he was retired, pre-occupied with writing a weekly article for the *Gazette,* and more comfortable with the anecdotal than the larger social history of the cemetery, he progressed only slowly.

Yet not all cemetery decisions were consistent with this increasing attention to cultivating the public image of the cemetery. As we have seen, the decision in 1979 to clear-cut Mount Murray – and the ill-advised defence of this action by Donald Roy – revealed the entent to which an attitude of entitlement still prevailed over support for the public interest and the preservation of green space. Ironically, in 1977, two years before the clear-cutting on Mount Murray, cemetery minutes showed a strong awareness of the public's interest in the mountain:

Over the last number of years, it would seem, both Cemeteries but particularly Mount Royal are being visited not only by those attending specific graves but also by the general public as peaceful sanctuaries for weekend walks and leisurely drives. The public's increasing appreciation of the natural beauty of the Cemetery's outstanding display of flowering shrubs, blossoming trees, peonies and roses etc. is most welcome and notable. Also, Mount Royal through all seasons of the year has become a favourite locale for birdwatchers. To encourage the pheasant population, the Cemetery provides feed at two locations.[8]

Although sensitive to the natural beauty of the site under their charge and what they were describing as the pleasures of "weekend walks" and "leisurely desires," the cemetery company had difficulties conveying these changing sympathies to the public. Stung by bad press, the trustees were forced to step in. In 1982 they discussed implementation of a "formal tree replacement scheme" and considered asking McGill faculty to assess and catalogue plant and animal life on the cemetery grounds.[9] They did not, however, cancel the original development plan for Mount Murray. Consequently, they found themselves dragged into ongoing conflict, particularly with a citizen's group formed in the late 1980s, l'Association des Citoyens d'Outremont. The trustees were not at all pleased to find the cemetery in court for breaches of both a City of Outremont tree-cutting bylaw and a provincial environmental law. This disastrous scenario would prove critical in their shift to transparency in their relations with the public.

In addition to this problem of appearing isolated and insensitive, the Mount Royal Cemetery faced new competition from the private sector. Opened in 1934, Montreal Memorial Park was a memorial-park cemetery modelled loosely on the highly successful Forest Lawn Memorial Park in California. Rural cemeteries like Mount Royal had been established on the basis of selling lots that would provide for the burial over time of established families and succeeding generations. Memorial parks democratized this principle. Profit-making enterprises, they marketed "pre-need," employing salespeople to convince much broader segments of the population of the need to purchase burial lots for later use. With simple religious statues, flush-to-the-ground bronze markers, a lawn-plan look, and a pragmatic association of burial and profit, memorial parks benefited from postwar consumer and entrepreneurial culture expanding rapidly across the North American suburban landscape. Instead of the gated sobriety, granite vistas, and a certain Protestant stuffiness perceived at Mount Royal Cemetery, memorial parks in Montreal marketed a familiar suburban environment, handy access from highways, carefree maintenance, and one-stop visitation, chapel, and burial space. By the 1960s, memorial parks had been joined in their sale of what was now more judiciously called "pre-arrangement," by funeral homes like Alfred Dallaire, a company that specialized in moderatey priced funerals across the English, French, and ethnic communities.

Mount Royal Cemetery also faced new competition at its crematorium, a business that had enjoyed a monopoly in Quebec since its opening in 1902. This changed after 1975 with the opening of crematoria by both the Montreal Memorial Park and Notre-Dame-des-Neiges Cemetery. These were soon joined by other crematoria as funeral-home operators like Alfred Dallaire followed customers into the suburbs, opening crematoria on the south shore and on the island of Laval.

The Mount Royal's response to this competition was at first muted. Consistent with its non-profit status, the cemetery had always indignantly rejected the aggressive sales techniques of memorial parks. Disdainful of the hard sell,

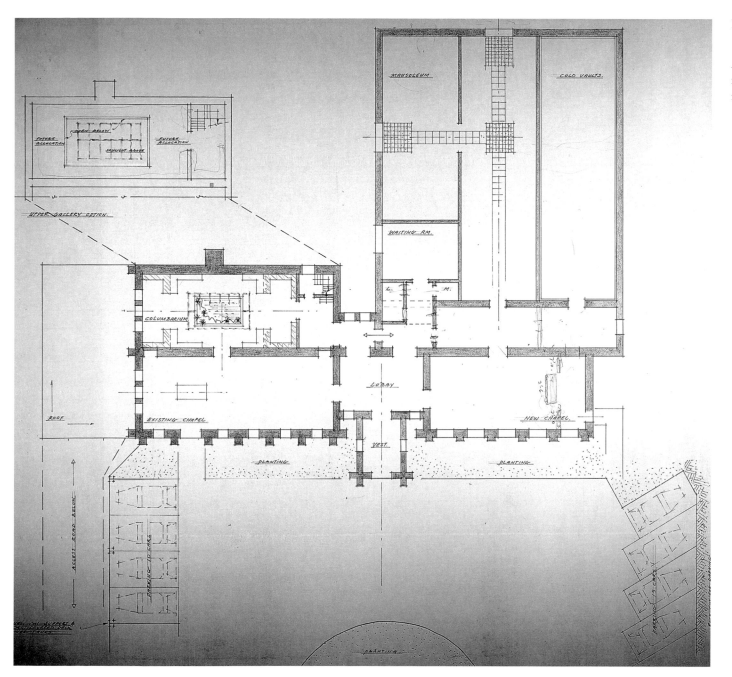

Plan of crematorium expansion, 1982–4.

As part of renovations in the mid-1980s, the storage vaults were replaced by crypts for urns.

Merle Christopher, executive director

In the early 1980s major renovation of the crematorium was also undertaken with one eye on the competition. Expansion consisted of building a second chapel to the right of the entrance, a columbarium to the rear of the old chapel, and "garden crypts," which replaced the old storage vaults. Not to be confused with upstarts nearby, the Mount Royal Crematorium had become, in the trustees' words, "among North America's Finest."[12] Despite these changes, cemetery management was slow to fight the competition on its own terms, preferring to trade on a reputation of reliability, civility, and service.[13] Since the company was most comfortable with English Montreal, its burial and crematorium operations remained rooted in good relations with funeral homes and, thanks to its trustees, its networks with the major Protestant churches.

In the late 1980s, competition for funeral, burial, and cremation markets in Montreal intensified with the arrival of multinational "death-care" corporations. New trustees on the Mount Royal board expressed concern that, as a non-profit company, the cemetery was not sufficiently sensitive to modern business techniques; they suggested that the board itself should be more involved in the running of the cemetery, something that had been largely left to management since the time of Ormiston Roy.[14] Above all, the cemetery's image as a closed, Anglo-Protestant institution had to be transformed if the company were to flourish in a changing Quebec. Its clientele had already changed dramatically over the previous generation. Not only was the overall character of the cemetery considerably more multicultural, but among the English-speaking community, which formed the company's traditional market, increasing numbers no longer belonged to a specific Protestant church. Burial registrations clearly indicate this trend. In 1971, only 1.3 per cent of registrations indicated that the deceased was a Protestant without a declared church affiliation; by 1998,

Donald Roy put it this way: "I didn't like the word 'advertising.'"[10] At the same time, Mount Royal management moved to protect its market and to expand revenue in different forms. The crematorium's service of picking up remains was improved for funeral homes outside the Montreal area. Merle Christopher, who had sales experience with the trustees of the Toronto General Burying Grounds, was hired as assistant manager in 1974, and, in a major policy change, he brought the company into the sale of monuments, inscriptions, and bronze plaques. These sales, which began in 1975, now represent 50 per cent of the cemetery's revenues.[11]

this category had risen to 11.8 per cent of registrations. Only 2.8 per cent of burial registrations in 1971 indicated no religious affiliation whatsoever; by 1998, fully 26 per cent of registrations were in this category. If, in the light of this secularization of its clientele, the company had to reshape its image at the Mount Royal location, the situation was even more dramatic at Hawthorn-Dale. With its unilingual, Protestant character, it could hardly function in a part of the island of Montreal that was overwhelmingly Roman Catholic and French speaking.

In 1990, with Donald Roy's imminent retirement as manager, the trustees reorganized management, replacing the office of manager with that of executive director, thus bringing direction of the company into what they called the "current usage in non-profit organizations."[15] Merle Christopher, the company's assistant manager since the early 1980s, was promoted into the new position. The trustees, determined to be more involved in the day-to-day workings of the cemetery and to enjoy a good working relationship with the executive director, agreed to a system of visitation whereby, in rotation, one or two trustees would tour the cemetery, examining particular sites like the crematorium, shops, or development of Mount Murray.

As part of a new attitude towards the public, the cemetery hired a francophone public relations firm, Le Cabinet de Relations Publiques National. In their campaign to improve the company's image, these advisers encouraged the cemetery to run radio advertisements. To permit evening visits, the cemetery gates were left open later during summer hours. Birdwatching and walking tours were introduced. In May 1990, two busloads of delegates to the International Lilac Society Conference who were welcomed at the cemetery responded by donating a plaque recognizing the company "for preserving a fine landscaped park containing many lilacs."[16] The reference to "park" on

the plaque represented a small but significant change in language and perceptions. This openness served to counter the image, as the minutes put it, that the Mount Royal Cemetery was "uncooperative to the concerns of outside interest groups."[17]

After years of intransigence, willingness to admit environmental error was chosen as the best means of resolving the legal issues arising from the development of Mount Murray. In July 1990, the company pleaded guilty to violating a provincial environmental law by dumping brick and building rubble and was fined $1,500; a few months later, Merle Christopher met municipal officials in Outremont, assuring them that the stability of Mount Murray's steep slope would be ensured by tree plantings undertaken by the cemetery and that the result would give a forest effect. Christopher was soon able to tell the trustees to breathe easier: "we are well on our way to 'quenching the fires' in the community."[18]

An early act of Christopher's administration was the hiring of landscape architect Malaka Ackaoui. Her mission was two-fold: to re-evaluate development on Mount Murray and to consider educational and tourism possibilities across the entire cemetery. The resulting master development plan was a clear departure from the earlier insistence on the rights of private property.[19] Taking a holistic approach, Ackaoui examined landscape, traffic, and development possibilities across the grounds. Turning away from earlier landscape regimes with their focus first on graves and then on lawn, she emphasized natural growth that might unify the site visually and ecologically. Whereas first the carriage and then the automobile had dominated transport within the cemetery's earlier phases, she proposed that the summit of Mount Murray privilege walking.

Since 1977 and the adoption of French as the official language of Quebec, language has been the very crucible

Hors du temps.

This Mountain View sculpture by Charles Daudelin was erected on the Outremont Summit of Mount Royal and was dedicated on 20 June 1993. The sculpture garden and look-out columbarium respond to changing forms of the family and evolving conceptions of burial.

The children's section was created in 1999 to offer a special place where children and stillborn or miscarried babies could be buried. The granite sculpture by Pascale Archambault suggests children playing.

of the "national question," with battles over access to English schools, the legality of bilingual signs, and the changing of English place names serving to marginalize the English-speaking community. Although it was, historically, a confidently unilingual anglophone institution, the cemetery in the Christopher regime quickly introduced bilingual signs across the grounds and in business correspondence. On the issue of whether the summit's name was Mount Murray, after the cemetery's Protestant founder, or the more politically acceptable le Sommet d'Outremont, the cemetery, even before the 1990s, avoided controversy by opting for the benign appellation "Mountain View." As well as being a burial site, Mountain View was landscaped to maximize public accessibility, to preserve native shrubs and native trees," and to fulfill what Ackaoui's report called "l'esprit du Mont Royal." Mountain View combines a striking lookout and reflective surroundings with effective land use of the

site as a burial area for two of the cemetery's growing constituencies. On the terraces leading up to the summit, "burial gardens" for casket burial have been constructed. Circular in design, these gardens have proven to be particularly attractive to Orthodox and Asian families. On the summit itself, central sculptures, a cremation garden, and a belvedere respond to the growing demand for urn burial. Emphasizing cultural openness, the sculptures were chosen in a competition held by the cemetery in collaboration with the Conseil de la sculpture du Québec and the Quebec Ministry of Cultural Affairs.[20]

Other directions suggested in the master plan have also been largely carried out. A tree-identification program was introduced, and in 1997 a horticulturist – by profession, a landscape architect in the tradition of Ormiston Roy – was hired to oversee the planting and maintenance of flowers and shrubs. Birdwatching is a natural public activity for

Landscape architect's drawing.

Malaka Ackaoui's plan integrated changing burial needs with sculpture and environmental concerns for views, walking, and birdwatching.

**Daily Checklist
of the Birds in
Mount Royal Cemetery**

◆ For each species, always indicate a quantity; even if approximate - an estimate is more accurate than a check mark.

◆ Use a new checklist for each visit and please remember to leave the *completed* checklist at the information board. *Thank you for your cooperation.*

"Daily Checklist of the Birds in Mount Royal Cemetery."

The use of its logo on birdwatching documents and the site's favour with cyclists and walkers are part of the cemetery's increasing association with mountain and environmental activities deemed compatible with the cemetery's main function. The cemetery is also renowned among horticulturalists, in part for its cultivation of rare trees in the Montreal region, such as the metasequoia.

cemetery grounds, compatible with the atmosphere of a rural cemetery, respectful of nature and life, and encouraging of a traditional Protestant behaviour – as the National Geographic Society points out, "experienced birders know how to move quietly and to stand patiently still."[21] It was, significantly, the cemetery's first female trustee, Elsie Norsworthy, who produced and promoted a birdwatching brochure, "Birdwatching in the Mount Royal Cemetery," as well as encouraging construction of bluebird houses and the posting of sightings. The board's second female trustee, Anne Pasold, president of the Atwater Library and prominent in McGill University's Redpath Museum, convinced the cemetery to contribute $7,000 to sponsor an indoor "cemetery walking tour" as part of a Redpath Museum exhibit. Executive director Christopher, reflecting back, explained this initiative as a "marketing plan to inform the public about our property" and as an act of "good corporate citizenship."[22] The favourable public response to these initiatives by female trustees convinced Christopher of the value of investing in public relations, and in 1995 Myriam Cloutier, a graduate in communications from Laval University was named communications coordinator. Promoted to director of public relations in 1997, she played a major role in cataloguing historical personages buried in the cemetery, in fielding genealogical questions, in conducting walking tours, and in establishing contact with the francophone press.

Central in this public relations strategy was the idea that legitimacy in the community could be based on the cemetery's historical place. By the 1970s, governments, institutions, and corporations had become increasingly conscious of the political and marketing mileage in associating themselves with cultural phenomena like art galleries, historical exhibitions, or museums. The Manufacturers Life Insurance Company sponsored an academic history of Canadi-

an business while, for readers of popular history, Pierre Berton's *The National Dream* anchored the achievements of the Canadian Pacific Railway to the positive feeling of a new Canadian nationalism.[23] In Montreal, a broad range of companies emphasized their roots in their clients' constituencies. As early as 1965, for example, Eaton's department store sponsored Museum Week in Montreal. As concepts of heritage began to replace narrower, bookish definitions of history, new emphasis was given to interpretation centres and sites with connections to local identity. In Ottawa, multiculturalism became official policy, bringing with it federal measures "to nurture our cultural heritage": not to be outdone, the Quebec government published a White Paper that gave prominence to heritage.[24] Established in Quebec in 1992, the Economuseum network took as its motto the phrase, "Heritage That Earns Its Keep" and advocated "the blending of a vibrant culture and a very legitimate economic ambition."[25] By the 1990s there were over 2,000 museums in Canada, all devoted in one form or another to cultivating public memory. For their part and from their very office windows, Mount Royal officials musing over how to improve the cemetery's public image could not miss the significance of the acres of material culture before them: their business location coincided with a major heritage site!

By the 1990s, a newly formed History Committee at the cemetery had published an historical walking-tour brochure. This was followed up by weekend walking tours. Organized by the director of public relations around specific historical themes – McGill University, Montreal street names, or shipwrecks – the tours attracted hundreds of visitors. Led in either English or French by popular personalities or historians, the tours were repeated the next day in the other language. In 1998, the cemetery established a bilingual charitable organization, The Friends of the Mount

Royal Cemetery/Les Amis du cimetière Mont Royal. Emphasizing that the cemetery was an institution of public interest, it established heritage and environmental activities that were supported by tax-deductible donations. The result of these initiatives was that, instead of being limited to an image of mausoleums and wealthy Protestants, the full, rich political and cultural history of the cemetery was promoted. The focus could be federal stalwarts like J.C.C. Abbott and Alexander Tilloch Galt, municipal politicians, such as Honoré Beaugrand, who opted for cremation, hockey star Howie Morenz, or the German victims of a nineteenth-century train wreck. The cemetery archives, particular burial sections, or specific headstones, enable students or specialists to study themes concerning architecture, women, infant mortality, work, poverty, Native people, or slavery. For those interested in genealogy, the cemetery is a fascinating source of information on individuals and families who have hundreds of thousands of descendants across the continent.

This link to local history became a principal tool in the efforts of independent cemeteries like Mount Royal and older funeral homes to offset international competitors. Lépine Cloutier, then a Quebec City group of funeral homes, unabashedly used Quebec nationalism in a newspaper advertisement: "The Lépine Cloutier group remains an entirely Québécois enterprise. Entirely, totally, uniquely Québécois … When you contact funeral homes in the Lépine Cloutier group you are dealing with local people, people like yourself, which we have been for 140 years, and which we will continue to be."[26]

The consolidation of funeral enterprises in the United States began in the 1960s and their acquisition of Canadian funeral homes dates from the mid-1980s. In 1998, the three largest multinationals – Service Corporation International, the Loewen Group (a Vancouver-based corporation), and Stewart Enterprises – controlled 5,242 funeral

Opening the cemetery gates.

Another sign of the cemetery's recent public relations initiatives are its walking tours and establishment of the Friends of the Mount Royal Cemetery.

F.R. Scott

Monument of Marian and F.R. Scott
(394, Section C)

Poet, professor of constitutional law,
and one of the founders of the
Canadian socialist movement, Frank Scott is buried with his wife,
artist Marian Dale Scott. In the next grave are his parents, Amy and
Canon Frederick George Scott. The epitaphs on the two graves emphasize changing forms of commemoration between generations: the older
underlines the faith of an Anglican priest, while the more recent com-
memorates secular values of love – "The Dance Is One."

Last tribute to Howie Morenz, Montreal Forum
11 March 1937 (L2037-G, Section L2).

In Montreal, hockey stars are accorded the funerals
of heroes. Thousands of fans paid their respects when
William Howard Morenz, who died at the age of
thirty-four, was laid out in the Montreal Forum.

homes, 1,158 cemeteries, and over 225 crematoria around the world.[27] Publicly traded companies, they brought capital, international experience, and political influence to bear on the markets that they wished to enter. Service Corporation International paid former U.S. president George Bush $70,000 for a speech to the International Cemetery and Funeral Association and donated $100,000 to his presidential library.[28] These are not overwhelming public relations expenses for a corporation that, in 1998, had 3,300 funeral home locations, 35,000 employees and $2.5 billion in revenues. In that year, Service Corporation International controlled 15 per cent of the British market; in addition, through their ownership of the largest death-care conglomerate in Europe they ran 950 funeral homes in France. In the United States, the affiliated funeral homes of their competitor Stewart Enterprises held one out of every nine funerals.[29]

Through their construction of highly competitive crematoria and cemeteries, these international corporations represented powerful threats to non-profit cemeteries like Mount Royal. In 1998, Service Corporation International controlled 430 cemeteries. While maintaining the family names and local management of the funeral homes they bought, they were able to cluster services such as hearses, equipment, and accounting, and were able to direct business from their funeral operations to their cemeteries and crematoria. Along with centralized management and economies of scale in purchasing, they devoted large budgets to advertising, marketing in particular the benefits of pre-arrangement. In 1988, the Lépine Cloutier funeral home of Quebec City, family run for five generations, was sold to Urgel Bourgie of Montreal. In turn, Urgel Bourgie, Quebec's most important funeral home, with seventy-seven parlours and five cemeteries, was sold in 1996 to Stewart Enterprises. Cemeteries also represent excellent sites for multi-service funeral complexes. Montreal's Notre-Dame-des-Neiges Cemetery found that 75 per cent of the individuals it consulted favoured the uniting at the cemetery of multiple functions: viewing, chapel, reception, cremation, and burial facilities.[30] In Los Angeles, Stewart Enterprises made a leasing arrangement with Roman Catholic authorities that allowed them to build mortuaries at six of the archdiocese's eleven cemeteries.

The Mount Royal Company's burial and cremation business depended in good measure on its longstanding relationships with funeral parlours throughout the area. This network was threatened with collapse when all three of the major international companies moved into the city, buying well-known funeral homes like Collins Clark MacGillivray, White and Wray-Walton-Wray (Service Corporation International), Paperman and Son (Loewen), and Urgel Bourgie and Feron's (Stewart). Some twenty-eight independent funeral companies operated in the Montreal area in the late 1970s; twenty years later this had been reduced to six. By 2000, the multinationals controlled about three-quarters of the funeral services in Montreal. In addition, since 1994, Service Corporation International has operated a crematorium on the south shore. Not surprisingly, the effects on the Mount Royal Cemetery were dramatic: there were, for example, 23 per cent fewer cremations at Mount Royal in the three-year period 1996–8 than in 1993–5.[31] As in the United States, the multinational corporations made arrangements with Roman Catholic authorities in Montreal to establish funeral homes on their cemetery properties. In 1997, the Centre Funeraire Côte-des-Neiges, owned by Service Corporation International, was built alongside Notre-Dame-des-Neiges Cemetery, with a separate gate facilitating access between the two.

In the United States, cemeteries, particularly memorial parks, long ago entered the mortuary business. In the suburbs of Los Angeles, for example, Forest Lawn Memorial Park opened its own funeral chapel in 1934. In the most important policy change since construction of the crematorium a century earlier, the Mount Royal Cemetery Company entered the funeral business in the 1990s. In the preceding decade, the company had acquired a funeral director's licence in order to conform to provincial regulations concerning operation of a crematorium. By 1990, the company applied to the Department of Social Affairs to have its licence extended to include removals – that is, the right to transfer bodies from the place of death – a prerogative reserved for certified funeral directors. Almost immediately, Mount Royal Cemetery began offering funeral services in its chapel-crematorium complex, initially using the M.A. Blythe Bernier Funeral Home for embalming services. Blythe Bernier, described in cemetery minutes as "a low key estab-

lishment which serves the community with care and understanding," was a well-known local business; indeed, its elderly owner was receiving offers from international funeral-home corporations.[32] Established in 1928, it was first located on Sherbrooke Street at the corner of Ste Famille, then a middle-class English-speaking neighbourhood near the McGill University campus. In the late 1930s, it moved a few blocks north to Park Avenue near Pine, an attractive location for immigrants living and working along nearby St Lawrence Boulevard. It had a particular clientele among German Protestants, many of whom were buried from the nearby Lutheran Church. In the 1980s, it followed the immigrant communities north, eventually relocating on Ogilvy Avenue in the Park Extension neighbourhood. Early in 1992, the trustees voted to buy Blythe Bernier and to continue its operations as a local enterprise in a multi-ethnic neighbourhood. Today, Blythe Bernier clients are 40 per cent Protestant, 40 per cent Catholic, and about 20 per cent Greek Orthodox.[33]

Organigram.

The 1990s brought the most important shift in the company's organization since construction of the crematorium a century ago.

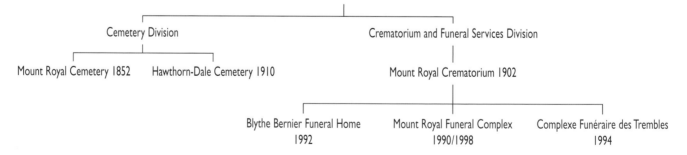

MOUNT ROYAL COMMEMORATIVE SERVICES
ORGANIZATIONAL STRUCTURE

THE MOUNT ROYAL CEMETERY COMPANY 1847

Cemetery Division — Crematorium and Funeral Services Division

Mount Royal Cemetery 1852 — Hawthorn-Dale Cemetery 1910

Mount Royal Crematorium 1902

Blythe Bernier Funeral Home 1992 — Mount Royal Funeral Complex 1990/1998 — Complexe Funéraire des Trembles 1994

Purchase of this funeral home was only part of the company's expanding business operation. Casket and urn sales were reorganized into showrooms in the new complex. Management was reorganized to reflect these changing operations: in 1997, Andrew Roy, son of former manager Donald Roy, was appointed director of funeral and cremation operations while Allan Job assumed a parallel position as director of cemetery operations. A Sales and Marketing Division was opened, expanded advertising was undertaken, and a cemetery Web site was initiated.[34] By 1998, the cemetery's office staff had increased to thirteen, double its size two decades earlier. Reflecting its enlarged business interests, its sense of marketing, and its bilingualism, Mount Royal Commemorative Services/Services Commémoratifs Mont-Royal, was adopted as an umbrella business name.

Adjustments were also made to improve Hawthorn-Dale's viability. In the early 1990s, the east-end grounds were costing the company as much as $50,000 a year to maintain; on several occasions, the company had considered selling the undeveloped portion of the site below Sherbrooke Street to housing developers.[35] Yet by the late 1980s the site's potential as public green space began to attract municipal interest. Authorities began denying the company building permits to construct new facilities, and in 1988 part of the cemetery's undeveloped land was placed under an "avis de réserve" by the City of Montreal with a view to its transformation into a park.[36] Three years later, the city moved to expropriate the land, awarding the company $6,400,000 compensation. This arrangement allowed public access to parkland that had been hitherto inaccessible because it lay behind the cemetery. Apparently pleased with this integration into a larger park system, the trustees referred to the arrangement as "co-existence."[37] Expropriation money was used to enhance the company's ability to offer competitive funeral operations. A modern funeral and

Far left The crematorium complex.

Taken from the site of the Jewish cemeteries, this winter photo recalls the devastating effects of the ice storm of 1998 on the cemetery.

Left The crematorium furnace, 2002

Above The offices.

At the main gates, the offices in the converted superintendent's house reflect an emphasis on traditional architecture
and the cemetery's cultural roots.

Top left Interior of the funeral complex, 2002

Left The columbarium, 2002

crematorium facility was constructed at Hawthorn-Dale. Opened in 1994, it was first named the Complexe Commémoratif Hawthorn-Dale. To emphasize the location's further identification with the community of Pointe-aux-Trembles, this was later changed to the Complexe Funéraire des Trembles. Today, 97 per cent of clients at this site are Catholic.

Money from the expropriation also went into a major addition to the crematorium complex at Mount Royal. By the spring of 1998, the complex had been transformed into a modern multiservice funeral, burial, and cremation facility that included elegant reception rooms, two chapels, and new columbaria. While this facility emphasized modernity and the efficiency and service of an upscale funeral parlour, other public activities were maintained in their traditional architectural and landscape setting near the cemetery's main entrance: administration, offices, grieving centre, and reception areas where the public is first received were strategically kept in the old superintendent's house.

A paradox is apparent in the striking changes introduced by the Mount Royal Cemetery Company since 1990. Alongside the entry into the funeral business, the utilization of new business and marketing tools, the construction of new landscapes, and the active soliciting of non-British clienteles, heritage and memory have regained their place of honour. One might say that the use of history has come full

circle. Crucial in the original conception of the cemetery and in its shaping as a distinctive part of Protestant culture in Montreal, history is now being marshalled to help the Mount Royal Company remain competitive, reminding Montrealers that the cemetery – and by association, its various facilities – is unique. Its history, beautiful site, and material culture distinguish the company from homogenized memorial parks and international competitors. In the democratized lingo of its publicists, the cemetery represents "a history of people" or, as another company brochure puts it, a "homeland for family memorials," a place where "memories are made tangible – and love is undisguised."[38]

Would these changing business strategies or the new respectability emanating from the effective use of heritage and the environment have surprised the cemetery's founders? They were themselves men caught in paradox, torn between grimy profits from canals, clocks, or ship-bottoms and profound sentiments for mountains, vistas, memory, and loved ones. In its third phase, it may be that Mount Royal Cemetery has come full circle, returning to its original overlapping of private company and public service, of burial ground and statuary art, of Romantic attempts to link the end of life to the course of Nature, and of an undiminished historic Protestant mission of somehow making Death instructional of Life.

NOTES

INTRODUCTION

1 Robert W. Habenstein and William M. Lamers, *The History of American Funeral Directing* (Milwaukee: Bulfin, 1955), 411.

2 W. Slater Lewis, *Royal Victoria Hospital, 1887–1947* (Montreal: McGill-Queen's University Press, 1969), 116.

3 The reader will discover a series of names – the Cemetery, the Protestant Cemetery, the Mount Royal Cemetery – used to describe the cemetery. While a certain liberty is taken in the text, the legal name is The Mount Royal Cemetery Company.

4 *Montreal Star*, 11 August 1934.

CHAPTER ONE

1 Alan Stewart, "Settlement, Commerce, and the Local Economy," in *Opening the Gates of Eighteenth-Century Montreal*, ed. Phyllis Lambert and Alan Stewart, (Montreal: Canadian Centre for Architecture, 1992), 46.

2 *Appendix to the Eighth Volume of the Journals of the Legislative Assembly of the Province of Canada* (1849), Appendix B; *Appendix to the Ninth Volume of the Journals of the Legislative Assembly of the Province of Canada* (1850), Appendix ZZ.

3 Louise Dechêne and Jean-Claude Robert, "Le choléra de 1832 dans le Bas-Canada: mesure des inégalités devant la mort," in *Étude méthodologique des crises démographiques*

du passé, ed. H. Charbonneau and André Larose (Liège: Ordina Éditions, 1979), 230.

4 *Appendix to the Eighth Volume*, Appendix B.

5 Writing of mid-nineteenth-century Flanders, Marguerite Yourcenar recalled that her grandmother gave birth to her children in her bedroom. Before the birth of each, she carefully laid out a mortuary dress for use if she died in childbirth. *Souvenirs pieux* (Paris: Gallimard, 1974), 129.

6 Risa Barkin and Ian Gentles, "Death in Victorian Toronto, 1850–1899," *Urban History Review* 19, no. 2 (1990): 20–1.

7 Michael Bliss, *Plague: A Story of Smallpox in Montreal* (Toronto: HarperCollins, 1991), 277.

8 *Montreal Gazette*, 31 January 1861.

9 *Montreal Herald*, 2 November 1816.

10 Anglican Church Archives, Montreal, James Jones, missionary, Bedford, to Rev. F. Fulford, 1852, in letters to Rev. Fulford, 1852–9, 299.

11 Charles Mappin, "The Evolution of Montreal's Cemetery Space from 1642 to the Present" (Master of Urban Planning, McGill University, 1995), 20.

12 *Montreal Gazette*, 16 September 1872.

13 Mappin, *Evolution*, 31, 28–29.

14 Murray Greenwood, *Legacies of Fear: Law and Politics in Quebec in the Era of the French Revolution* (Toronto: Osgoode Society, 1993), 6.

15 Mount Royal Cemetery Archives (hereafter MRCA), Notary

Chabouillez N.P., no. 2525, deed of sale, 26 July 1797; *Montreal Gazette*, 7 June 1846.

16 MRC, Minutes, 7 May 1799, 26 July 1801.

17 *Montreal Gazette*, 6 August 1960.

18 *Revised Acts and Ordinances of Lower Canada* (Montreal, 1845).

19 McCord Museum, McCord Papers, vol. 854, Protestant Burying Ground of Montreal, "1825 Rules."

20 MRC, Minutes, 5 August 1853.

21 Ibid., 7 May 1799, 17 June 1818.

22 "1825 Rules."

23 Ibid.

24 James Berry, *The Glasgow Necropolis* (Glasgow: Glasgow City Council, 1985), 22.

25 Information from the archives of the Church of St Andrew and St Paul was provided by the Reverend J.S.S. Armour.

26 "1825 Rules."

27 An Act to Vest in the Mount Royal Cemetery Company, the Old Protestant Burial Grounds in the City of Montreal, *Statutes of Quebec* (1872).

28 J.M. LeMoine, *Quebec Past and Present* (Quebec: Coté, 1876), 441–42.

29 Dechêne and Robert, "Le cholera," 236; cited in Walter Sendzik, "The 1832 Montreal Cholera Epidemic" (MA thesis, McGill University, 1997), 2.

30 *Revised Statutes of the Province of Quebec*, vol. 1 (Quebec, 1888), ss. 3847, 3848, 3070.

31 Geoffrey Bilson, *A Darkened House: Cholera in Nineteenth-Century Canada* (Toronto: University of Toronto Press, 1980), 36.

32 *Montreal Transcript*, 27 July 1847; 15 April 1847; Jean-Rémi Brault, *Montréal au XIXe siècle*, (Montreal: Leméac, 1990), 138; Other estimates put the burials in Point St Charles at 6,000. Anon, "Le Typhus de 1847," *Revue Canadienne, 1898–99*, 257.

33 MRC, Minutes, 12 June 1843.

34 MRC, Minutes, 5 September 1845.

35 *Montreal Gazette*, 19 May 1831.

36 *Montreal Transcript*, 1 September 1847; Robert Prévost, *Montreal: A History* (Toronto: McClelland and Stewart, 1993), 288.

37 Bilson, *Darkened House*, 117.

38 *Montreal Transcript*, 6 February 1847.

39 For the changing attitude to odour see Alain Corbin, *The Foul and the Fragrant: Odour and the Social Imagination* (London: Papermac, 1996).

40 Cited in Colin Coates, "Monuments and Memories: The Evolution of British Columbian Cemeteries, 1850–1950," *Material History Bulletin* 25 (spring 1987): 12.

41 J. Jay Smith, *Designs for Monuments and Mural Tablets Adapted to Rural Cemeteries, Church Yards, Churches, and Chapels* (New York: Bartlett and Welford, 1846), 19, 5.

42 "An Act respecting the practice of Physics and Surgery, and the Study of Anatomy," Canada, *Consolidated Statutes* (1859).

43 R.D. Gidney and W.P.J. Millar, *Professional Gentlemen: The Professions in Nineteenth-Century Ontario* (Toronto: University of Toronto Press, 1994), 156.

44 36th Annual Report of the Montreal General Hospital, 1858; H.E. MacDermot, *History of the Montreal General Hospital* (Montreal: Montreal General Hospital, 1950), 15.

45 F.J. Shepherd, "Reminiscences of Student Days and Dissecting Room" (unpublished manuscript, 1919) 25; cited in Caroline Schoofs, unpublished history paper, McGill University, 1999.

46 *Montreal Gazette* 26, 28 January 1861.

47 McCord Papers, vol. 854, "Protestant Burying Ground of Montreal," handwritten note by John Samuel McCord, n.d.

48 McCord Papers, vol. 857, "Miscellaneous Reports re: Mount Royal Cemetery, Questions submitted by the committee of the Legislative Assembly, appointed to consider … the necessity of legislating with regard to interment in

large towns or their precincts" (1852).

49 See Richard L. Bushman, *The Refinement of America: Persons, Houses, Cities* (New York: Knopf, 1992); Mariana Valverde, *The Age of Light, Soap, and Water: Moral Reform in English Canada, 1885–1925* (Toronto: McClelland and Stewart, 1991), 30.

50 William Wordsworth, "Lines Composed on the Banks of Wye Above Tintern Abbey." *The Poetical Works of Wordsworth*, ed. Paul Sheato (Boston: Houghton Mifflin, 1982), 92.

51 Quoted in Leonore Davidoff and Catherine Hall, *Family Fortunes: Men and Women of the English Middle Class, 1780–1850* (London: Hutchison, 1987), 409.

52 Boston Athaneum, "Mount Auburn Cemetery Circular" (Boston, 1832).

53 Downing cited in David Schuyler, "The Evolution of the Anglo-American Rural Cemetery: Landscape Architecture as Social and Cultural History," *Journal of Garden History*, 4, no. 3 (1985): 595; H. Dearborn, *A Concise History of and Guide through Mount Auburn* (Boston, 1843), 1.

54 Mary Macaulay Allodi and Rosemarie L. Tovell, *An Engraver's Pilgrimage: James Smillie in Quebec, 1821–1830* (Toronto: Royal Ontario Museum, 1989), xix; *Mount Auburn Illustrated in Highly Finished Line Engravings from Drawings Taken on the Spot with Descriptive Notices* (New York, 1847); James Smillie, *Green-Wood Illustrated* (New York, 1847).

55 Paul King, "A Brief History of the Cataraqui Cemetery," *Historic Kingston* 28 (1979): 11–24.

56 McCord Papers, vol. 856, Henry Scott to John Samuel McCord, 17 April 1851; the McCord Papers also include form letters from the Toronto Necropolis. See vol. 857, "Miscellaneous Reports re; Mt. Royal Cemetery." For Mount Hermon see LeMoine, *Quebec*, 441–42.

57 Linden-Ward, *Silent City*, 199.

58 Smith, *Designs for Monuments*, 7.

CHAPTER TWO

1 John Stuart Mill, *On Liberty*, cited in Jürgen Habermas, *The Structural Transformation of the Public Sphere: An Inquiry into a Category of Bourgeois Society* (Cambridge: MIT Press, 1999), 133.

2 *Montreal Gazette*, 7 June 1846.

3 William Westfall, *Two Worlds: The Protestant Culture of Nineteenth-Century Ontario* (Kingston and Montreal: McGill-Queen's University Press, 1989), 195.

4 See T.W. Acheson, *Saint John: The Making of a Colonial Community* (Toronto: University of Toronto Press, 1985); and *Saint John Rural Cemetery Company: Act of Incorporation* (Saint John: W.L. Avery, 1848), 5.

5 Roy Bourgeois, "La commercialisation de la mort à Moncton, 1856–1914" (PhD diss., Université Laval, 1999), 166.

6 *Montreal Gazette*, 30 January 1846.

7 Mount Royal Cemetery (MRC) Minutes, 7 April 1846.

8 MRC Minutes, 7 April, 11, 18 August 1846.

9 MRC, "Circular of 24 October 1846 by Joshua Pelton."

10 *Montreal Transcript*, 11 January 1847.

11 MRC Minutes, 18 August 1846

12 *Montreal Gazette*, 23 June 1846

13 An Act to Incorporate the Montreal Cemetery Company, *Statutes of Canada*, 10 & 11 Vic., c. 67 (1847), ; *Montreal Transcript*, 11 January 1847; Edgar Andrew Collard, 'Garden in the Sun' (unpublished ms), ch. 8.

14 *Montreal Gazette*, 6 July 1846

15 The Moncton Rural Cemetery, chartered in 1856, took similar form as a private but non-profit company (Bourgeois, "La commercialisation," 165). Brooklyn's Green-Wood Cemetery was apparently organized in 1838 as a joint-stock company that would turn a profit but was reorganized as a trust. D.C. Sloane, *The Last Great Necessity: Cemeteries in*

American History (Baltimore: Johns Hopkins University Press, 1991), 59.

16 *Montreal Gazette*, 7 April 1851

17 McCord Papers, vol. 410, J.S. McCord diary, 1 April 1851, newspaper clipping; MRC Minutes, Annual Meeting, 1852.

18 MRC Minutes, 26 September 1851.

19 The choice of a northern sloping site higher than the city conformed to public health criteria formulated first by the French. An 1804 French law was specific that new cemeteries should be located with northern exposures, where putrid air would be blown away. Thomas A. Kselman, *Death and the Afterlife in Modern France*, (Princeton, NJ: Princeton University Press, 1993), 169–70; an American cemetery manual agreed on the need for elevated and airy sites but preferred southern exposures on which snow would melt quickly. J. Jay Smith, *Designs for Monuments and Mural Tablets Adapted to Rural Cemeteries, Church Yards, Churches, and Chapels* (New York: Bartlett and Welford, 1846), 7.

20 MRC *Annual Report*, 1852.

21 Ibid.

22 MRC Minutes, 3 June 1853; *Annual Report*, 1854.

23 An Act to Incorporate the Mount Hermon Cemetery, *Statutes of Canada*, 12 Vict., c. 191 (30 May 1849).

24 An Act to Incorporate the Montreal Cemetery Company, *Statutes of Canada*, 10 & 11 Vict., c. 67 (1847).

25 An Act to amend the Act incorporating the Mount Royal Cemetery Company, *Statutes of Canada*, 16 Vict., c. 118 (22 April 1853).

26 Archives of the Anglican Diocese of Montreal, Cemetery File, Sentence of Consecration, 15 June 1854.

27 MRC *Annual Report*, 1853.

28 MRC *Annual Report*, 1865.

29 Annual Report, 1874. For the use of national memory see Pierre Nora, ed., *Les lieux de mémoire* (Paris: Gallimard,

1997), 2: 1729–54.

30 MRC Minutes, 16 July 1816, 18 October 1819, 7 April 1859.

31 MRC *Annual Report*, April 1858; *Montreal Gazette*, 1 March 1861.

32 Smith, *Designs for Monuments*, 18.

33 In Quebec City, English emigrant William Treggett was working as gardener on timber merchant John Gilmour's estate, where he was well known for his skills in horticulture, landscaping, and drawing. In 1865, Gilmour, himself a trustee of Mount Hermon Cemetery, was instrumental in hiring Treggett as superintendent, a post he held for forty-three years. Treggetts have served as superintendents of Mount Hermon Cemetery to the present day. The Moncton Rural Cemetery first hired "a sexton and caretaker" to supervise its grounds but in 1881 replaced him with a gardener. Bourgeois, "La commercialisation," 168.

34 MRC *Annual Report*, 1853.

35 *Mount Royal Cemetery Company Acts of Incorporation and By-Laws* (Montreal: Bentley and Co., 1879), 34–8.

36 Sloane, *Last Great Necessity*, 207–8.

37 "By Laws of the Montreal Cemetery Company as amended," in Minutes, vol. 2, 1852.

38 MRCA, Charter of 1847; according to section 5 of the 1847 charter, "each such denomination shall be entitled to elect a number of Directors bearing such proportion to twenty-one as the sum subscribed by persons of such denomination shall bear to the whole amount of the Capital Stock subscribed."

39 MRC Minutes, 6 January 1854.

40 *Règlement concernant le Cimetière de Notre-Dame-des-Neiges* (Montreal: Beauchemin and Valois, Libraires-Imprimeurs, 1877).

CHAPTER THREE

1 Letter from Alexander Reford to author 14 July 2002. Reford letterbook 12, Robert Reford to McIntosh Granite Company, 26 May 1909.

2 Mount Royal Cemetery (hereafter MRC), *Annual Report*, 1887.

3 John Langford, *The Stranger's Illustrated Guide to the City of Montreal* (Montreal: Chisholm, 1868).

4 McCord Museum, McCord Papers, vol. 855, "Regulations concerning Visitors to the Mount Royal Cemetery" (1852).

5 Quebec, *Sessional Papers*, vol. 30, part 2 (1896), annex 1, 5.

6 MRC *Annual Report*, 1886.

7 MRC *Annual Report*, 1854.

8 Ibid.

9 MRC *Annual Report*, 1855. See also McCord Museum, McCord Papers, J.S. McCord diary, 3 April 1854. The other means of identifying a grave site outside the free ground was by consulting records in the cemetery office.

10 MRC *Annual Report*, 1894.

11 *Annual Report of the St Andrew's Society of Montreal* (Montreal, 1867), 5–6.

12 William Orme McRobie, *Fighting the Flames, or Twenty-Seven Years in the Montreal Fire Brigade* (Montreal: Witness Printing House, 1881), 29. For the early years of the fire brigade see Huguette Charron and Françoise Lewis, *Les débuts d'un Chef, Zéphirin Benoit. La naissance d'une ville, Saint-Henri 1875–1888* (Montreal: Private Publication, 2000).

13 Bryan Palmer, *Working Class Experience: Rethinking the History of Canadian Labour, 1800–1991* (Toronto: McClelland and Stewart, 1992), 128; Lynne Marks, *Revivals and Roller Rinks: Religion, Leisure, and Identity in Late-Nineteenth-Century Small-Town Ontario* (Toronto: University of Toronto Press, 1996), 117.

14 MRC *Annual Report*, 1868.

15 David Charles Sloane, *The Last Great Necessity: Cemeteries in American History* (Baltimore: Johns Hopkins University Press, 1991), 84.

16 Archives nationales du Québec à Montréal, American Presbyterian Church, Envelope entitled "Com. Receipts 1830–1839," Joshua Pelton to Rev. Mr. Perkins, Minister of the American Presbyterian Church, 20 April 1833; document provided by Rosalind Trigger.

17 MRC Minutes, 5 August 1853.

18 MRC *Annual Report*, 1896.

19 MRC *Annual Report*, 1906.

20 McCord Papers, clipping in J.S. McCord diary, 19 January 1857.

21 *Journals of the Legislative Assembly of the Province of Canada*, 1849, Appendix TTTT to vol. 8, reimbursement to C.H. Linter, 30 March 1847; "Tariff of Fees" included in Minutes, 1853; winter burials (December to April), presumably if the ground could be opened, cost 12s. 6d., as did the removal of burials or the blasting of rock.

22 MRC Minutes, 13 May 1865.

23 MRC burial cards, 31 July 1866, 28 July 1862, 25 July 1865, 9 January 1895.

24 Anny Duchaine, Walter Forsberg, and Marie-Laure Mahood, "'The Forgotten Free Ground': A Research Project on Plot G-450 of the Mount Royal Cemetery" (McGill undergraduate essay, December 2001). 4.

25 Ibid., Appendix 15.

26 MRC *Annual Report*, 1868.

27 Janice Harvey, "The Protestant Orphan Asylum and the Montreal Ladies Benevolent Society: A Case Study in Protestant Child Charity" (PhD diss., McGill University, 2001).

28 *Annual Report of the Montreal Protestant House of Industry and*

Refuge (Montreal: Herald Press, 1864, 1865, 1869).

29 Richard Allen, The Social Gospel: Religion and Social Reform in Canada, 1914–28 (Toronto: University of Toronto Press, 1973).

30 Thomas Laqueur, "Bodies, Death and Pauper Funerals," *Representations* 1, no. 1 (1983): 120.

31 *Montreal Gazette*, 11 February 1936.

32 *La Presse*, 16 October 1907.

33 MRC Minutes, 3 August 1871.

34 Collard, *The Irish Way: The History of the Irish Protestant Benevolent Society* (Montreal: Price-Patterson, 1992), 57; *Annual Report* of the Irish Protestant Benevolent Society of Montreal (Montreal, 1889).

35 Denise Helly, *Les Chinois de Montréal, 1877–1951* (Quebec: IQRC, 1987), 278; for the eugenics movement in Montreal, see Angus McLaren, *Our Own Master Race: Eugenics in Canada, 1885–1945* (Toronto: McClelland and Stewart, 1990), 24–5.

36 Peter S. Li, *The Chinese in Canada* (Toronto: Oxford University Press, 1988), 59; for racism see Constance Backhouse, *Colour Coded: A Legal History of Racism in Canada, 1900–1950* (Toronto: University of Toronto Press, 1999) 132–72.

37 *The Favorite*, 3 May 1873, 269.

38 Helly, *Les Chinois*, 173.

39 MRC Minutes, 14 September 1903. For a description of a Chinese burial, see *Montreal Gazette*, 1 May 1858.

40 MRC Minutes, 5 January 1904.

CHAPTER FOUR

1 Mount Royal Cemetery (MRA), Minutes, 12 September 1856.

2 Ibid., 2 April 1861.

3 Ibid., 6 April 1858.

4 Ibid., 1 March 1863; 5 April 1864; MRC *Annual Report*, 1875.

5 MRC Minutes, 4 April 1871.

6 MRC *Annual Report*, 1875, 1877.

7 McCord Museum, McCord Papers, vol. 855, "Regulations concerning visitors to the Mount Royal Cemetery," November 1852; vol. 857, "Misc. Reports re; Mt. Royal Cemetery," Rules of Mount Auburn Cemetery.

8 MRC *Annual Report*, 1864.

9 Ashton Oxenden, *The History of My Life* (London: Green, 1891), 177–8.

10 John Langford, *The Stranger's Illustrated Guide to the City of Montreal* (Montreal: Chisholm, 1868); Adrien Leblond de Brumath, *Guide de Montréal et de ses environs* (Montreal: Granger, 1897), 72; *The Traveler's Guide for Montreal and Quebec* (Montreal, 1861), 9; *The Albion Hotel Visitor's Guide to Montreal and River St Lawrence* (Montreal: Decker, Stearns and Murray, n.d.), 15.

11 MRC Minutes, 5 April 1870, 6 November 1873, 5 February 1874, 1 June 1876. The gate was presumably removed with the extension of Bleury Street / Park Avenue to this point later in the 1870s.

12 Chaarlotte Hutt, *City of the Dead: The Story of Glasgow's Southern Necropolis* (Glasgow: Glasgow City Libraries and Archives, 1996), 21.

13 *Montreal Gazette*, 31 January 1851

14 McCord Papers, vol. 855, "Regulations concerning visitors to the Mount Royal Cemetery," November 1852.

15 Ibid.

16 MRC *Annual Report*, 1864.

17 "A Proprietor," *Montreal Gazette*, 23 May 1865.

18 MRC Minutes, 1 June 1876; for the importance of moral regulation see Mariana Valverde, *The Age of Light, Soap, and Water: Moral Reform in English Canada, 1885–1925* (Toronto:

McClelland and Stewart, 1991).

19 *Montreal Gazette*, 6 November 1865; McCord Papers, vol. 420, diary, 21 September 1863.

20 Cited in Edgar Andrew Collard, "Garden in the Sun" (unpublished ms), Phase II, 8.

21 *Mount Royal Cemetery Company Acts of Incorporation and By-Laws* (Montreal: Bentley and Co., 1879), 37.

22 *Montreal Gazette*, 10 September, 3 December 1866.

23 *Montreal Daily Witness*, 11 September 1912.

24 *Montreal Gazette*, 2 May 1877.

25 Hereward Senior, *Orangeism: The Canadian Phase* (Toronto: McGraw-Hill, 1972), 47, 62.

26 *Montreal Daily Star*, 16 July 1877.

27 Ibid. Mary Ryan has best reminded us of the expansion of public ceremonies in the period 1825–50. She also notes the extent to which public rites were "clearly marked by masculine signs, most often crafted by male hands": *Women in Public: Between Banners and Ballots, 1825–1880* (Baltimore: Johns Hopkins University Press, 1990), 23.

28 Senior, *Orangeism*, 76

29 *Montreal Daily Star*, 16 July 1877.

30 MRC Minutes, 2 May 1878, 1 March 1881; *Mount Royal Cemetery Company Acts*, 41.

31 *Montreal Gazette*, 24 December 1866. Three generations of the family of cemetery president McCord were prominent masons.

32 Peter DeLottinville, "Joe Beef of Montreal: Working-Class Culture and the Tavern, 1869–1889," *Labour/Le Travailleur* 8/9 (Autumn/Spring 1981/82), 23.

33 Ibid., 28. For the place of the tavern and its contradiction with cemetery culture see Roy Rosenzweig, "The Rise of the Saloon," in *Rethinking Popular Culture: Contemporary Perspectives in Cultural Studies*, ed. C. Mukerji and Michael Schudson (Berkeley: University of California Press, 1991), 121–56.

34 *Montreal Gazette*, 19 January 1889; *Montreal Star*, 16, 18 January 1889; *Montreal Herald*, 16 January 1889.

35 Robert Ross, *Status and Respectability in the Cape Colony, 1750–1870* (Cambridge: Cambridge University Press, 1999), 25.

36 *Montreal Gazette*, 19 January 1889; *Montreal Star*, 16, 18 January 1889; *Montreal Herald*, 16 January 1889.

37 MRC Minutes, 4 October 1877, 4 July 1878.

38 *Mount Royal Cemetery Company Acts*, 38; *Annual Report*, 1887.

39 Newspaper clipping, (n.d.) in MRC Minutes, November 1880.

40 Newspaper clipping, (n.d.) in MRC Minutes, 15 April 1901.

41 MRC, "Superintendent's Report," included in *Annual Report*, 1899. His report does not mention any provision for women.

42 MRC Minutes, 7 March 1872.

43 MRC, Deed by notary F.J. Durand no. 7000, 22 January 1878.

44 Frederick Law Olmsted, *Mount Royal, Montreal* (New York: Putnam's Sons, 1981), 26

45 MRC Minutes, 6 February 1894, 31 December 1895.

CHAPTER FIVE

1 At the entrance to Père Lachaise Cemetery in Paris, for example, lists are posted of gravesites due for repossession unless heirs pay for renewal.

2 *Montreal Cemetery Company* (Montreal: D. Bentley and Co., 1879), 40–1.

3 McCord Museum, McCord Papers, vol. 855, "Regulations concerning visitors to to the Mount Royal Cemetery," November 1852.

4 McCord Papers, vol. 855, "Mount Royal Cemetery, Conditions, Limitations and Privileges," 1852.

5   *Montreal Gazette*, 17 July 1856.

6   Montreal *Directory* (Montreal: John Lovell, 1851); Lovell's *Business Directory*, 1877–8, 215.

7   *Montreal Gazette*, 29 June 1864.

8   Mount Royal Cemetery (MRC), "Report of Committee on Establishment of Department," MRC Minutes, 14 March 1875.

9   "Consolidated Charter of the Mount Royal Cemetery Company" (1955), s. 5, included in the Minutes, vol. 12.

10 J. Jay Smith, *Designs for Monuments and Mural Tablets Adapted to Rural Cemeteries, Church Yards, Churches, and Chapels* (New York: Bartlett and Welford, 1846), 14.

11 MRC *Annual Report*, 1880.

12 See, for example, the Minutes of the Annual Meeting, 1855.

13 Quebec, An Act for the Preservation of the Public Health, By-law, Rules and Regulations (1885); Minutes, 2 April 1872, 7 May 1874.

14 McCord Papers, vol. 855, "Regulations concerning visitors."

15 Smith, *Designs for Monuments*, 14; author's interview with Brian Treggett, superintendent of Mount Hermon Cemetery, 10 April 2000.

16 MRC *Annual Report*, 1893.

17 Smith, *Designs for Monuments*, 24.

18 MRC *Annual Report*, April 1860. At the Moncton Rural Cemetery, a Permanent Care Fund was not introduced until 1907. Bourgeois, "La commercialisation de la mort à Moncton, 1856–1914" (PhD diss., Université Laval, 1999) 178. In the oral-history tradition of Mount Hermon Cemetery, the introduction of perpetual care in 1880 was directly related to the arrival of the railway in Quebec City and the subsequent exodus of many Protestant lot-owners.

19 MRC, 1879 by laws.

20 MRC *Annual Report*, 1893; the horse-drawn mower is mentioned in the *Annual Report*, 1899.

21 MRC *Annual Report*, 1905.

22 "Superintendent's Report," *Annual Report*, 1899.

23 MRC Minutes, 8 December 1908.

24 "Report of the Trustees and the Executive Director for the Year 1999," 27 April 2000. See the similarities with other professions in Magali Sarfatti Larson, *The Rise of Professionalism: A Sociological Analysis* (Berkeley: University of California Press, 1977), 199.

25 MRC Minutes, 14 January 1919.

26 "Report of Landscape Architect and General Superintendent," in MRC *Annual Report*, 1915.

27 Ormiston Roy to Grounds Committee, included with MRC Minutes, 19 March 1918.

28 "Report of Manager John F. Roy, 3 February 1930," in MRC *Annual Report*, 1930.

29 "Superintendent's Report," MRC *Annual Report*, 1899.

30 MRC *Annual Report*, 1899, 1904.

31 Archives nationales du Québec à Montréal, American Presbyterian Church, P603, S2, SS14, letter of Kirk Session, St Paul's, to Rev. Caleb Strong, 30 August 1841. Document provided by Rosalyn Trigger.

32 "Superintendent's Report," in MRC *Annual Report*, 1908.

33 MRC *Annual Report*, 1908.

34 "Superintendent's Report," in MRC *Annual Report*, 1918.

35 MRC *Annual Report*, 1919; Minutes, 9–12 November 1918.

CHAPTER SIX

1   John Langford, *The Stranger's Illustrated Guide to the City of Montreal* (Montreal: C.R. Chisholm, 1868).

2   Jonathan Hodgson (1880–1914), Thomas E. Hodgson (1914–26), C.J. Hodgson (1926–52), T.W. Hodgson (1953–4).

3   James Stevens Curl, *The Cemeteries and Burial Grounds*

of Glasgow (Glasgow: Strathclyde Council, 1974) 5.

4   *Canadian Horticultural Magazine*, November 1898, 193.

5   Mount Royal Cemetery (MRC) Minutes, 17 June 1938.

6   "Report of the Landscape Architect, 1 February 1935," MRC *Annual Report*, 1935.

7   Ibid.

8   David Charles Sloane, *The Last Great Necessity: Cemeteries in American History* (Baltimore: Johns Hopkins University Press, 1991), 111.

9   MRC *Annual Report*, 1899.

10 Ibid.

11 MRC *Annual Report*, 1899.

12 See Sarah Schmidt, "'Private' Acts in 'Public' Spaces: Parks in Turn-of-the-Century Montreal," in Tamara Myers et al., eds., *Power, Place and Identity: Historical Studies of Social and Legal Regulation in Quebec* (Montreal: Montreal History Group, 1998), 129–50.

13 "Progress of Rural Cemeteries," *Park and Cemetery and Landscape Garden* 33, no. 9 (1923): 234

14 Author's interview with Donald Roy, 29 April 2000.

15 MRC *Annual Report*s and "Superintendent's Reports," 1891, 1892, 1893, 1896.

16 MRC *Annual Report*, 1890.

17 MRC Minutes, 23 March 1897.

18 MRC Minutes, 3 March 1890.

19 MRC *Annual Report*, 1890.

20 MRC *Annual Report*, 1906.

21 Ibid.

22 MRC *Annual Report*, 1909.

23 "Superintendent's Report," MRC *Annual Report*, 1906.

24 Letter posted in MRC Minutes, 1907, George Irving to Chairman of Mount Royal Cemetery Company, 20 December 1906; MRC *Annual Report*, 1907.

25 MRC *Annual Report*, 1907. In its first years, the cemetery was known as both Riverview and Bellevue. In 1909, Hawthorn-Dale was chosen: the Hawthorn is a tree of the rose family. Dale, ironically in light of the flatness of the site, recalls the gentle valleys so vaunted by advocates of the older rural cemetery.

26 "Report of the Landscape Architect, 1 February 1945," MRC *Annual Report*, 1945.

27 MRC Minutes, 16 October 1906.

28 V.A. Linnell, quoted in Edgar Andrew Collard's column, *Montreal Gazette*, 29 May 1982; see also MRC, Jean-Paul Viaud, conservateur, Musée ferroviaire canadien, to Myriam Cloutier, 24 October 1995.

29 The funeral car can now be seen in the Musée ferroviaire canadien in Carignan, Quebec.

30 MRC, Report of the Ground Committee of the Mount Royal Cemetery Company, 16 June 1908.

31 *Montreal Gazette*, 21 June 1908.

32 Ibid.

33 Ibid. Digging an adult's grave on the Mountain cost $5, or $7.50 with a shell.

34 MRC *Annual Report*, 1918.

35 *Montreal Gazette*, 2 February 1934.

36 MRC *Annual Report*, 1912.

37 MRC *Annual Report*, 1910.

38 MRC *Annual Report*, 1914.

39 These Roman Catholic burials without service were contrary to canon law, by which the poor had the right to a funeral and a decent and free burial, and were the subject of complaints in the press. *Le Devoir*, 4 January 1952 and *Le Matin* (Montreal), 14 January 1952.

40 *Montreal Gazette*, 11 February 1936.

41 *Montreal Gazette,* 11 March 1955.

42 MRC *Annual Report*, 1915.

43 Mallarmé, *Collected Poems* (Berkeley: University of

California Press, 1994), 53.

44 "Superintendent's Report, 19 December 1899," MRC *Annual Report, 1899*

45 MRC *Annual Report*, 1899; "Superintendent's Report," *Annual Report, 1906*.

46 "Report of the Landscape Architect," *Annual Report* 1917, 1919.

47 "Report of the Landscape Architect" *Annual Report*, 1945, "Report of the Landscape Architect," *Annual Report*, 1954.

48 "Superintendent's Report," *Annual Report*, 1906.

49 "Report of the Landscape Architect," *Annual Report, 1932*.

50 "Report of the Landscape Architect," *Annual Report, 1925*.

51 "Report of the Landscape Architect," *Annual Report*, 1945.

52 *Annual Report*, 1936; Collard, "Garden in the Sun," (unpublished ms) Phase III, 43.

53 "Report of the Landscape Architect," *Annual Report*, 1935.

54 Ibid.

55 *Annual Report*, 1898.

56 *Conseil des Arts et Manufactures de la Province de Quebec* "École de Montréal" (1888–9).

57 *Montreal Gazette*, 3 August 2002.

58 Author's interview with Donald Roy, 29 April 2000.

CHAPTER SEVEN

1 Kenneth Macleod, *Report on the Burial Grounds in Glasgow* (Glasgow: Anderson, 1876), 44.

2 See, for example, William Tegg, *The Last Act* (London, 1876), and the *Canadian Illustrated News*, 5 December 1874.

3 James Farrell, *Inventing the American Way of Death, 1830–1920*, (Philadelphia: Temple University Press, 1986), 164.

4 Hugo Erichsen, *The Cremation of the Dead Considered from an Aesthetic, Sanitary, Religious, Historical, Medico-Legal, and Economical Standpoint* (Detroit: D.O. Haynes, 1887), 50.

5 *Cremation: Its History, Practice and Advantages* (Montreal:

Mount Royal Cemetery Company Crematorium, 1902), 12.

6 Robert Nicol, *At the End of the Road: Government, Society, and the Disposal of Human Remains in the Nineteenth and Twentieth Century* (London: St Leonard's Allen and Union, 1994), 172.

7 Augustus Cobb, *Earth-burial and Cremation. The History of Earth-burial with Its Attendant Evils, and the Advantage Offered by Cremation* (New York: Putnam's, 1892), 88.

8 Erichsen, *Cremation of the Dead*, 229–30.

9 Cobb, *Earth-burial and Cremation*, 132.

10 Nicol, *At the End of the Road*, 81.

11 "Crematoria in Great Britain and Abroad," *Canadian Architect and Builder* 19, no. 4 (1906): 52.

12 Stephen Prothero, *Purified by Fire: A History of Cremation in America* (Berkeley: University of California Press, 2001), 165.

13 Ibid., 137.

14 Erichsen, *Cremation of the Dead*, 251; Cobb, *Earth-burial and Cremation*, 157, 159; Prothero, *Purified by Fire*, 131–2; Macleod, *Report*, 44.

15 Cobb, *Earth-burial and Cremation*, 161.

16 Mariana Valverde, *The Age of Light, Soap, and Water: Moral Reform in English Canada, 1885–1925* (Toronto: McClelland and Stewart, 1991), 46.

17 Macleod, *Report*, 44.

18 Mount Royal Cemetery (MRC) *Annual Report*, 1899.

19 Prothero, *Purified by Fire*, 119.

20 Erichsen, *Cremation of the Dead*, 138–9.

21 Ibid., 86.

22 Molson's copy can be examined in the Osler Medical Library, McGill University.

23 Cited in David Charles Sloane, *The Last Great Necessity: Cemeteries in American History* (Baltimore: Johns Hopkins University Press, 1991), 145.

24 George A. Baynes, *Disposal of the Dead: By Land, by Water,*

or by Fire (Montreal: Witness Printing House, 1875), 9.

25 Shirley E. Woods Jr, *The Molson Saga, 1763–1983* (Toronto: Doubleday, 1983), 191.

26 MRC Minutes, 6 March 1888.

27 *Annual Report*, 1896.

28 Prothero, *Purified by Fire*, 75; C.J. Cuming, *A History of Anglican Liturgy* (London: St Martin's Press, 1969), 89; Louise A. Winton, ed., *Handbook of Burial Rites* (Toronto: Commemorative Services of Ontario, 1985).

29 Woods, *Molson Saga*, 190.

30 *Montreal Daily Star*, 1 June 1898.

31 "Superintendent's Report," *Annual Report*, 1899.

32 Cited in Donald Roy, "The History and Growth of Cremation in Canada" (paper delivered to Cremation Association of North America, 1980), 6.

33 George Durdy, "The Cremation Movement in Canada," *Canadian Cemetery Service*, June 1958, 2.

34 Cited in Sébastien St-Onge, *L'industrie de la mort*, (Quebec: Éditions Nota bene, 2001), 29–30. My translation.

35 Roy, "History and Growth," 2.

36 *Cremation: Its History, Practice and Advantages* (Montreal: Mount Royal Cemetery Company Crematorium, 1902), 6; MRC Crematorium Minutes, 1905.

37 See, for example, Ormiston Roy in *Montreal Gazette*, 2 February 1934.

38 MRC Minutes, 8 July 1902.

39 "Letters Patent to the Crematorium," Secretary of State, 22 October 1903, included loose in MRC Crematorium Minutes; MRC Minutes, 3 July 1900; Stanley Brice Frost and Robert H. Michel, "Sir William Christopher Macdonald," *Dictionary of Canadian Biography*, 14: 693, 690; Mount Royal Cemetery Archives unclassified, Donald M. Rowat N.P. #6015, 25 August 1914; also unclassified, "Will of William Macdonald."

40 "By-laws" n.d., The Crematorium Limited, loose in MRC Crematorium Minutes.

41 Ibid.

42 *Cremation: Its History*, 20–21; *Le Petit Journal*, 27 February 1938.

43 Author's interview with Donald Roy, 29 April 2000.

44 Ormiston Roy to President, Crematorium Ltd., 8 March 1911, loose MRC in Crematorium Minutes; author's interview with Donald Roy, 29 April 2000.

45 "By-laws" n.d., The Crematorium Limited, loose in Crematorium Minutes.

46 MRC Crematorium Minutes, 28 March, 16 September 1960.

47 Sloane, *The Last Great Necessity*, 228.

48 MRC Crematorium Minutes, 2 December 1918.

49 *Montreal Gazette*, 1 October 1951.

50 MRC Crematorium Minutes, 2 December 1918.

51 "Report of Landscape Architect," *Annual Report*, 1936.

52 *Montreal Gazette*, 5 February 1949.

53 *Montreal Herald*, 23 May 1914; *Le Petit Journal*, 18 July 1965; MRC Crematorium Minutes, 1 January 1965.

54 *Montreal Gazette*, 2 February 1934.

55 *Montreal Gazette*, 5 February 1949; MRC Crematorium Minutes, 2 December 1918.

56 "Législation et directives concernant l'incinération. Document approuvé par le Comité exécutif de l'A.E.Q.," *L'Église Canadienne* 9, no. 7 (1976): 196–7; Louise A. Winton, ed., *Handbook of Burial Rites* (Toronto: Commemorative Services of Ontario, 1985), 8.

57 Calculations by Brian Fitzgerald, "The Roman Catholic Church and Its Reaction to Cremation at Mount Royal Cemetery" (unpublished essay, McGill University, 1998).

58 Figures from the Cremation Association of North America cited in St-Onge, *L'industrie de la mort*, 139.

CHAPTER EIGHT

1 Pierre Nora, ed., *Les lieux de mémoire* (Paris: Gallimard, 1997) vol. 2.

2 *Montreal Gazette*, 15 April 1942.

3 *La Presse*, 25 May 1940.

4 *Montreal Star*, 24 May 1902, 20 October 1937.

5 Ibid., 24 May 1902; Edgar Andrew Collard, "Garden in the Sun" (unpublished ms) phase III, p. 22.

6 *Montreal Gazette*, 28 December 1908.

7 For the Last Post Fund see Serge Marc Durflinger, *Lest We Forget: A History of the Last Post Fund, 1909–1999* (Montreal: Last Post Fund, 2000).

8 Mount Royal Cemetery (MRC), loose clipping in Minutes, Last Post Fund, "Fifth Annual Report."

9 MRC Minutes, 5 April 1910.

10 David Charles Sloane, *The Last Great Necessity: Cemeteries in American History* (Baltimore: Johns Hopkins University Press, 1991), 233; cited in Durflinger, *Lest We Forget*, 19.

11 MRC *Annual Report*, 1918.

12 MRC Minutes, 9 April 1918.

13 Ibid.

14 Nora ed., *Les lieux de mémoire*, 1775.

15 Cited in Jonathan Vance, *Death So Noble: Memory, Meaning, and the First World War* (Vancouver: UBC Press, 1997) 100.

16 Vance, *Death So Noble*, 63; "Trustees' Report," February 1917, Canadian Patriotic Fund to Secretary, Mount Royal Cemetery, 9 February 1915, included in MRC Minutes, 9 February 1915.

17 MRC *Annual Report*, February 1918.

18 Edwin Gibson and G. Kingsley Ward, *Courage Remembered: The Story behind the Construction and Maintenance of the Commonwealth's Military Cemeteries and Memorials of the Wars of 1914–1918 and 1939–1945* (Toronto: McClelland and Stewart, 1989), 47, 57, 241. The commission identified the burial or cremation site of 584,967 war dead in the First World War and commemorated another 529,808 on memorials to the missing. The Second World War gave it a renewed mandate. By 1989, the commission, renamed the Commonwealth War Graves Commission in 1960, had 1,400 employees around the world and an annual budget of £18 million. Custodian of some 2,500 war cemeteries and 200 memorials, it has commemorated 1,694,857 war dead, including 110,088 Canadians. Commonwealth countries paid a percentage of the commission's budget calculated in proportion to the number of their graves in its sites; in 1937 the Canadian government paid 7.8 per cent of the commission's budget, a figure that had risen to 9.9 per cent by the 1980s.

19 Vance, *Death So Noble*, 60–1.

20 Gibson and Ward, *Courage Remembered*, 67.

21 "Report of Landscape Architect and General Manager," MRC *Annual Report*, 1922.

22 "Report of Landscape Architect and General Manager," MRC *Annual Report*, 1923.

23 MRC Minutes, 24 January 1909.

24 Gibson and Ward, *Courage Remembered*, 81, 83

25 Vance, *Death So Noble*, 61. MRC, Minutes of meeting of Grounds Committee, 8 March 1921; Agreement, Mount Royal Cemetery Company and Dominion of Canada, 12 April 1921, loose in MRC Minutes, 1921. Granite was to be used in preference to the standard Portland stone quarried in southern England and used in the commission's European cemeteries.

26 MRC, Agreement, Mount Royal Cemetery Company and Dominion of Canada, 12 April 1921.

27 The numbers in the respective cemeteries are taken from Gibson and Ward, *Courage Remembered*, 244.

28 Durflinger, *Lest We Forget*, 19.

29 "Report of Landscape Architect and General Manager,"

MRC *Annual Report*, 1923.

30 David Charles Stone, *The Last Great Necessity: Cemeteries in American History* (Baltimore: Johns Hopkins University Press, 1991), 183–4.

31 "Report of Landscape Architect and General Manager," MRC *Annual Report*, 1925.

32 Mappin, "The Evolution of Montreal's Cemetery Space from 1642 to the Present" (Master of Urban Planning, McGill University, 1995), 53; Collard, "Garden," phase III, 23; *Montreal Gazette*, 15 April 1942. In 1944 as part of a road- improvement project, the City of Montreal purchased the Papineau Military Cemetery. The $35,000 purchase price was used by the Last Post Fund to transfer remains to Pointe Claire.

33 "Report of the Landscape Architect," MRC *Annual Report* 1934; Vance, *Death So Noble*, 70.

34 A sketch of the Currie monument by A.T. Galt Durnford, and presented by his daughter Mrs W. Ralph Lewis, hangs in the cemetery office.

35 Vance, *Death So Noble*, 70.

36 "Report of the Landscape Architect," MRC *Annual Report,* 1937.

37 "Private Supplementary Report of the Landscape Architect," MRC *Annual Report,* 1937.

38 MRC Minutes, 9 January 1951.

CHAPTER NINE

1 Mount Royal Cemetery (MRC), John F. Roy to Board of Trustees, 28 February 1966, *Annual Report*, 1967.

2 MRC Minutes, 5 November 1948.

3 MRC Minutes, 6 September 1955.

4 MRC, Report of Manager, February 1962.

5 MRC Minutes, 14 September 1962, 21 October 1958, 21 November 1961.

6 David Charles Sloane, *The Last Great Necessity: Cemeteries in American History* (Baltimore: Johns Hopkins University Press, 1991), 238–9.

7 MRC, unidentified newspaper clipping, n.d., Gordon Mesley, "Pheasants Prosper atop Mount Royal."

8 Author's interview with Merle Christopher, 8 August 2000.

9 Sloane, *Last Great Necessity*, 222.

10 Ibid., 169.

11 MRC Minutes, 24 October 1913, 12 March 1935.

12 MRC Minutes, 12 March 1935, *Montreal Gazette*, 14 August 1940.

13 Author's interview with Donald Roy, 29 April 2000.

14 "Report of the Landscape Architect," MRC *Annual Report,* 1932.

15 Ibid., January 1933.

16 Manager John F. Roy to H.T. Duath, Inspector, Unemployment Insurance Company, 8 July 1941, included in MRC Minutes, 1941.

17 "Pensions Plan for Employees," 15 November 1955, included in MRC Minutes, 1955.

18 MRC Minutes, 9 June 1953.

19 Sloane, *Last Great Necessity*, 208.

20 Ibid., 239.

21 MRC *Annual Report*, 1967.

22 MRC *Annual Report*, 1977.

23 MRC *Annual Report*, 1978.

24 MRC Minutes, 20 May 1969; MRC *Annual Report*, 1975.

25 J.I. Cooper, *Montreal: A Brief History* (Montreal: McGill-Queen's University Press, 1969), 124, 177.

26 Ad in Montreal *Churchman*, July 1939, in Advertising file, MRC.

27 Simon Langlois, *La société québécoise en tendances, 1960–1990* (Quebec: Institut québécois de recherche sur la culture, 1990), 351.

28 Peter Stathopoulos, *The Greek Community of Montreal* (Athens: National Centre of Social Research, 1971), 25.

29 This grave was later transferred to the father of the child buried there.

30 "Report of Landscape Architect" MRC *Annual Report,* 1930, 1931.

31 "Report of Landscape Architect," MRC *Annual Report,* 1937, 1938.

32 MRC *Annual Report,* 1977.

33 *Montreal Gazette,* 11 January 1955.

34 MRC Minutes, 2 May 1953.

35 Bill 243: An Act respecting the Mount Royal Cemetery Company and certain territorial limits of the city of Outremont and the city of Montreal, Quebec, Legislative Assembly, 9–10 Elizabeth II, c. 102 (10 June 1961); MRC Minutes, 21 November 1960; MRC *Annual Report,* February 1972, March 1975.

36 MRC Minutes, 6 September 1955, 12 May 1959.

37 Léandre Bergeron, *The History of Quebec: A Patriote's Handbook* (Toronto: NC Press, 1971), iv.

38 MRC Minutes, 16 October 1959.

39 Author's interview with Donald Roy, 29 April 2000; author's interview with Merle Christopher, 28 January 2002.

40 *La Presse,* 8 August 1979.

41 *La Presse,* 1 February 1980. My translation.

CHAPTER TEN

1 Mount Royal Cemetery (MRC) Minutes, 9 September 1952.

2 *Montreal Gazette,* 18 October 1952

3 MRC Minutes, 13 September 1959.

4 MRC Minutes, 12 September 1966.

5 MRC Minutes, 21 March 1961.

6 MRC Minutes, 27 June 1973.

7 MRC Minutes, 19 September 1973, undated clipping of letter to *Montreal Gazette.*

8 MRC *Annual Report,* 1977.

9 MRC Minutes, 29 September 1982.

10 Author's interview with Donald Roy, 29 April 2000.

11 Author's interview with Merle Christopher, 29 January 2002.

12 MRC *Annual Report,* 1986.

13 *Montreal Gazette* 17 June 1954.

14 Author's interview with Merle Christopher, 28 January 2002.

15 MRC Minutes, 22 February 1990.

16 MRC Minutes, 31 May 1990.

17 MRC Minutes, 26 April 1990.

18 MRC Minutes, 28 June 1990.

19 MRC Minutes, 22 February, 25 October 1990; author's interview with Malaka Ackaoui, 18 August 2000.

20 *Le cimetière Mont-Royal. Un jardin pour la vie* (Montreal: Williams, Asselin, Ackaoui et Associés, 1995), 30.

21 *Field Guide to the Birds of North America* (Washington: National Geographic Society, 1992) 14.

22 Author's interview with Merle Christopher, 28 January 2002.

23 Michael Bliss, *Northern Enterprise: Five Centuries of Canadian Business* (Toronto: McClelland and Stewart, 1987; Pierre Berton, *The National Dream: The Great Railway, 1871–1881* (Toronto: McClelland and Stewart, 1970).

24 Stanley Haidaz, House of Commons, *Debates,* 30 May 1973, 4264; for the White Paper statement see Pierre Mayrand, "A New Concept in Museology in Quebec," *Muse* 11, no. 1 (1984): 33.

25 "Économusée" (Quebec: Société internationale des entreprises Économusée, n.d).

26 Cited in Sébastien St-Onge, *L'industrie de la mort* (Quebec: Édition Note bene, 2001), 53. My translation.

27 "Consolidation of Funeral Enterprises" unpublished report, Mount Royal Cemetery, 20 October 1998.

28 Thomas Lynch, "Last Rites," *Harper's Magazine*, June 2000, 168.

29 "Consolidation of Funeral Expenses."

30 St Onge, *L'industrie de la mort*, 61, 127.

31 "Consolidation of Funeral Enterprises."

32 MRC Minutes, 31 October 1991.

33 McGill University History Department, research dossier compiled by Sophie Mathieu.

34 www.mountroyalcem.com

35 Author's interview with Merle Christopher, 28 January 2002.

36 MRC *Annual Report*, 1989.

37 MRC Minutes, 18 November 1991.

38 "This Is a Cemetery," Mount Royal Cemetery Company brochure, n.d. For more on cemeteries as heritage sites see regular issues of the *Newsletter* of the Écomusée de l'Au-Delà.

BIBLIOGRAPHY

Mount Royal Cemetery has extensive archives dating back to the establishment of the Protestant Cemetery in 1799. Included in these are maps, deeds, and some correspondence. Of great importance are the burial records themselves, along with the minutes of the annual meetings of the Mount Royal Cemetery Company and the Crematorium Company.

For a general history of Quebec across the period see John A. Dickinson and Young, *A Short History of Quebec*, 3rd ed. (Montreal and Kingston: McGill-Queen's University Press, 2002). There is an extensive literature on the Protestant elite that founded the cemetery and runs it to this day. A good starting place is Ronald Rudin, *The Forgotten Quebecers: A History of English-Speaking Quebec, 1759–1980* (Quebec: Institut québécois de recherche sur la culture, 1985). Many of the leading figures have biographies in the *Dictionary of Canadian Biography*. The lives of the elite are discussed in Donald McKay, *The Square Mile: Merchant Princes of Montreal* (Vancouver: Douglas and McIntyre, 1987). The life of the founder, John Samuel McCord, is described in P. Miller, B. Young, D. Fyson, D. Wright, and M.T. McCaffrey, *The McCord Family: A Passionate Vision* (Montreal: McCord Museum of Canadian History, 1992). Of particular importance in understanding English Montreal's development of Mount Royal is Roderick MacLeod, "Salubrious Settings and Fortunate Families: The Making of Montreal's Golden Square Mile, 1840–1895" PhD diss., McGill University, 1997. The different Protestant denominations have played a crucial role in Mount Royal's history. For the Anglican community see J.I. Cooper, *The Blessed Communion: the Origins and History of the Diocese of Montreal, 1760–1960* (Montreal: Diocese of Montreal, 1960); Methodists are treated in Neil Semple, *The Lord's Dominion: The History of Canadian Methodism* (Montreal and Kingston, McGill-Queen's University Press, 1996). The best history of the Presbyterians in Montreal remains Robert Campbell's *A History of the Scotch Presbyterian Church in St Gabriel Street* (Montreal: W. Drysdale, 1887). For the evolution of Protestantism in the early twentieth century see in particular Michel Gauvreau, *College and Creed in English Canada from the Great Revival to the Great Depression* (Montreal and Kingston: McGill-Queen's University Press, 1991), Richard Allen, *The Social Passion: Religion and Social Reform in Canada, 1914–1928* (Toronto: University of Toronto Press, 1973), and Ramsay Cook, *The Regenerators: Social Criticism in Late Victorian English Canada* (Toronto: University of Toronto Press, 1985). The implications of Roman Catholicism and burial are treated in Raymond Lemieux and Jean-Paul Montminy, *Le catholicisme québécois* (Quebec: Les Éditions de l'IQRC, 2000). For issues of commemoration and public memory see Pierre Nora, ed., *Les lieux de mémoire* (Paris: Gallimard, 1997), vol. 2. Extremely important for its perspective on the influence of the First World War on memorialization and attitudes towards death is Jonathan F. Vance's, *Death So Noble: Memory, Meaning, and the First World War* (Vancouver: UBC Press, 1997). For the history of the Last

Post Fund see Serge Marc Durflinger, *Lest We Forget: A History of the Last Post Fund, 1909–1999* (Montreal: Last Post Fund, 2000). Also important in the construct of the twentieth-century landscape of memory is H.V. Nelles, *The Art of Nation-Building: Pageantry and Spectacle at Quebec's Tercentenary* (Toronto: University of Toronto Press, 1999). The larger implications of professionalism are effectively treated in Burton Bledstein, The Culture of Professionalism: *The Middle-Class and the Development of Higher Education in America* (New York: Norton, 1976).

For cholera and its effects on the Montreal population see Louise Dechêne and Jean-Claude Robert, "Le cholera de 1832 dans le Bas-Canada: mesure des inégalités devant la mort," in *Étude méthodologique des crises démographiques du passé*, edited by H. Charbonneau et André Larose (Liège: Ordina Éditions, 1979) and Geoffrey Bilson, *A Darkened House: Cholera in Nineteenth-Century Canada* (Toronto: University of Toronto Press, 1980). The Montreal smallpox epidemic of 1885 is treated in Michael Bliss, *Plague: A Story of Smallpox in Montreal* (Toronto: HarperCollins, 1991). A intriguing study of changing middle-class attitudes to odours is in Alain Corbin, *The Foul and the Fragrant: Odour and the Social Imagination* (London: Papermac, 1996).

For death in Quebec see Serge Gagnon, *Mourir hier et aujour-d'hui* (Québec: Les presses de l'Université Laval, 1987), Réal Brisson, *La mort au Québec. Dossier exploratoire* (Quebec: CELAT, 1988) and Lorraine Guay, *Le cimetière vide* (Cahier du CRAD, 13, no. 1 [1991]). For cemeteries in the Montreal area see Charles Mappin, 'The Evolution of Montreal's Cemetery Space from 1642 to the Present' (Master of Urban Planning thesis, McGill University, 1995). Cemeteries as heritage can be examined in the *Newsletter* and other publications of the Écomusée de l'Au-Delà, a non-profit organization in Montreal whose objectives are to preserve the natural, cultural, and historical heritage of Quebec cemeteries. The development of the "death care industry" in contemporary Quebec is treated in Sébastien

St-Onge, *L'industrie de la mort* (Quebec: Éditions Nota bene, 2001). Of particular importance for the Mount Royal Cemetery itself is Edgar Andrew Collard's unpublished manuscript (available at the cemetery) 'Garden in the Sun' (n.d.). For recent development of the cemetery see Malaka Ackaoui, *Le cimetière Mont-Royal. Un Jardin pour la vie* (Montreal: Williams, Asselin, Ackaoui et Associés, 1995). For a variety of information on the cemetery and its activities, its website should be consulted (www.mountroyalcem.com).

The most influential book on death in western society is Philippe Ariès's *Western Attitudes toward Death from the Middle Ages to the Present* (Baltimore: Johns Hopkins University Press, 1974). Of great importance for the historical context of death is Michel Vovelle, *Mourir autrefois. Attitudes collectives devant la mort aux XVIIe et XVIIIe siècles* (Paris: Gallimard, 1974). The social history of nineteenth-century death is treated in Pat Jalland, *Death in the Victorian Family* (Oxford: Oxford University Press, 1996). Death in England in the sixteenth and seventeenth centuries is effectively described in David Cressy, *Birth, Marriage and Death: Ritual, Religion, and the Life-cycle in Tudor and Stuart England* (Oxford: Oxford University Press, 1999). See also Vanessa Harding, *The Dead and the Living in Paris and London 1500–1670* (Cambridge: Cambridge University Press, 2002). For the history of English funerals see Julian Litten, *The English Way of Death: The Common Funeral since 1450* (London: Robert Hale, 1991). Dissection and the poor is effectively described in Ruth Richardson, *Death, Dissection and the Destitute* (London: Routledge and Kegan Paul, 1988). For contemporary funerary practice see Joachim Whaley, *Mirrors of Mortality: Studies in the Social History of Death* (London: Europa, 1981). An important Canadian case study that concentrates on funeral directors but has an important section on the Moncton Rural Cemetery is contained in the thesis of Roy Bourgeois, 'La commercialisa-tion de la mort à Moncton, 1856–1914' (PhD diss., Université Laval, 1999). For a readable, popular history of burial see Penny

Colman, *Corpses, Coffins, and Crypts: A History of Burial* (New York: Henry Holt, 1997).

The most important study of American cemeteries is David Charles Sloane, *The Last Great Necessity: Cemeteries in American History* (Baltimore: Johns Hopkins University Press, 1991). Also of great importance for its American comparisons was James Farrell, *Inventing the American Way of Death, 1830–1920* (Philadelphia: Temple University Press, 1980). In the United Kingdon, Julie Rugg of the Cemetery Research Group at the University of York has published several works on burial. See for example, "A New Burial Form and Its Meanings: Cemetery Establishment in the First Half of the Nineteenth Century," in *Grave Concerns: Death and Burial in England 1700–1850*, edited by Margaret Cox (York: Council for British Archaeology, 1998), 44–53. For the place of cemeteries in American society, see Richard Meyer, ed., *Cemeteries and Grave-markers: Voices of American Culture* (London: Research Press, 1989).

For the practices of rural cemeteries see J. Jay Smith, *Designs for Monuments and Mural Tablets Adapted to Rural Cemeteries, Church Yards, Churches and Chapels* (New York: Bartlett and Welford, 1846). For war graves see Edwin Gibson and G. Kingsley Ward, *Courage Remembered: The Story Behind the Construction and Maintenance of the Commonwealth's Military Cemeteries and Memorials of the Wars of 1914–1918 and 1939–1945* (Toronto: McClelland and Stewart, 1989). The influence of Frederick Law Olmsted is described in Witold Rybczynski, *A Clearing in the Distance: Frederick Law Olmsted and North America in the Nineteenth Century* (Toronto: HarperCollins, 1999).

Cremation is effectively described in the cemetery's own 1902 publication, *Cremation: Its History, Practice and Advantages*. For recent treatments see Robert Nicol, *At the End of the Road: Government, Society, and the Disposal of Human Remains in the Nineteenth and Twentieth Century* (London: St Leonard's Allen and Union, 1994) and Stephen Prothero, *Purified by Fire: A History of Cremation in America* (Berkele:, University of

California Press, 2001). Particularly useful because of their effect on cremation practice at Mount Royal Cemetery are Hugo Erichsen, *The Cremation of the Dead Considered from an Aesthetic, Sanitary, Religious, Historical, Medico-Legal, and Economical Standpoint* (Detroit: D.O. Haynes, 1887) and Augustus Cobb, *Earth-burial and Cremation: The History of Earth-burial with Its Attendant Evils, and the Advantage Offered by Cremation* (New York: Putnam's, 1892). Cremation and other burial rites are described in Louise A. Winton, ed., *Handbook of Burial Rites* (Toronto: Commemorative Services of Ontario, 1985).

Many excellent histories of individual cemeteries have been written. Among the best are David Weston, *The Sleeping City: The Story of Rockwood Necropolis* (Sydney, Australia: Southwood Press, 1989). One of my favorites for British cemeteries is Michael T.R.B. Turnbull, *The Edinburgh Graveyard Guide* (Edinburgh: Saint Andrew Press, 1991). Among the liveliest histories of graveyards in Canada are Nancy Millar, *Once upon a Tomb: Stories from Canadian Graveyards* (Calgary: Fifth House, 1997) and John Adams, *Historic Guide to Ross Bay Cemetery* (Victoria: Heritage Architectural Guides, 1983). For Kingston's Cataraqui Cemetery see Paul King, "A Brief History of the Cataraqui Cemetery," *Historic Kingston*, 28 (1979): 11–24. With important similarities to the history of Mount Royal, Quebec City's Mount Hermon is described in Brian Treggett and Sylvie Bergeron, *The Silent Records of the Past: Mount Hermon Cemetery* (Sillery: Mount Harmon Cemetery, 1988). The most professional cemetery guidebook that I have seen is Susan Wilson's *Garden of Memories: A Guide to Historic Forest Hills* (Boston: Forest Hills Educational Trust, 1998).

For the significance of the Mountain to Montrealers see Bernard Debarbieux and Claude Marois, "Le mont Royal. Forme naturelle, paysages et territoriales urbaines," *Cahiers de géographie du Québec* 41, no. 113 (1997): 171–87.

ILLUSTRATION CREDITS

MAPS

INDEX

WALKING THROUGH THE CEMETERY:

GRAVE LOCATION MAPS

Location Maps of the Mount Royal Cemetery

1 Gate House
2 Office
3 Old receiving vaults
4 Lilac knoll
5 Crematorium complex
6 Molson mausoleums
7 South entrance
8 Department of Veterans Affairs lot
9 Children's section (G3)
10 Imperial War Graves Commission lot
11 Gate to Notre-Dame-des-Neiges Cemetery
12 Last Post Fund lot
13 New Free Ground
14 Chinese Colony lot
15 Sheds and workers' residences

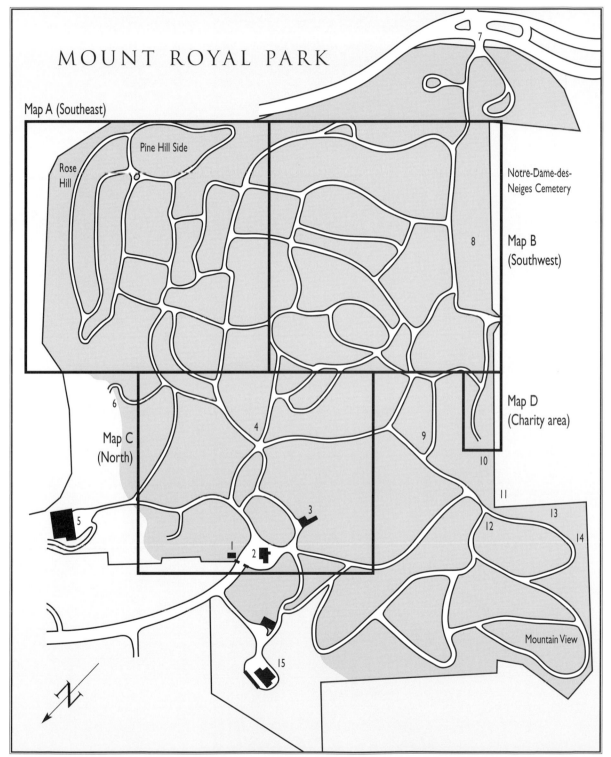

MOUNT ROYAL PARK

Map A (Southeast)

Rose Hill

Pine Hill Side

Notre-Dame-des-Neiges Cemetery

Map B (Southwest)

Map C (North)

Map D (Charity area)

Mountain View

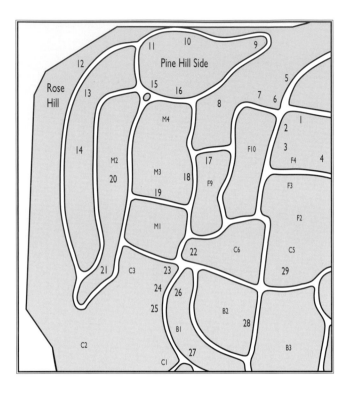

Location Map A: Southeast

1 Redpath family
2 Roddick family
3 Birks family
4 Gault family
5 Mackay family (founders of the Mackay School for the Deaf)
6 Torrance family
7 William Workman Mausoleum
8 Alexander Tilloch Galt (Father of Confederation)
9 Ormiston Roy
10 Elsie Reford
11 Richard B. Angus
12 John F. Roy
13 C.D. Howe
14 Mordecai Richler
15 Herbert Holt
16 Charles Melville Hays
17 Anna Leonowens
18 Sise family
19 Edward Maxwell (architect of the Montreal Museum of Fine Arts)
20 Edwin Holgate
21 John William Dawson
22 Grand Trunk train wreck victims
23 Abbott and Bethune families
24 Frank Scott
25 McCulloch family
26 George Browne (architect of the Molson Mausoleums)
27 Stanley Ryerson
28 Joe Beef
29 David Thompson

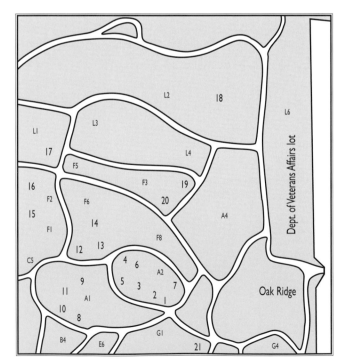

Location Map B: Southwest

1 William Squire
2 Joseph Onesakenrat
3 Peter McGill
4 William Dow
5 Bishop Francis Fulford
6 McCord family
7 Benaiah Gibb
8 John Williams Hopkins (architect of the cemetery gates)
9 James Ferrier
10 William Murray
11 John Young
12 John Rowan (fur trader for the Hudson's Bay Company)
13 George Simpson (head of the Hudson's Bay Company)
14 William Christopher Macdonald
15 John Lovell
16 William Notman
17 William Clendinneng
18 Howie Morenz
19 McGill donors
20 Honoré Beaugrand
21 Sarah Maxwell

Location Map C: North

1 Thomas Storrow Brown
2 Richard Sprigings
3 Hannah Lyman
4 Firemen's monument
5 J.H.R. Molson and the
   Frothingham family
6 Masonic Lodge monuments
7 Hugh Allan

8 Arthur Currie
9 Henry Wilson and
   Henry Teuscher
10 Charles Chiniquy
11 Frank Roy
12 Thomas Hackett
13 Mortimer Davis
   (Temple Emanu-el)

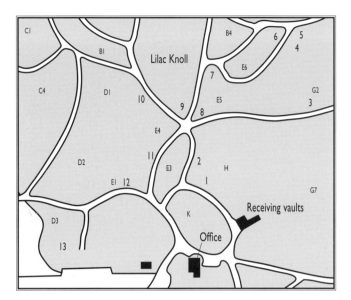

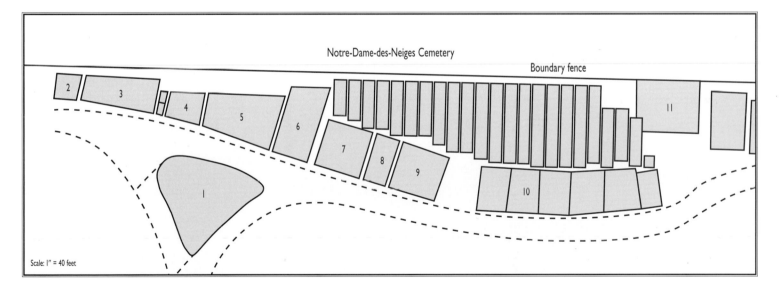

Location Map D: Charity area

1 Montreal Sailors' Institute
2 St Margaret's Home for Incurables
3 Montreal Sailors' Institute
4 Boys' Home
5 YMCA
6 Irish Protestant Benevolent Society

7 Protestant House of Industry and Refuge
8 Protestant Orphan Asylum
9 Ladies Benevolent Society
10 St George's Society
11 Old Free Ground

Plan
OF
MOUNT ROYAL
CEMETERY
NEAR
Montreal
LAID OUT BY
SIDNEY AND NEFF
CIVIL ENGINEERS
PHILADELPHIA
1852

SCALE